CRITICAL DIALOGUES IN SOUTHEAST ASIAN STUDIES

Charles Keyes, Vicente Rafael, and Laurie J. Sears, Series Editors

Critical Dialogues in Southeast Asian Studies

This series offers perspectives in Southeast Asian Studies that stem from reconsideration of the relationships among scholars, texts, archives, field sites, and subject matter. Volumes in the series feature inquiries into historiography, critical ethnography, colonialism and postcolonialism, nationalism and ethnicity, gender and sexuality, science and technology, politics and society, and literature, drama, and film. A common vision of the series is a belief that area studies scholarship sheds light on shifting contexts and contests over forms of knowing and modes of action that inform cultural politics and shape histories of modernity.

Imagined Ancestries of Vietnamese Communism: Ton Duc Thang and the Politics of History and Memory
by Christoph Giebel

Beginning to Remember: The Past in the Indonesian Present
edited by Mary S. Zurbuchen

Seditious Histories: Contesting Thai and Southeast Asian Pasts
by Craig J. Reynolds

Knowing Southeast Asian Subjects
edited by Laurie J. Sears

Making Fields of Merit: Buddhist Female Ascetics and Gendered Orders in Thailand
by Monica Lindberg Falk

Love, Passion and Patriotism: Sexuality and the Philippine Propaganda Movement, 1882-1892
by Raquel A. G. Reyes

Gathering Leaves and Lifting Words: Intertextuality and Buddhist Monastic Education in Laos and Thailand
by Justin Thomas McDaniel

The Ironies of Freedom: Sex, Culture, and Neoliberal Governance in Vietnam
by Thu-hyong Nguyen-vo

Submitting to God: Women and Islam in Urban Malaysia
by Sylva Frisk

Submitting to God
Women and Islam in Urban Malaysia

SYLVA FRISK

University of Washington Press
Seattle

Published simultaneously in the United States and Denmark.

University of Washington Press
PO Box 50096
Seattle, WA 98145-5096, USA
www.washington.edu/uwpress

Published in Denmark by NIAS Press
Nordic Institute of Asian Studies
Leifsgade 33, 2300 Copenhagen S, Denmark

Library of Congress Cataloging-in-Publication Data

Frisk, Sylva.
   Submitting to God: women and Islam in urban Malaysia / by Sylva Frisk.
      p. cm. — (Critical dialogues in Southeast Asian Studies)
   Includes bibliographical references and index.
   ISBN 978-0-295-98925-9 (pbk. : alk. paper)
   1. Women in Islam. 2. Women in Islam—Malaysia. 3. Muslim
   women—Malaysia—Social conditions. I. Title.
   BP173.4.F75 2009
   297.082'09595—dc22   2009008139

Typeset by NIAS Press
Produced by SRM Production Services Sdn Bhd and printed in Malaysia
Printed on acid-free paper

Contents

Figures

Figures 1.1.–4.1. by Sylva Frisk; Figure 4.2. by Jan Mellqvist

Preface and Acknowledgements

My research interest in the religious practices of Muslim women in Malaysia started in the early 1990s when I had the opportunity, as a fresh doctoral student, to visit Dr Wil Burghoorn, a senior researcher and also close friend, while she was doing her fieldwork on Malay factory women in one of the Free Trade Zones in the Klang valley, west of Kuala Lumpur. During this first visit I came across religious study groups formed by women and I met women who expressed a strong sense of self esteem and value in relation to religious commitment and studies. They were eager to introduce me to Malay traditions and practices and emphasized the fact that women were allowed to take an active part in all aspects of society; they could work side by side with men, they earned their own money, they were visible in public space and they could contribute to the religious life of the community. The importance that women placed on religious practice in their everyday life and the roles that women played in religious education showed me a different dimension of the wave of Islamization movement that had swept over the country since the early 1970s. What I had read thus far on Islamization in Malaysia had a clear focus on men's activities and roles and women were usually presented in terms of victims of Islamization or as passive followers of the movement. When I, during my first visit to the country, met women who guided me through their religious practices and introduced me to female religious spaces it opened up a wide field of research questions concerning gender, Islam and agency that I have ever since tried to grapple.

In 1995, a couple of years after my first visit to Malaysia, I embarked on a field work in Kuala Lumpur with the intention of collecting data for my dissertation with a focus on women's religious practices in urban Malaysia. Over the next 12 months I spent most of my days in mosques, in Koran study groups and in Arabic classes together with women who were driven by a desire to learn more about their own religion or the desire to teach and inspire other women to learn more about Islam. During this field work I formed relationships as an anthropologist with individual women as interlocutors. These contacts have extended beyond the initial PhD project as I have, as a researcher, been able to return to Kuala Lumpur on a fairly regular basis up until this date. New research questions have been in focus, but I have been able to keep contact with many of these women: to follow their daily lives but also participate in the religious study groups that they are engaged in. The data that I present in this book have thus been collected over an extensive period of time beginning with my dissertation project in the mid-90s and ending with my latest field trip in January 2009.

Many of these relationships that I formed during my first long term field work have transformed, over time, into relationships of friendship: I have stayed close with them long after the field work, and eventually the dissertation, were finished. As friends, these women, have a deep concerng for my personal religious beliefs. Firdaus, my adopted sister and dear friend, has ever since we met the first time in 1995 nurtured a hope that I would see the beauty and truth in Islam the same way that she does. She has explained the verses of the Koran to me hundreds of times, she has introduced me to female sessions of devotion, always making me aware of the spiritual aspects of everyday life and how the words of God may be experienced in any small detail. She does not give up on me and has never shown any disappointment or frustration over my personal inability or ignorance to see the world as she does. 'You are simply not ready yet', is her calm comment to my lack of personal commitment.

Other women have worked equally hard to guide me both as an anthropologist trying to understand the meaning of religious practice in this particular context, but also as a friend who, as they see it, is in need of guidance from God. I owe these women my deepest gratitude for sharing their knowledge, their experiences and spirituality with me. I have already mentioned Firdaus and I want to include Siti Zubaida, my adopted mother and also my *ustazah*, along with my dear friends Ainon, Noorley, and Hanim. I know that they have hoped and desired that I, personally, would discover the truth in Islam along the way. While I have disappointed them on that point, I have written this book with deep respect for the religious lives that they lead and for their willingness to open them up to me.

I am obliged to a large number of people and institutions without whose assistance and support this book would not have been completed or published. As mentioned above, Dr Burghoorn introduced me, not only to Malaysia and to the magic of fieldwork, but also to social anthropology as a field of study and for this I owe her my deepest gratitude. The encouragement, enthusiasm and support that she has shared with med over the years leave traces on each page of this book.

A number of persons have contributed with critical reading, of the entire, or parts of the manuscript. I would like to thank, in particular, Professor Don Kulick who gave constructive critique of the theoretical discussion and Dr. Datuk Professor Sharifah Zaleha Syed Hassan who helped me fine tune the ethnographic analysis through her very careful reading of the manuscript and was a also a valuable support during fieldwork, and, finally, the four anonymous reviewers of University of Washington Press and NIAS Press. I extend my warmest thanks to all of you.

I am also indebted to the editors of the Gendering Asia series at NIAS Press, Dr Wil Burghoorn, Senior Researcher Cecilia Milwertz and Professor Helle Rydstrøm; to Gerald Jackson, Editor in Chief at NIAS Press; and to Professor Charles Keyes, editor of the series 'Critical Dialogues in Southeast Asian Studies' at University of Washington Press for support and assistance in the publishing process. Ms Dayaneetha De Silva of Firefly Books edited the manuscript with great professionalism and care. I was in safe hands with Senior Editor Leena Höskuldsson of NIAS Press, who managed the entire project, and Editorial Assistant Samantha Pedersen. Thank you so much.

This research project was made possible with the financial support from several sources: SIDA/SAREC, the Centre for Asian Studies and the Faculty of Social Science at University of Gothenburg. The fieldwork was financially supported by Knut och Alice Wallenbergs Stiftelse, Stipendiefonden Viktor Rydbergs minne, Wilhelm och Martina Lundgrens Vetenskapsfond, Kungliga och Hvitfeldtska Stipendieinrättningen, NIAS – Nordic Institute for Asian Studies, and the Swedish School of Advanced Asia Pacific Studies. The Swedish School of Advanced Asia Pacific Studies was also generous in financing the printing of the book.

Glossary

ad-deen	Islam as a way of life
adat	customary law
adat perpatih	matrilineal law; matrilineal kinship system
adat temenggung	patrilineal law; bilateral kinship system
air Yasin	water which has aquired healing powers when the chapter Yasin in the Koran has been recitied over it
akad nikah	religious marriage ceremony
akal	reason
akikah kenduri	child's hair-cutting ritual
amal salleh	good deeds
assalamualaikum	peace be upon you
aurat	parts of the body that should not be exposed
azan	call to prayer
baju kurung	Malay women's tunic
baju Melayu	Malay men's traditional dress
bangsa	race, nation
bersanding	traditional Malay wedding
bomoh	Malay ritual specialist
buka	open
buka puasa	breaking of the fast
ceramah agama	religious talks
dakwah	responding to the call; Islamic resurgence groups

dakwah songsang	deviant *dakwah*
din	religion
doa	prayer
Fatiha	opening verse of the Koran
fatwa	rulings on religious matters
fidiah	small fine for not fasting due to ill health
hadith	Koranic exegesis
haji	man who has performed the Hajj
hajj	pilgrimage to Mecca
hajjah	woman who has performed the Hajj
halal	meat prepared according to Muslim dietary laws
hantu-hantu	ghosts and spirits, non-Islamic
haram	forbidden
hidayat	guidance
hudud	Islamic penal code
ibadah	religious duties (also *ibadat*)
Iblis	Satan
ilmu hitam	bad (black) magic
ilmu putih	good (white) magic
imam	prayer leader and head of mosque
iman	belief
jalaseh	Iranian women's home-based religious gathering
jemaah	informal religious grouping
jinn	spirits
kadi	judge
kafir	non-believers, those who reject the truth

kebaya	two-piece, figure-hugging traditional Malay women's dress
kenduri	communal feast, celebration, often involving prayer
keramat	sacred; saint; used to denote saint worship
khatam Koran	complete the reading of the Koran
khutbah nikah	recitation of the marriage service
kursus perkahwinan	preparatory marriage class
layan suami	to comply with, be attentive to, one's husband
laylat al-qadr	night on which the Koran was first revealed to Muhammad
madrasah	reformed *pondok* school system based on Western principles
maghrib	evening prayer
majlis doa	religious gathering
mandi	traditional bath
mas kahwin	marriage money
masuk Melayu	to become Malay
Melayu Baru	New Malay
Minah karan	Malay girls working in factories
mini-telekung	small scarf covering head and neck
muezzin	man who calls Muslims to prayer
mufti	Islamic legal expert
Muharram	the first month of the Muslim calendar
mukmin	person with conscious, embodied desire to submit to God's will
nafsu	the drive to satisfy basic needs
neraka	hell

niat	intention
noor	light
orang dakwah	*dakwah* person
pahala	merit
pawang	traditional Malay healer or sorcerer
pondok	traditional village religious (boarding) school
puasa	fasting
puasa enam	commendable fasting, lit. six-day fast
puasa sunna	commendable fasting following the sunna
rakaat	ritual cycles
Ramadan	ninth month of the Muslim calendar, the fasting month
rendang	a spicy, dry coconut-based curry
selendang	sheer scarf worn with Malay dress
sembahyang	ritual prayers
shahada	declaration of faith
sharia	Islamic legal code
solat	the five daily ritual Muslim prayers
Sunna	way of the Prophet
sura	a chapter or part of the Koran
surau	village prayer hall
Syawal	the month following Ramadan
syukur	gratitude to God
syurga	heaven
tafsir	interpreting the meaning of Koranic verses
tahlil	repetition of God's name
tajwid	Arabic classes for Koran reading and recitation

takwah	God-fearing
tarbiya	religious education
tarikat	path to truth through experience
tauhid	unity
telekung	small scarf covering the hair, neck and shoulders
terawih	evening congregational prayer during Ramadan
tudung	combination of a *baju kurung* worn with the mini-*telekung*
tutup	to cover or close; to adopt the veil
ulama	religious teacher
ummah	community of Muslim believers
umrah	(performing the) lesser pilgrimage
usrah	small study group
ustaz	male village religious teacher
ustazah	female village religious teacher
waalaikumsalam	and upon you, be peace
zakat	yearly tithe or almsgiving
zakat fitrah	compulsory tax for Muslims

Abbreviations

ABIM	Angkatan Belia Islam Malaysia, Muslim Youth Movement of Malaysia
DAP	Democratic Action Party
IRC	Islamic Republic Council
ISA	Internal Security Act 1960
KeADILAN	Parti KeADILan Rakyat, People's Justice Party
NEP	New Economic Policy
MARA	Majlis Amanah Rakyat
MCA	Malaysian Chinese Association
MIC	Malaysian Indian Congress
NGO	non-governmental organization
PAS	Parti Islam Se-Malaysia
PERKIM	Pertubuhan Kebajikan Islam Malaysia
SIS	Sisters in Islam
UMNO	United Malays National Organization
YADIM	Yayasan Dakwah Islam Malaysia, Dakwah Foundation of Malaysia

1

Introduction

WOMEN IN THE MOSQUE

Once a week, in the hours between noon and late afternoon, the mosque in one of the more affluent neighbourhoods in Kuala Lumpur attracts a large number of women. The small parking lot within the mosque grounds becomes crowded, and the male mosque caretaker tries to prevent traffic jams by directing the cars as they enter the gates. Other arrivals are dropped off just outside the entrance and the women who step out of the cars quickly move into the shade of the mosque. Most of the women are dressed in traditional *baju kurung* – a full length two-piece garment with long sleeves. They have dressed with care, choosing headscarves in colours to match their bright batik outfits. The stream of women entering the mosque forms a colourful contrast to the white mosque and the hard, white light of the afternoon.

The mosque has a women's section, which can be reached from the side of the building. From there, the women have access to the lecture hall where religious talks (*ceramah agama*) and classes are held. The women's washroom, for pre-prayer ablutions, is near the lecture hall, as are the stairs leading up to the women's prayer area, which consists of a balcony above the main hall used by the men. Around the corner, there is a class under way for children. Their voices, as they practise pronouncing the Arabic alphabet, fill the mosque yard with the puffs and clicks of consonants and soft breathy vowels.

The lecture hall is furnished with about a hundred sets of individual tables and chairs, with a larger desk at the front of the room, where there is a blackboard. The floor is covered with synthetic rugs; shoes are slipped off and left on wooden racks outside the hall. On the floor just next to the doorway is a large, transparent box where women can drop their donations. There is no fee for attending the religious talks, but participants give voluntary contributions. The money is used for activities organized by the women's committee, for community welfare and also for the mosque generally.

Before sitting down at their small tables, some women place tape recorders along the edge of the front desk. Greetings are exchanged and the room fills with chatter. Sometimes there is a bit of commerce in headscarves or costume jewellery at the back of the room, although this activity is somewhat frowned upon by the organizing committee. Information about forthcoming talks and other events are written on the blackboard and invitations to collective rituals held in private homes are announced.

As the hall fills with people before the speaker arrives, some of the women in the organizing committee distribute sheets of paper with a text in Arabic consisting of the 99 names of God. A tape recorder is turned on and the crowd chants along, repeating the names of God, until the speaker of the day walks in. The recording is stopped and the speaker is greeted. Someone in the first row quickly switches on all the tape recorders placed on the front desk. The speaker takes a seat behind the desk, leads the crowd in the recitation of Fatiha, the opening verse in the Koran, and introduces the topic for the day.

I witnessed such a gathering during one of my initial encounters with the women who have come to open up their religious lives to me, first during my year-long fieldwork in Kuala Lumpur in 1995–1996, and then subsequently on frequent visits over the years since. This scene also represents my first impression of the Malaysian mosque as a public space, animated by the bustle of women teaching, studying, praying and doing charity work. This first impression of the mosque as a female space stayed with me, and was intensified, during the course of my fieldwork.

Such classes are part of a wide variety of informal religious courses initiated by and for women in Kuala Lumpur and its suburbs, as well as in other urban areas in Malaysia. Attending this class, as well as a wide range of other classes and study groups regularly, formed the point of departure for my fieldwork: by participating in religious studies, I learnt about these

Figure 1.1. Mosque group

women's spiritual concerns, how they crafted themselves as pious subjects through performing religious duties and acts of worship, and through collective rituals that they organized and performed independently of men, in their homes and in mosques.

In the course of my fieldwork, I realized that women usually outnumbered men in such religious education activities. Some of the women I met within this context also showed a stronger commitment to Islam than their husbands, a commitment going far beyond the basic religious duties such as praying and fasting. This commitment to Islam took on different forms in their lives. Those who worked outside home tried to fit in religious studies in their limited spare time. Others had made the choice to quit their professional careers and become full-time 'housewives' in order to spend more time on studying Islam. Describing their family lives, many women said that a husband's duty to fill the role of household provider consumed much of his time and, therefore, men had difficulty finding time for religious studies. These women saw their own commitment to the faith as a way for them to assume the role of transmitter of religious knowledge to their families: not only to their children, but also to their husbands.

MALAY WOMEN AND ISLAMIZATION

Throughout Malaysia, religious education has flourished and grown in popularity since the 1980s, developing out of a broad current of Islamization of society. This current has been driven by the collective activities of a wide range of urban Islamic resurgence groups, locally referred to as 'the *dakwah* movement', aimed at strengthening the Islamic identity and religious practices of Malays, along with increasing state-level Islamization policies.[1]

Janet Bauer (1997) notes that while politicized religious movements often appear male-dominated from a distance, closer observation usually shows large numbers of active female participants and members. Women in the Malaysian *dakwah* movement have generally been described as followers and supporters, whereas men, in their capacity as political leaders or religious ideologues, are presented as initiators (Zainah 1987; Norani 1998). Relatively little has been said about women's participation in the process of Islamization from the perspective of women themselves. The present book was written to address this gap by providing an ethnographic account of women's religious activities in urban Malaysia, focusing on religion as an everyday, lived practice. My aim has been to investigate how Malay women have come to understand themselves: as religious/pious subjects, or rather as gendered, religious subjects, since the construction of the self also involves a process of construction of gendered identity (Moore 1994). Through this account of how Malay Muslim women have become active participants in the increased religiosity, the book also explores the motivations and meanings women ascribe to their emerging roles in the religious sphere and within the Islamization process.

As we will see, Islamization in the Malaysian case has opened up possibilities for women to enter into religious debate and education, through which they produce, recreate and transform Islamic discourse and practice. Anthropologists have been paying increasing attention to the evolution of this transformation in particular contexts. A number of recent studies from other societies attest to the ways in which women have been assuming active positions as critical mediators and interpreters of Islamization in everyday life, even in terms of religious practices classified as 'high' Islam (Allès 2003; Kamalkhani 1993, 1996; Horvatich 1994; Jaschok and Shui 2000; Mahmood 1998, 2001a; Torab 1996; Whalley 1996). Taking its cue from this research, the present book critically examines the kind of agency that the women concerned develop in the course of their religious lives. What kind of agency may we ascribe to Malay women who are actively involved in Islamization both on a personal and social level?

ISLAM, GENDER AND RESISTANCE

Raising questions about women's agency means stepping into an ocean of discussions and debates about the relationship between structure and agency, and between society and the individual, familiar to all social sciences in general and to feminist theory and gender studies in particular. In her inspiring introduction to the book *The Agency of Women in Asia*, the Australian anthropologist Lyn Parker remarks that feminist anthropology has been at the forefront of social science research when it comes to representing women's active agency. Anthropology has lent itself easily to the feminist project to give women voices and provide ethnographic evidence of women's activities in contexts where, traditionally, they have not been seen and heard. Anthropologists were thus early supporters of feminist scholars'critique in the 1970s and 1980s of the androcentric bias in the social sciences.

Within the field of religious studies, feminist scholarship has challenged the implicit but dominant assumption that, since women are excluded from many formal religious roles, they either are not religious practitioners, or their practice is not interesting or important for understanding the religious life of their communities. Out of this critique has emerged a body of studies in which the religious lives of women within different faiths are investigated and made visible, showing that women's religious lives are far more complex than earlier, androcentric accounts had suggested.[2]

Feminist scholars dealing with women in fundamentalist traditions have found the concept of agency particularly useful. A focus on agency enables women involved in fundamentalist movements to be seen and described as being active rather than passive participants. Using the perspective of agency also offers an escape from what Sandra Harding (1991) calls a totalizing or uncritical opposition between fundamentalism and the modern. The cross-cultural studies of gender and fundamentalism in *Mixed Blessings* (Brink and Mencher 1997) are an important contribution to the study of women's active agency in such male-dominated and fundamentalist religious contexts. Significantly, again with reference to Harding (1991), the essays of *Mixed Blessings* resist an image of fundamentalists as culturally backward 'others'.

Recent work on Muslim societies has produced some insightful ethno-graphic examples of how women successfully develop their own religious practices and traditions within the frame of 'customary' or 'popular' religion, as opposed to 'orthodox' or 'normative' Islam.[3] Studies of women as agents within customary religion show that women, through their religious practice, can challenge or resist male dominance encouraged by 'orthodox' versions of Islam (Abu-Lughod 1986; Boddy 1989; Hegland 1998).

The understanding of Muslim women's agency as resistance against patriarchal structures that sanction male religious authority is also found in studies of women in societies characterized by both modernization and Islamization. A major field of inquiry in this regard has been how Muslim women are affected by, and how they respond to modernization and Islamization in various contexts. Muslims in many post-colonial societies have found in Islam a forceful medium for identity politics and for legitimizing political power. Discourses produced in such contexts, however, are often highly gendered. Political, religious and cultural revivalist movements have assigned to women the role of bearers of cultural values and made them symbols of the community/nation. This has expressed itself in an urgency to gain control over women's bodies. Women's responsibility as mothers and reproducers of the group has been emphasized, together with a powerful discourse on women's modesty through dress, behaviour and restrictions in movement (Kandiyoti 1991; Mernissi 1975; Moghadam 1993, 1994).

In Malaysia, the 1970s *dakwah* movement was successfully co-opted by the government, and Islamic reform has grown into a broad and decisive process with clear ethnic, gendered and social consequences. The strong convergence between the state's Islamization project and that sought by resurgent Islamists has drawn much scholarly attention.[4] The government and the *dakwah* movement may have disagreed in their visions of the modern Malaysian state and on economic development, but both were equally eager to offer alternatives to Western modernization – alternatives that made powerful claims on women's bodies and their minds. The *dakwah* movement explicitly urged women to veil, and to guard their modesty. The *dakwah* emphasis on a woman's domestic, maternal role is also found in the state's discourse on the role of women in modernizing the country.

Academic interest in women and Islamization in Malaysia has mainly focused on the effects that Islamization and modernization have had on women's lives (Ong 1995; Stivens 1998). The social anthropologist Aihwa Ong (1995) has argued that male authority has been strengthened as a result of Islamization. Indeed, her work has produced an image of Malay women as victims of patriarchal structures and practices in both public and private spheres. Such an approach obviously raises questions about how women themselves have been dealing with, or responded to, the strengthening of Islamic practices and ideals.

The readiness of modern women, in various Muslim contexts, to dress and act in accordance with Islamic ideals, in particular the practice of veiling, has subsequently attracted much scholarly attention, with undertones ranging from fascination and bewilderment to alarm. There has been a tendency to favour the meaning of the practice of veiling as a kind of resistance against patriarchal structures and male dominance. For example, women in the Arab world have been understood to use the veil as a way of claiming the rights and mobility traditionally denied them (Jansen 1998; MacLeod 1992). The use of the veil is then understood to create a morally safe space, enabling women to move about in public more easily. Women's agency in this context is understood to embrace veiling as a strategic way to effect social change. Although Southeast Asian Muslim women have not been excluded historically from the public sphere (at least not married women), the contemporary phenomenon of veiling amongst Muslims in the region has been analysed in much the same terms. It has been understood largely as a moral, gendered and ethnic response to the claims on femininity embedded in the processes of modernity and industrialization (Ong 1987; Stivens; Ackerman 1991; Lindqvist 2002).

Although the emphasis on women's agency is affirmed in studies of women's involvement in Islamization, or in 'fundamentalist' movements in general, it is important to understand that this affirmation takes place against the hegemonic representation of women as victimized subjects who, to a very large extent, are constituted by subjection only (Bracke 2003). When the perception of women as victims is abandoned in favour of the notion of women as agents, the shift is also made from subordination to resistance. This analytical shift brought about by feminist theory goes hand in hand with a desire to liberate women from male dominance, which is essential to feminism as a political project. In feminist theory, that desire can easily become naturalized, universalized and normative (Mahmood 2001). In fact, resistance to gendered relations of domination has become a presupposition for feminist notions of women's agency. It is important to see that such a presupposition may also hide other notions and expressions of agency. This book provides evidence that women's religious commitment and practice have dimensions other than resistance or subordination.

FEMINISM, AGENCY AND SUBJECTIVITY

The claim on women's agency, as it has been formulated within feminist theory, is closely linked to a long-standing debate over notions of the subject. The debate expresses the tension between the notion of the Cartesian constituting subject, and the constituted subject of the social constructivists. This tension has structured the treatment of subjectivity and agency within feminism for a long time (Hekman 1991, 1995).

The Cartesian, modern notion of the transcendental, constituting subject has been attacked in various ways. Feminist critique of the modern subject, of which the work of Simone de Beauvoir in *The Second Sex* (1972) has been profoundly influential, has been that it is conceptualized as inherently masculine and thus has been a significant factor in maintaining the inferior status of women. In order for the subjection of women to change, de Beauvoir saw the necessity for an opening-up of the category of the subject to include women, and in her notion that one is not born, but becomes, a woman she introduces the *idea* of the constituted subject.[5]

This tension between the ideas of the constituted and the constituting subject, and between voluntarism and determinism, is in many ways embodied by the work of Michel Foucault. Despite his notorious lack of interest in feminist theory, Foucault's work has become one of the most important influences upon how feminists have addressed questions about the connection between gender identity and agency.

Foucault's ideas on the effects of power upon the body, developed in *Discipline and Punish* (1979) and in the first volume of *The History of Sexuality* (1981), have been particularly useful for feminists in their efforts to explain aspects of women's oppression (McNay 1992; Sawicki 1991). Nonetheless, these books have also been criticized by feminists for reducing social agents to passive bodies and for lacking an explanation of how individuals may act autonomously. Foucault himself recognized the analytical limitations of his earlier work and later developed the notion of the self, as a complement to his studies on the body and power. In *The Use of Pleasure* (1985), the second volume of *The History of Sexuality*, Foucault shifts from the idea of individuals as docile bodies to the idea of individuals as agents with a capacity for autonomous action, and thereby, he shifts from an analysis of technologies of domination to an analysis of technologies of subjectification (McNay 1996). In this volume, Foucault develops a notion of the self through a study of classical Greek society. He asks how individuals (in this case, male citizens) in ancient Greece came to understand themselves as moral, desiring subjects. Foucault argues that Greek men actively constituted themselves as subjects through a number of practices and techniques of the self (arts of existence), which he situates at the level of ethical practice. Arts of existence are described as '...those intentional and voluntary actions by which men not only set themselves rules of conduct, but also seek to transform themselves, to change themselves in their singular being, and to make their life into an oeuvre that carries certain aesthetic values and meets certain stylistic criteria' (Foucault 1985: 10–11).

For Greek male citizens, moral conduct was constituted by the intensity of practice (between restraint and excess) and by the distinction between activity and passivity.[6] Through self-mastery and restraint and through a stylization of asymmetrical relations of power with respect to other people, the individual acquired a condition characterized as freedom. To be free in relation to one's pleasures meant not being their slave. Freedom is also described, by the Greeks, as the power that the individual has over himself and over others.[7]

In *Gender and Agency*, the feminist philosopher Lois McNay (2000) shows that Foucault's ideas of the self or an aesthetics of existence in *The Use of Pleasure* are useful for the generative notion of agency that she proposes, in that it gestures towards the autonomous and creative element inherent to action. The problem, according to McNay, is that this creative element is asserted rather than elaborated upon in Foucault's work. He does not account for the status of the self-fashioning subject which appears to precede an ethics of the self. His work also fails to distinguish with more precision between practices of the self that are imposed on individuals through cultural sanctions and those that are more freely adopted.[8]

McNay argues that recent theoretical work on gender identity offers only a partial account of agency because it remains within an essentially negative understanding of subject formation. What is at the core of the negative paradigm of subjectification is the idea that the individual emerges from constraint. The subject is understood in passive terms as an effect of discursive structures and actions, which means that the subject's agency is mainly understood as resistance to or dislocation from dominant norms. McNay acknowledges that the negative paradigm of subjectification has been very useful for feminist theory '...because it offers a way of analysing the deeply entrenched aspects of gendered behaviour while eschewing reference to a pre-social sexual difference' (McNay 2003: 140). The conceptualization of agency as resistance or disclocation from dominant norms has been used successfully in describing situations where individual practices do not conform to those norms, something which has been powerfully formulated, for example, in the work of American philosopher Judith Butler (1990, 1993) on the inherent instability of gender norms and the consequent possibilities that this throws up for resistance, subversion and the emancipatory remodelling of identity. Nonetheless, while affirming the usefulness of the negative paradigm of subjectification for feminist theory, McNay is critical of the tendency for the negative paradigm to become an exhaustive explanation of all aspects of subjectivity and agency.

Instead of highlighting the retentive dimension of the sedimented effect of power upon the body, emphasized in the negative paradigm, McNay suggests a more generative understanding of subject formation and agency. She call for a more precise and varied account of agency, including a more '...dialogical understanding of the temporal aspects of subject formation' (2000: 4) and an emphasis on '...the protensive and future oriented dimension of praxis as the living through of embodied potentialities, and as the anticipatory aspects inherent within subject formation' (ibid. 4–5). She also suggests that we understand the subject formation as '...a lived relation between embodied potentiality and material relations' (ibid. 16).

The main implication of this generative logic for a theory of agency, according to McNay, is that it yields an understanding of a creative or imaginative substrate to action. She says: 'It is crucial to conceptualize these creative or productive aspects immanent to agency in order to explain how, when faced with complexity and difference, individuals may respond in unanticipated and innovative ways which may hinder, reinforce or catalyze social change' (ibid. 5). A generative understanding of subjectification and agency is necessary in order to explain the differing motivations and ways in which individuals and groups struggle over, appropriate and transform cultural meanings and resources.

In the present study of Malay women's active participation in Islamization, the generative notion of agency suggested by McNay is necessary in order to avoid seeing women's actions simply as resistance to a male-dominated social order, or, in more negative terms, as false consciousness or internalized patriarchal oppression. A generative account of Malay women's religious subjectivity and agency requires that we go beyond an account of the discursive effects of the Islamic movement and modernization on women's lives. The historical and political processes of Islamization in Malaysia have put women in discursive positions that require them, for example, to guard their modesty through veiling or to practise the religious duty of praying more diligently. Those practices, however, also generate intellectual and embodied experiences and attitudes that are highly significant for how they come to understand themselves as religious subjects who consciously and actively submit to God's will.

Piety and agency: creative aspects of submission

Recent studies exploring the creative aspects of submission within both Muslim and Christian traditions have adopted this more generative approach to women's agency. They observe that there are serious limitations to the secular and liberal notion of agency within feminist theory for our understanding of the agency of pious women. The American anthropologist Saba Mahmood (1998) has worked with the emerging women's mosque movement in Cairo where women, for the first time in history, meet publicly in their local mosques to teach and study Islam with each other. Mahmood argues that when feminist theory gives priority to resistance and the pursuit of female autonomy as primary areas of investigation, this set of desires becomes universalized and naturalized, while others (like cultivating submission to God) are viewed as artefacts produced by the imposition of patriarchal power (2001a: 155). She stresses that forms of desire are always socially constructed. Therefore, it is necessary to investigate the conditions under which different forms of desire emerge. She analyses how women seek to cultivate Islamic virtues such as modesty, shyness and patience. Those virtues are associated with feminine passivity, inaction and submissiveness, which, from a feminist point of view, sit uncomfortably with the idea of agency. Mahmood, however, shows us that they may very well be understood as a form of agency.[9] The cultivation of Islamic virtues, in the context of pious Egyptian women, enables certain ways of being and forecloses others. It does not mark a reluctance to act in the women, but is integral to the constructive project of becoming pious, which involves considerable investment, struggle and achievement.

Phyllis Mack's (2003) historical work on eighteenth-century Quaker women is also interesting in this respect. Mack documents how Quaker women invariably insisted that their actions were done not as acts of will but as acts of obedience – that they acted as instruments of divine authority at the same time as they acted as authorities of the community. She writes:

> If we think of agency as comprising both the capacity for effective action and the free choice to act, we might say that Quaker women's actions were effective but not intentional (or, more accurately, that they saw their intentions as inspired by and identical with God's). Quaker women defined agency not as the freedom to do what one wants but as the freedom to do what is right. Since 'what is right' was determined by absolute truth or God as well as by individual conscience, agency implied obedience as well as the freedom to make choices and act on them. And since doing what is right inevitably means subduing at least some of one's own habits, desires, and impulses, agency implied self-negation as well as self-expression. The goal of the individual's religious discipline was to shape her personal desires and narrow self-interest until they became identical with God's desire, with absolute goodness. The sanctified Christian wants what God wants; she is God's agent in the world. (Mack 2003: 156–157)

Marie Griffith's *God's Daughters*, a work within religious studies, explores the creative aspects of submission in Christian worship within a North American Pentecostal organization. One important aspect of the discourse of submission discussed is the idea of wifely submission to male authority: women's submission to their husband's authority is here understood to be the will of God to which they surrender. In response to the assumption made by many outsiders that the conservative, Christian women of the organization are merely participating in their own victimization, internalizing patriarchal ideas about female submission that confirm and increase their sense of personal inferiority, Griffith argues that the women themselves claim that the doctrine of submission leads both to freedom and to transformation. They hold that, through submission, they become God's obedient daughters and, as such, God rewards them by healing their sorrows and easing their pain. Women's narratives also stress that wifely submission has improved their marriages in the sense that their husbands have drawn closer to Jesus and thereby become transformed into happy, loving husbands. In addition, women's stories recount that their submission also generates a feeling of freedom and power in the sense that they experience the capability to release divine power and effect change. Griffith suggests that these women retain a kind of 'mediated agency' through their reliance on the omnipotent God (2000: 180).

The women I met during my fieldwork at the mosque classes or other religious study groups were actively seeking to realize a personal life informed by Islam in all its various aspects. They did not express any desire to challenge male religious authority. On the contrary, as we shall see, they supported it in various ways. This did not mean that they avoided criticizing men, directly or indirectly, about their lack of knowledge about Islam. Men who failed to live up to the position of religious authority granted them by Islam were subject to criticism. Views expressed by men based on what women perceived to be misconceptions of Islam were openly met by arguments taken from the Islamic scriptures. However, this critique was not voiced with the aim of challenging male authority. On the contrary, it was given with the aim of buttressing male authority. Men were supposed to fill the positions of imam (prayer leader, head of the mosque) and *kadi* (judge), as well as of the religious head of the family. Women expected them to do a good job.

In order to develop a life lived in accordance to God's will, the women did call for change, but this change was primarily sought within women themselves and in their relationship with God. Their aim was to develop an active submission to God. However, as they went about this, they also elaborated and modified certain themes of the orthodox model. It is this process that I wish to capture in this book.

The important point that I hope to illustrate is that *women's religious practices as produced within an orthodox model of Islam do not necessarily, or in any simplistic fashion, challenge, oppose or resist, at least not as these terms are usually understood within a Western, feminist discourse.* However, this does not mean that women are passive victims of an Islamization produced somewhere else and by others. In fact, as we shall see, from the point of view of the women in this study, resistance and submission and the dichotomy between them appear as rather irrelevant when applied to the realm of their religious lives.

The aim of this book is thus twofold. With the material presented here I wish to contribute to an understanding of Malay women's agency by showing how they carve out a religious space for themselves in a modernizing Muslim society, thereby strengthening their Islamic identity. I will show how Malay women develop agency within the orthodox Islamic context where male dominance and authority are traditionally emphasized. Through this agency, women construct themselves as religious actors and as religious persons, and by this process transform the practice of Islam in Malaysia. Instead of focusing on the effects of Islamization on women's lives, the present book will account for women's Islamization: their religiosity and their spiritual development.

My second aim is theoretical. While feminist theory has deeply influenced the study of women and religion (King 1995; Gross 1996), the study of women's religious lives has, until very recently, had much less impact on feminist theory. This analysis of pious Muslim women's agency as an active submission to the will of God can contribute to a more nuanced account and reconfigured concept of agency within feminist thought, allowing for an understanding of women's agency in terms other than mere resistance or subjugation.

FIELDWORK

The book is based primarily on material collected during twelve months of anthropological fieldwork conducted in 1995 and 1996. During regular revisits to the field after 1996 until the present, I have also been able to continue data collection and follow up on individual women as well as study groups. However, it is important to say a few words about Malaysia in the mid-1990s, when the major fieldwork was done.

Politically, this was a period when the religious resurgence of the 1970s had already passed its peak and membership in *dakwah* organizations had declined notably. The Malaysian government had successfully implemented its own religious propagation, promoting what it called a 'moderate' version of Islam compared to what they labelled as the dakwah groups' more 'radical' one. The issue of Malaysia turning into an Islamic state had thereby been played down on the political agenda.

It is important to emphasize that the fieldwork predates later events of importance for the development of political Islam in Malaysia, in particular, the sacking of the deputy prime minister, Anwar Ibrahim, in 1998, a former Muslim youth leader whose presence in government strengthened Malaysia's reform-oriented Islamization policies. Anwar was generally (and still is) regarded as a person of great integrity and spirituality, and the accusations of corruption and sodomy directed at him, the extended trial and, later, the sentence of fifteen years in jail, caused discontent among Muslims as well as among non-Muslims. The 'Anwar affair' led to the formation of new political parties, a shifting of support of voters from UMNO (United Malays National Organization) – the Malay-based and dominant party in the coalition government – to the national Islamic party PAS (Parti Islam Se-Malaysia), and a rapidly growing Islamic assertiveness among the Malays. During my fieldwork, however, these events lay in the future and *dakwah* groups considered that they were suffering from a decline in support. When I was taken to religious talks organized by official *dakwah* organizations, my friends would comment that ten years ago the crowds had been much bigger. In Ong's summing up of the beginning of the 1990s:

> The Islamic resurgence of the 1970s, emerging in its black female garb and fiery criticism of Western consumerism, official corruption, and the spiritual hollowness of modern life, had settled down as a normalized cultural practice in which people carried on the daily affairs of life of an affluent, developing country. (1995: 160)

Islamization as a 'normalized cultural practice' comes very close to how I would like to describe the activities of the women in focus of this study. They did not, in general, express any explicit political aims. But, on the other hand, as this book will show, their religious commitment was not limited to a headscarf and the correct performance of the basic religious duties. I found the religious activities among ordinary Malay women in the city of Kuala Lumpur vivid, with their intense focus on individual religious practice and questions about morality and piety.

My position in the field

In her ethnography about Muslims in Bosnia, social anthroplogist Tone Bringa (1995) notes that she was very careful of how she presented her research to the villagers. She explained that she was studying 'Muslim traditions and customs' and she consciously avoided expressions like 'studying Islam' or 'Islamic customs'. The reason was that she had found that the latter prompted many Muslims to give the sharia version of Islamic practices rather than sharing their own interpretations or practices. To most of the villagers, this distinction was not a problem and did not create any confusion. My own experience in this area was rather different.

When I first tried to establish contact with various study groups, there was a negotiation between me and the women about my position and identity connected to the aim of my project, which I presented in terms of a desire to learn about the everyday religious practices of Muslim women. My efforts to convince the women that my research was not theological but rather about 'culture' or 'the Muslim way of life in Malaysia' were more or less rejected. One typical reaction was simply to declare that, if my research was not theological, then it definitely should be: there was no point in doing anything else.[10] Other women perceived my research as 'theological' no matter what I said, regarding it is as equivalent to the work of Islamic scholars.

The background to their reactions lies in a very strong and ongoing process of separating 'culture' from 'religion', in the sense of purifying Islam from Malay cultural elements that were considered 'non-Islamic'. There were frequent, continual and lively discussions about whether a certain custom was Islamic, or not Islamic but non-contradictory to Islam and maybe acceptable, or contradictory to Islam (and thus not acceptable). People seemed to be asking themselves what I was doing in the mosque if I was interested in 'culture'.

It was soon clear that the position offered to me by the women was the one of a potential convert.[11] This was, more or less, the only possible position that was made available to me if I was going to be able to go around asking questions about people's religious practices. It was never suggested that I ought to convert, to actually pronounce the declaration of faith, but I was encouraged to study the Koran and it was hoped that one day I would see the beauty of Islam. This hope provided me with the opportunity to participate in the religious study groups on roughly the same terms as the other women. They were in the process of learning more about Islam, and so was I, in a way. Instead of excluding me on the basis of my identity as a non-Muslim, I was included as a 'not-yet-Muslim'. From this point I could start letting go of my own expectations of what the fieldwork was supposed to be about to one where I could start listening to the expectations that the people I was seeking out had of me. I was, however, explicit about why I participated in the study groups, and I always corrected anyone who assumed that I was there with the intention of converting to Islam.

My first, brief, encounter with one woman at a religious class in a mosque exemplifies this. I introduced myself as usual, saying that I was in Malaysia to research women's involvement in the Islamization process and I explained that I was not a Muslim myself. Her first question was whether I wanted to convert to Islam and I responded that this was not my intention. She paused to reflect on this, then asked if I did the *tafsir* (interpretation of the meaning of Koranic verses) to which I answered yes, I did attend *tafsir* classes where we used an English translation of the Koran. This brightened her up and she said in a more confident voice that she was sure that I would see the truth of it. But then she hesitated and repeated her first question. Did I really not want to convert? She reacted to my negative answer in silence, busying herself with the notebook and pencil on her desk. After a minute, she spoke again and this time it was with renewed confidence. She said that I had not been given the *hidayat* (guidance) from God yet, reassuring me that it would only be a matter of time; once I received God's guidance, I would come to love God, just like all other Muslims.

As the fieldwork proceeded and I became enmeshed in Islamic studies and Koran reading, people were less and less concerned with my religious identity. They were content with the fact that I was anxious to study Islam.

Towards the end of the fieldwork, some women still expressed a desire for me to convert to Islam, but at this point, the desire was no longer attached to a fear of me getting it all wrong, but was instead expressed as something they wanted for me as a friend. In particular, the women I had become closer to during fieldwork wished that I would embrace Islam because they cared for me as a friend and they wanted me to have a life after death.

Although this fieldwork has made a profound impact on me as a person, it has not changed my religious beliefs. The voice with which I write is thus of a non-Muslim. As an anthropologist, my duty is to try and represent the Muslim point of view in this case, but ultimately, it is my voice that you hear.

Fieldwork in Kuala Lumpur: the fieldworker 'on the move'

Kuala Lumpur was founded as a mining camp for Chinese immigrants in the 1840s; by the 1890s the town had become a centre for the British colonial administration as well as a commercial centre for the expanding rubber industry on the west coast of the peninsula. It was made the capital of the Federation of Malaya in 1948 and then the capital of independent Malaysia in 1957. As Kuala Lumpur grew in political importance during the 1950s, the city began to fill with Malay migrants from other states. Over the past 150 years, Kuala Lumpur has been through a dramatic transformation and it is now a modern, multiethnic city of almost a million inhabitants. It is still steadily expanding, both in terms of population[12] and area.

Through its development into the country's economic and political heart and as an important recipient of rural to urban migration, Kuala Lumpur, or KL, as Malaysians prefer to refer to their capital, has played a key function in this transformation. Social anthropologist Eric Thompson describes KL as an ahistorical city – 'the forward looking capital of a forward looking nation' (2000: 24). The nationalist discourse has been distinctly future-oriented, as expressed in former Prime Minister Mahathir Mohamad's vision of Malaysia becoming a fully developed nation by the year 2020. There is an apparent link between this vision of modernity and cityscape changes (Goh 1998). Kuala Lumpur mirrors the futurism of Malaysian nationalism and the city is constantly changing as large new projects spring up when old ones, such as the famous Petronas Twin Towers, are barely finished. In tandem with modernization projects, one of the chief aims of the government has been to Islamize urban space in Malaysia, which is achieved through the construction of a large number of mosques and suraus as well as through the architectural aesthetics of important buildings such as the Twin Towers.

The fieldwork carried out for this book demanded mobility. It entailed moving about much of the time, travelling from one end of town to the other daily. The people that I wished to meet did not come to me. Instead, I had to go to them. I rented a house in one of the middle- to upper-middle-class areas in Kuala Lumpur and I followed the mosque activities and religious gatherings that took place within the community of Malays living there. A lot of the material was also collected during religious classes and gatherings in various parts of Kuala Lumpur and its sprawling metropolitan area, which extends down the Klang River valley through the satellite towns of Petaling Jaya, Subang Jaya and Shah Alam right through to the port of Klang and its hinterland. While most of the classes and study groups that I followed took place in Kuala Lumpur itself, participants did not always live near the mosques or houses where classes were held. Location influenced women's choice of which class to attend as much as other factors such as the popularity of the class, the reputation of the teacher and who the participants were (generally, whether their friends had joined up). Like my own life in the field, the daily lives of the women I studied involved a great deal of commuting between various places and activities: their homes, workplaces, religious classes, visits to relatives and friends, as well shopping. Since participants in the various groups did not necessarily have relationships with each other outside the religious classes, I ended up with a very dispersed network of sorts, with women living in different areas, and with different occupations and family situations. At first I saw only the irregularities. In time though, I realized that my network of contacts were actually more closely connected to each other than I had imagined. As fieldwork progressed, it became increasingly common for me to meet women in a context other than our original place of encounter.

Over time, I came to know some women better than others, and I would spend time with them outside the religious sphere, getting to know their families. The language used with informants was primarily

English. Even though Bahasa Malaysia, or Malay, is the national language, English, the language of the former colonizers, still holds a central place in communication, particularly in the city of Kuala Lumpur. The religious activities of the women also involved Arabic, the language of the Koran, and everyday conversation also contained Arabic phrases or concepts. The majority of women I met had been educated when English was still the medium of instruction in schools, and some had even studied, or lived, in the United Kingdom or other English-speaking countries. Among these women there was a demand for religious classes conducted in English. Such classes were provided primarily by *dakwah* organizations that also tried to attract non-Malay Muslims and converts. Activities in the mosque and in religious classes held in workplaces, in contrast, were held in Malay. My knowledge of Malay was fairly rudimentary, allowing me to follow and engage in simple, everyday conversation. My ability to follow classes in religion in Malay was limited, although my classmates assisted me with translations. Outside the classes, the women themselves preferred to use English with me and my conversations with them were generally in that language.

For the most part I used informal and non-structured forms of interviews. Most women felt uncomfortable with formal interviews and the presence of a tape recorder. Participant observation was by far the most successful method. It should be noted, however, that the women themselves defined the space for participant observation by imposing limits and boundaries. Many women pointed out to me that they were not authorities on Islam, and expressed concern that I would take their understanding of Islam as the Truth. They were still in the process of learning and they were well aware of their limited understanding of Islam. If I would take their words too seriously and those words were not 'correct', not only would it lead me to portray a distorted image of Islam in the West; they would, in the end, be responsible for the misconceptions that I might disseminate. Better then not to say anything and direct me to safer sources such as the scholars at the International Islamic University of Malaysia.

It is important to point out here that religious authorities did not encourage individual interpretation of the Islamic sources. There were regular newspaper reports about cases of religious teachers or groups being accused of 'deviation' from 'True Islam'. Fear of being spied on by religious authorities was evident among the people I met. In everyday conversation about something having to do with religion, it was not uncommon for women to hesitate and ask me to confirm what they had just told me with an authority before taking notes. Another example was a group of women whose study activities took place within the space of the mosque. They had started out independently, as a group of neighbours getting together at each other's homes to read the Koran and learn Arabic. Soon they were meeting on a regular basis and the group was growing. Concerned by how their gatherings could be perceived by religious authorities,[13] the group decided to make public their activities and asked the local mosque if they could use the facilities there instead. They were granted this request.

Here, I defer to Malaysian religious sensitivities by using identity-concealing techniques. Although the women whose lives are presented and discussed here did not practise Islam in a politically controversial way, most of them wished to remain anonymous. All names in the text are therefore pseudonyms. In addition to this, since I find a change of name an inadequate means of concealing someone's identity, I have avoided giving too detailed information about the women who appear in the text. Even in the more in-depth case studies, I have tried to make individuals unrecognizable by altering aspects of their backgrounds and families. This also means occasional changes in environment and context. I have, however, been careful not to change things that have a direct bearing on the analysis that I develop.

OUTLINE OF THE BOOK

The next chapter provides an introduction to the development of Islamization in Malaysia with a focus on the religious reform movement – the *dakwah* movement. This chapter forms a background to Chapters 3, 4and 5, which describe the religious activities and discussions of the women in this study.

Chapter 3 shows urban Malay women appropriating mosques for the purpose of studying, teaching and debating Islamic scriptures. I also describe how women come together in study groups outside the home, in the workplace or within *dakwah* organizations. The aim is to show how the study of the scriptures forms a central part in women's increasing commitment to Islam.

Chapter 4 is organized along Islam's five pillars and focuses on the meaning that women attribute to their religious duties. I argue that it is important to know about these duties in general, and about prayer in particular, in order to understand the creative aspects of submission.

Chapter 5 focuses on issues and discussions that surfaced within the religious study groups. Daily religious practices and duties and bodily comportment were discussed and negotiated from the desire to create a strong relationship with God, to achieve a life lived in accordance with God's will. Chapter 5 also describes women's hosting of collective rituals, often performed exclusively by and for women. Women have thus taken on the religious authority necessary for the performance of these rituals. This is a relatively new, urban phenomenon. In the Malaysian case, collective rituals are still performed in homes, but women are now performing them independently of men. I argue that these rituals have been 'Islamized' and participants are now drawn from both the mosque and kin networks.

Chapter 6 shows some of consequences that women's acquired knowledge about Islam have on gender relations. When women assume the identity of *mukmin*, that is, of a pious person, they emphasize the equal responsibility of men and women towards God. I argue that women, through the Islamic discourse on piety, are able to negotiate and transform gender relations and actively shape their lives in correspondence to ideals found in orthodox Islam.

The last chapter summarizes the main arguments in the book and concludes with a discussion on the relationship between feminist theory and anthropology with reference to the question of the agency of pious Muslim women.

NOTES

1   The development of, and different forms taken by, contemporary Malaysian Islamization will be treated more extensively in Chapter 2. It should, however, be noted here that the *dakwah* movement has been largely understood as an ethnic response to economic, political, social and cultural changes.

See, for example, K. S. Jomo and Ahmad Shabery Cheek (1992), Chandra Muzaffar (1986) and Judith Nagata (1984). Nagata (1984) and Chandra (1987) have convincingly analysed the Islamic resurgence of the 1970s as a way of redrawing the blurred ethnic boundaries between Malays and non-Malays caused by the New Economic Policy, in terms of industrialization, migration and modernization.

2   A list of relevant references would be very long. I have to mention *Unspoken Worlds: Women's Religious Lives in Non-Western Cultures* (Falk and Gross 1980) as well as no. 13–14 of the journal *Études Orientales* (1994). Susan Sered's 1992 discussion is an important one. Within anthropology, there are many – Abu-Lughod (1993), Mazumdar and Mazumdar (1999), Gemzöe (2000), Allès (2000), Raudvere (2002) and Falk (2008) – just to mention a few. The first volume of the *Encyclopedia of Women in Islamic Societies*, edited by Suad Joseph (2003) is also an important compilation of articles on women's religious activities.

3   These dichotomies, derived from Robert Redfield's (1956) distinction between Great and Little traditions, have been used as analytical tools in the anthropology of Islam when dealing with Islam as a universal religion with certain elements shared by all Muslims and practised in particular local settings. There are various ways of expressing the dichotomy, but the content of the distinction remains the same. One type of Islam, the true faith, scriptural, normative, formal, official Islam, is set off from popular, alternative, folk, rural or informal Islam (Holy 1991). The list of dichotomies used could be made longer, but the relationship between the two is always the same. In Robert Launay's words it is a means to '...distinguish between constant and variable components of Islamic beliefs and practices in different communities. Constant components would constitute the essential 'core' of Islam, whereas variable features could be explained in terms of local social and cultural peculiarities' (1992: 6).

4   See, for example, Nagata (1994), Aihwa Ong (1995), Shamsul Amri Baharuddin (1994), Maila Stivens (1998) and Norani Othman (1998) for explorations of the relationship between the state and the *dakwah* movement with respect to discourses on women, modernity and Islam.

5   See feminist philosopher Susan Hekman (1991) for a more extensive discussion on the feminist critique of the constituting subject.

6   Foucault says: '...in the way in which the subject constitutes himself in an active fashion, by the practice of the self, these practices are nevertheless not something that the individual invents by himself. They are patterns that he finds in his culture and which are proposed, suggested and imposed in him by his culture, his society and his social group' (1985: 154).

7   Foucault (1985) shows us that the relationship between codes of behaviour and forms of 'subjectivization', that is how individuals come to understand themselves as subjects, varies from era to era and he carefully reminds the

reader that ancient Greek ethics cannot be transported into contemporary society as a blueprint for behaviour in any simple way. In classical Greek thought, the relationship between a system of laws and an individual's actual ethical behaviour is very flexible. Individuals appear to have been relatively free to interpret the norms of behaviour in their own style, rather than conform exactly to these norms.

8   Judith Butler's *The Psychic life of Power* (1997) also addresses this problem in Foucault's work.

9   See Sarah Coakly (2002) for a related discussion on the Christian concept of vulnerability within feminist theology.

10   I think that this comment was as much directed to me as a person – meaning that if I did take a theological interest, then I would see the Truth – as to me as an anthropologist, in the sense that no other research about Islam was of value.

11   Catharina Raudvere (2002) writes about a similar experience as a non-Muslim researcher during her fieldwork among Sufi women in Istanbul. In her case, as in mine, informants tended to downplay the analytical purpose of the study and instead anticipated conversion.

12   Migration from the countryside to the city (and in particular to the capital) is itself a radical transformative process. Eric Thompson (2000) has explored the evolving relationship evolving between one rural village and Kuala Lumpur.

13   Among other things, Malaysia's Internal Security Act 1960 (ISA) makes it illegal to hold, without a permit, public gatherings of five or more persons, and gives the police power to arrest and detain such persons without trial.

2

Islamization in Malaysia

In the opening lines of a speech delivered at UMNO's 55th General Assembly in Kuala Lumpur, on 23–25 September 2004, Malaysian Prime Minister Abdullah Badawi made a comment on UMNO's victory in the 2004 elections:

> The success of the United Malays National Organization (UMNO) is a victory for moderation. It is the success of a struggle that gives priority to development and a realization that Muslims must become a progressive and forward-looking people. Muslims must achieve success in this world and, at the same time, equip themselves to face the Hereafter. UMNO has now proven to the world the success of a progressive approach to Islam. UMNO must therefore enhance its understanding of the concept of development that we propagate through *Islam Hadhari* (Civilizational Islam). (Abdullah 2006: 1)

Islam Hadhari undoubtedly represents Abdullah Badawi's attempt to conceptualize ideas and visions developed by his predecessor Mahathir Mohammad, Malaysia's leader for more than two decades, rather than a radically new idea on the political role of Islam in Malaysia.[1] It could also, possibly, be seen as an attempt by Abdullah Badawi to clarify the contours of his own leadership in relation to that of his predecessor. What is more interesting here is the manner in which the assumed equation made between the concepts 'Malay' and 'Muslim' is taken for granted, as is the more explicit role for Malays/Muslims to take up in the nation's development. The way that ethnic identity and religious affiliation are linked to each other in the form of a 'metonymic singularization of the Malays and Muslims' (Willford

Figure 2.1. Outside the National Mosque in Kuala Lumpur

2006) in political discourse is also at the heart of the history of Islamization and modernization in Malaysia. It is this history that this chapter aims to sketch.

MALAYSIA: A PLURAL SOCIETY

Malaysia has come to be associated with ethnic conflict and tension, in particular between the Malays and Chinese. Ethnicity has played a key role in social, religious and political developments since independence and has been the focus of scholarly attention (Nagata 1984; Chandra 1987; Ackerman and Lee 1988; Kahn and Loh 1992).

Nonetheless, with four major ethnic groups, none of them in an absolute majority, Malaysia is often said to be a truly plural society. It is multiethnic, multilingual and multireligious. The significant categories used in population censuses and in legislation as well as in everyday usage are 'Malay', 'Chinese', 'Indian' and 'Other'. These categories are used to define a person's ethnic identity, or 'race' at birth, and coded into his or her identity card, and referred to throughout life. Children are consequently obliged to indicate their 'race' when taking examinations – success in receiving a scholarship for higher education or even employment after school may be dependent on ethnic identity, since ethnicity is politically and administratively deployed to meet official quotas of various kinds.

The Malays, who make up 50.8 per cent of the population, are the largest single ethnic group. Of the remainder, the Chinese form the second largest group, with 26.3 per cent of the population, and Indians represent a significant minority at 7.4 per cent. Last, but not least, 15.5 per cent of the population is categorized as 'Other' – including all the numerous groups of original inhabitants/indigenous people (Orang Asli) of peninsular and East Malaysia, and Eurasians and Europeans.[2]

According to these figures, Malays form the largest group, but their numerical majority is evened out slightly when the group of Malays/Muslims is contrasted to non-Malays as a group. The Malays have been Muslim since the fifteenth century and they belong to the Sunni branch of Islam, following the Shafi'i school of Islamic law. Islam became the official religion at independence in 1957. At this official level, Islam has a unifying function amongst the Malays,[3] although, as we shall see later, the development of the *dakwah* movement has created fissures in the community. Among the non-Malays, there is a relatively loose relationship between religion and ethnicity. The Chinese are typically Buddhist-Taoists and the Indians are Hindus, but many among the non-Muslims are followers of various Christian denominations and new religious movements.[4] Freedom of worship is guaranteed in the constitution, although, in reality, Muslims are prevented from attending non-Muslim religious gatherings and ceremonies, whereas non-Muslims are welcome to join Muslim activities.

MALAY NATIONALISM, THE CREATION OF A MALAY BANGSA

Malay identity, in Malaysia, is a politicized and contested arena where the relative emphases on religion, adat or language as defining elements have shifted over time. The idea of Malayness as a 'race' or 'ethnic identity' was largely created by various actors during the colonial era.

Ethnicity – a colonial construct

It was during the period of colonial governance that 'Malay', 'Chinese' and 'Indian' emerged as officially sanctioned ethnic categories. The historian Charles Hirschman (1987) argues that the racial ideology of today's Malaysia was, in fact, created with the help of the British colonial administration, which introduced European concepts of 'race' via the population census.[5] Put differently, the concept of 'race' was a break with the way people living on the peninsula had categorized themselves historically: before the colonial era, people distinguished themselves on the basis of religion, language or customs.

The census-constructed ethnic categories became the basis for a host of legal codes and enactments introduced by the colonial government (Shamsul 1998). These ethnic categories consequently became an idiom of both official and everyday discourse. Historians have shown how Malays themselves were agents in the invention of a particular 'Malayness' in relation to the other ethnic identities. Adrian Vickers (2004) argues that while the colonial invention of Malay identity was, at one level, negotiated between native rulers and Europeans in power, this construct could not have had such a huge impact without the co-option and consent of people at various levels. Anthony Milner (1998), analysing texts by Malay ideologues during the colonial era, similarly finds that they were not slow to adopt British concepts of race. Other social affiliations, such as being followers of individual royal houses or the wider Muslim *ummah* (community) were played down in favour of the Malay *bangsa* (race, nation). Milner shows that this trend was further strengthened in the beginning of the twentieth century as Chinese and Indian immigrants arrived en masse to work in tin mines, on oil-palm plantations and in the colonial civil service. Malay writers began to talk about this Asian immigration, particularly the large inflow of Chinese,[6] as a challenge to the existence of the Malay *bangsa*, which was therefore in need of strengthening.

Emergence of Malay dominance

At independence in 1957, the four categories of 'Malay', 'Chinese', 'Indian' and 'Other' continued to be used in official, political and social interaction at all levels. Ethnicity was, from the beginning, an organizing factor in politics, and the first national government consisted of a coalition of three ethnic-based parties – UMNO, the Malayan Chinese Association (MCA), and the Malayan Indian Congress (MIC) – together forming the Alliance. The Malay-based UMNO was the dominant party in the coalition government and has held that position ever since. Indeed, as reflected in the quote by Abdullah Badawi, UMNO has historically played, and still plays, a major role in the very constitution of Malays as an ethnic group, and in the consolidation of the Malay/non-Malay divide.

The national constitution, adopted after a long debate leading up to independence, defined a Malay as a 'person who professes the Muslim religion, habitually speaks Malay, conforms to Malay customs' (Mohamad Suffian 1972: 247, cited in Milner 1998: 162).[7] In addition, while Malaysian citizenship is not based on ethnicity, Malays were granted special constitutional rights and privileges (Shamsul 1998: 141). Malay dominance was, for example, articulated in government policies relating to economic development. Since the early days of independence, Malaysia has focused on achieving development through economic planning. In response to the World Bank's recommendations and to powerful Malaysian Chinese and foreign business interests, the colonial policies of liberal capitalism coupled with monetary and fiscal conservatism were continued. At the same time, the Alliance, the ruling coalition dominated by UMNO, saw a need to start rural development programmes. UMNO hoped to win the political support of Malays who lived outside the towns and cities by stimulating the rural economy. Despite these efforts, the majority of Malays remained economically backward peasants; control of the country's economy was still very much in the hands of Malaysian Chinese and foreigners (Shamsul 1998: 144). At the same time, unemployment rose (mainly among non-Malays) following independence, due partly to the fall in rubber prices and slow economic growth. A concrete result of this was a lack of support for the ruling Alliance in the 1969 national elections, something that caused celebration amongst the Chinese in the aftermath of the voting. The antagonism between Malays and Chinese turned violent in a watershed event known as 'May 13', when hundreds of people, mostly Chinese, were killed in confrontations with Malays in the streets of Kuala Lumpur. The dramatic events were seen as a breakdown of national unity. The underlying causes were believed to be, among the Malays, the culmination of frustration with their economic situation and, within the Chinese community, the decline in tolerance towards the special rights given to Malays. The May 13 riots triggered two important reactions. One was a political response in the form of the introduction of the New Economic Policy (NEP) in 1971, and the other was the birth of the modern Islamic revivalist movement, the *dakwah* movement.

The NEP

The NEP was the political response to the May 13 riots. Increased unemployment in the period between independence and the 1970s had been identified as one of the reasons for the violence between Malays and Chinese. The Second Malaysia Plan (1971–1975) had two important goals. The first was to reduce and eventually eliminate poverty for all Malaysians, regardless of ethnic identity. The second was to reduce and eventually eliminate the economic imbalances between the ethnic groups. Average Malay family incomes were at this point half of that of the non-Malays. This had to change without the non-Malays being deprived of anything. Economic growth was singled out as the most important means of achieving the NEP's goals. The NEP was, in its basic motives and strategies, a continuation of the ethnic policies first introduced by the colonial government and later expanded upon by the Malaysian state (Shamsul 1998).

The traditional employment of Malays was in the agricultural sector, and the Chinese in the manufacturing and commercial sectors. One of the NEP's targets was to move Malays from agricultural employment into manufacturing and commerce. The numbers of Chinese and Indians in these sectors were not to decrease, only their proportion in relation to Malays. Major efforts were therefore made to create opportunities for paid employment in the urban centres. One important outcome of the NEP was the establishment of Free Trade Zones to attract foreign companies to set up manufacturing operations in the country. This kind of state-intervened industrialization resulted in the dramatic economic growth that gave Malaysia the epithet 'one of the Asian mini-Tigers'.[8] The average growth rate in 1970–1990 was 6.5 per cent and later over 8 per cent in 1990–1995.[9] Unemployment has been very low, and the country continues to experience labour shortages, which is one reason for the large-scale labour immigration from Indonesia and Bangladesh in particular, in sectors such as the construction industry and domestic work (in affluent urban homes). Along with this has come illegal immigration.

The NEP did not rest at employment strategies. The overall aim was that the bumiputra (literally, sons of the soil, and a category virtually synonymous with Malay), within a period of one generation '... would own and manage at least 30 per cent of all commercial and industrial activities of the economy in all categories and scales of operation' (Milne and Mauzy 1999: 52).[10] This was to be achieved by increasing the numbers of Malay managers and entrepreneurs, which called for better training facilities. Financial organizations such as MARA (Majlis Amanah Rakyat) and Bank Bumiputra gave advice and financial help. The Malaysian social anthropologist Shamsul Amri Baharuddin (1986) notes that such measures resulted in some growth of Malay rural entrepreneurship from the early 1980s and onwards. But the real boom of Malay entrepreneurs has taken place in the urban areas. For example, the ferocious construction of housing areas and office buildings in and around Kuala Lumpur, particularly throughout the Klang Valley, has motivated Malays to become entrepreneurs in large numbers. The bumiputra share of corporate wealth increased from 2.4 per cent in 1970 to 19.3 per cent in 1990 (Gomez 2002: 84).[11]

Another important means of helping Malays out of poverty was through education. One way was to raise the intake of Malay students at local universities as well as to send large numbers of students for further studies abroad. Many Malay students sponsored to study at foreign universities, for example, in the United Kingdom and United States, became more devout. The Singaporean political scientist Hussin Mutalib (1994) suggests that this was a reaction grounded in a kind of culture shock. Most of these sponsored students had been brought up in a rural setting, and had difficulties in dealing with a Western lifestyle. Hussin emphasizes the sense of alienation and anomie experienced by these students. Many of these students started to view Malay society itself as 'un-Islamic' and they feared the 'ills' of Western life developing in Malaysia. Upon their return to Malaysia, many became supporters of the emerging *dakwah* movement. A substantial number of students were also sent to Islamic educational centres such as

Medina, Islamabad or Cairo. There they were inspired by a version of Islam that differed from the one they had grown up with. These students also became involved in *dakwah* activities when they returned to Malaysia.

Vision 2020

In 1981, Mahathir Mohamad became Malaysia's prime minister and would stay in office for the next two decades. Ten years later, in 1991, he proclaimed that Malaysia was to become an industrialized, modernized and fully developed country by the year 2020 – 'Vision 2020'. The Malaysian political scientist Khoo Boo Teik describes Mahathir's development programme as a '… nationalist project driven by capitalist impulses or a capitalist project imbued with nationalist aspirations' (2003: 5). Vision 2020 and its implementation has earned Mahathir the description of 'the man who set Malaysia on the world map' or labels such as *Bapa Pembangunan* (father of development) (Khoo 2003: 2). Mahathir's articulation of Vision 2020 was a departure from the old concerns of NEP. The goal of national unity that had informed the NEP had been more or less achieved, and Mahathir envisioned structural transformation from Malaysia's '…previous dependence on primary commodity production to having an industrialized economy that could advance towards post-industrial conditions' (Khoo 2003: 21).

The new middle class

State-led modernization and industrialization since the 1970s, and later Mahathir's liberalization and privatization project, have created a whole new layer of successful Malay entrepreneurs, capitalists who are part of an affluent middle class (the so-called *Melayu Baru* or the New Malay[12]) within a rapidly urbanizing country.[13]

The Malaysian sociologist Abdul Rahman Embong (2001) lists a number of salient characteristics of the 'new', expanding Malay middle class. His approach to the concept of 'middle class' is occupational: those who form the new middle class are salaried professionals along with managerial and administrative employees. The 'new' middle class is here defined in relation to the 'old' middle class, consisting of those who have some capital and may or may not have control over labour, and the 'marginal' middle class, made up of lower level white collar employees. Here I am more concerned with the group that Abdul Rahman (2001) defines as the 'new' middle class, as most of the women who are the subjects of this book could be placed in that category.

Abdul Rahman describes this middle class as new because those who are part of it are a first generation and it is thus characterized by upward social mobility, achieved largely through state-sponsored higher education. Credit and loans are a necessary supplement to their salaried income to keep up their highly consumerist lifestyle. The middle class gives priority to, among other things, comfortable housing and cars, computers, handphones, foreign holidays and leisure. Typically, the middle class owns their homes – double-storey linked or terrace houses, apartments and even bungalows.

At the time of my fieldwork in 1995–1996, Malaysia was still riding a wave of economic prosperity and the recession of 1997 lay ahead. There was a relaxation of the ethnic quotas hitherto applied in business and education, there was less overt ethnic tension than ten years before, and the government talked about the importance of creating a '*bangsa* Malaysia', a national identity of Malaysians embracing all ethnic groups. The idea of Malaysians being 'one big family' was enhanced in a slogan that the deputy prime minister of the time, Anwar Ibrahim, launched in Mandarin (*wo wee yi jia ren*).[14] In spite of the political rhetoric, Malaysia was still a society very much divided and organized along ethnic/religious lines, and ethnic boundaries still informed many aspects of everyday life in Kuala Lumpur. In the city and its constantly growing suburbs there was, for example, quite a clear tendency towards ethnically segregated living areas. There were entire neighbourhoods with predominantly Chinese inhabitants, and others with a majority of Malay families. People took the ethnic composition of a neighbourhood into serious consideration whenever they looked for a new house. This was also reflected in the composition of local shopkeepers and restaurants.

The economic crisis of 1997–1998

Speculative attacks on the Thai baht and other Asian currencies in 1997 precipitated economic collapses in Thailand, Indonesia, South Korea and Malaysia. The economic crisis hit all levels of Malaysian society, albeit differently. Abdul Rahman (2001) argued that the working class were the worst affected by the crisis. In a survey conducted in the Klang Valley in 1999, 14.8 per cent of the working-class respondents stated that they had lost their jobs, while middle-class respondents were more secure in comparison. The crisis did not diminish the size of the middle class significantly, but higher interest rates meant that some had to sell cars and houses; credit cards became a burden.

The economic crisis posed a threat to Malaysia's political leadership. Prime Minister Mahathir Mohamad responded on the international front by attacking globalization, and in particular the financial speculators who freely moved capital across borders. The crisis also spurred him to formulate plans for a K-economy or 'knowledge economy' (ibid. 2001) that could deal with globalization and liberalization. On the domestic front, the economic crisis turned political as Mahathir turned on his deputy, Anwar Ibrahim, and accused him of bowing down before foreign interests and organizations such as the International Monetary Fund (ibid.).[15] In September 1998, Anwar was arrested on charges of corruption and sodomy. He was sentenced to six years of prison in 1999 and later to another nine in 2000.

Anwar's political fall and imprisonment gave rise to the *Reformasi* (reformation) movement formed by individuals, opposition parties and non-governmental organizations (NGOs) in support of Anwar in particular and civil rights in general. One outcome of *Reformasi* was the birth of Parti KeADILan Nasional (KeADILan, National Justice Party), headed by Anwar's wife Wan Azizah.[16] KeADILan led the fight to free Anwar, took a stance against Mahathir's autocratic leadership style, and had democracy, transparency, civil rights and anti-corruption on its agenda. In the 1999 elections, many Malays left UMNO and instead voted for candidates from opposition parties such as PAS and KeADILan which, together with Democratic Action Party (DAP) and Parti Rakyat Malaysia, formed Barisan Alternatif (Alternative Front). UMNO's and Mahathir's setbacks were, however, short-lived. In 2000, the economy recovered significantly, with an annual growth rate of 8.5 per cent. By 2001, Mahathir had consolidated his position as Malaysia's leader and UMNO gained back some of the constituencies it had lost in 1999 (Martinez 2002). It was during this period of relative political and economic stability that Mahathir prepared to retire and hand over the leadership of UMNO, along with the premiership of the country, to his chosen successor Abdullah Badawi.

ISLAM, ADAT AND THE MALAYS

Islam has a long history in the Malay Peninsula and the early Islamic influences were varied. Muslim traders had been travelling through the region since the ninth century and in the fifteenth century, Islam started to spread to the local population. The earliest propagators of Islam in the peninsula are believed to have been Indian Muslims. This influence can be seen linguistically in the frequency of Sanskrit terms (instead of Arabic) used for religious notions such as *puasa* for fasting, *neraka* for hell and *syurga* for heaven (Mohd Taib 1989: 39). Along with Indian Muslims, however, there was also a strong, early Persian and Arab influence. Malaysian scholar Mohd Taib Osman has suggested that Muslims from India and Persia were responsible for the spread of pantheistic mysticism and other popular elements of Islam[17] whereas the Arabs brought more orthodox teachings to the Malays.

As a social, legal and conceptual system, Islam became highly integrated with its local counterpart, Malay adat (customary law, tradition). Over time, the two systems developed a relationship that at times is characterized by complementarity, and at others, by tension. Adat, of course, is a concept that exists throughout the Muslim world. It is an Arabic word, which generally refers to '...the total constellation of concepts, rules and codes of behaviour which are conceived as legitimate or right, appropriate or necessary' (Wazir 1992: 14). Adat, obviously, shows a high degree of variation in concept and interpretation over the Muslim world. For example, Malay adat holds a quite different set of ideas concerning gender than adat in the Arab-Muslim world. Indeed, Muslim societies in Southeast Asia have provided interesting material in this regard, since the gender segregation and male dominance characteristic of many other Muslim societies have not been as accentuated here.[18] An important feature of the relationship between Islam and adat, in general, is that it is historically dynamic with local variations.[19]

Within the Malay context, adat also shows variations. There are, for example, two kinship systems: the bilateral form of organization (adat *temenggong*), which dominates the Malay Peninsula, and the matrilineal one (adat *perpatih*). Although the matrilineal system has weakened over time (Peletz 1992), the coming of Islam and its patrilineal kinship system did not displace the bilateral component of Malay society. Bilateral features continue to form the fabric of Malay kinship, family and community relations (Wazir 1992).

In *Women and Culture: Between Malay* Adat *and Islam* (1992), Malaysian social anthropologist Wazir Jahan Karim explains that the foundation for the relatively equal relationship between Malay men and women is found in the bilateral norm in Malay adat, which exists parallel and intertwined with the Islamic system of ideas and laws. Hierarchical differences based on gender emphasized by Islam are reduced by the bilateral norm in adat. Wazir argues that

> ... the Malay ego-centred kindred system of patterning relationships underplays many modes of gender differentiation which are expressed in other Muslim communities maintained by institutions of patriliny-sexual segregation, marriage alliances, male authority and leadership, female domesticity and male-initiated divorce. (1992: 5)

In cases of the distribution and division of land and property, for instance, adat and Islamic law are seen as alternative choices and men and women are often given equal opportunities to inherit property. Other forms of hierarchy such as age, seniority and class are also recognized by adat but are simultaneously balanced out or reduced through central values of generosity, generalized reciprocity, cooperation and sharing.

Wazir further shows that the complementarity of Malay adat and Islam, in areas other than gender, dominated the precolonial Malay states. Islam was adopted as a formal political ideology, while fundamental institutions of adat guided people's day-to-day relationships. Islam thus never ruled out adat, but instead used the pre-existing system of social relations to gain legitimacy.

Furthermore, the general view is that the early phase of Islam in the region was characterized by tolerance and a tendency toward syncretism with existing beliefs. Thus, for instance, the introduction of Islamic monotheism did not mean a total displacement of indigenous animist notions of the supernatural, or ways of dealing with it.[20] Animistic notions were instead easily reinterpreted in terms of popular Islamic ideas.

The complementary relationship between Malay adat and Islam has, however, been challenged by historical and political changes. The syncretic relationship between religion and folk belief, for example, was attacked in the middle of the eighteenth century when the Wahhabi reform movement spread from the Arab world to the Indonesian archipelago (Mohd. Taib 1985). The Wahhabis propagated a return to a strict monotheism and a purification of religious practices and beliefs from pre-Islamic times. Islam in Malaysia has been influenced considerably by Wahhabism.

The tension between adat and Islam in Malaysia will run as a central theme throughout the material presented in this book. This chapter provides a brief overview of Malay Islamic reform movements and their development since the beginning of the twentieth century, with a focus on gender. In particular, I shall look at male and female roles in these movements and what kinds of discourses about gender have been developed through Islamization. The first part will deal with religious reform during the colonial period up to independence in 1957; the second part deals more explicitly with the *dakwah* movement of the 1970s, and the role it has played in the process of Islamization in Malaysia.

ISLAMIC REFORM IN COLONIAL TIMES:
THE KAUM MUDA MOVEMENT

The history of modern Malay Islamic reform is closely connected to the colonial history of the Malay Peninsula. As the British colonial power established itself on the peninsula in the second half of the nineteenth century, it followed a general principle of non-interference in religious affairs.[21] Still, it had deep effects on Islam in Malaya. The colonial rule has, in fact, been pointed out as one of the two major factors contributing to the emergence of the religious reform movement in the early decades of the twentieth century – Kaum Muda (Roff 1994; Mohd. Taib 1989; Sharifah Zaleha 1990). Kaum Muda means 'the young group' in Malay and this group was also referred to as 'modernists'. Kaum Muda is used in opposition to 'the old group', or the 'traditionalists' – Kaum Tua.

Kaum Muda

In his book *The Origins of Malay Nationalism* (1994), the historian William R. Roff provides an analysis of the relationship between colonial rule and the emergence of Kaum Muda. He argues that British policy contained an implicit preservation and reinforcement of the traditional bases of local authority and social organization. The colonial ideology of 'development' meant that the existing administrative and political systems were modified by the introduction of bureaucracy, which included the state council instead of sultan being recognized as the highest authority (Sharifah Zaleha 1990). The British also introduced a civil and criminal law system that was to regulate all departments of life except those regarding Malay religion and custom. As a consequence, the local rulers and traditional elite found themselves stripped of any real power to influence politics in their states and they took the opportunity to seize the only field left open to them – religion and custom (Roff 1994). By the second decade of the Twentieth century, most Malayan states had developed some kind of central organization which exercized overall control of religious matters and a more formal system of Islamic law was introduced. The tasks of the Councils of Religion and Custom in the various states were varied and far-reaching. Roff gives examples such as the appointment of the *kadi*, the certification of religious teachers, the consideration of points of Islamic law and practice, the appealing of cases from the lower courts, and the supervision and approval of religious publications.[22] He points out that few of the measures taken were really new, since a religious system of law to some extent had been practised ever since the arrival of Islam. What Roff sees as new, and a result of British policy, was the systematic application of Islamic law and the organization that lay behind it.

Besides British policy in Malaya, Malaysian social anthropologist, Sharifah Zaleha binte Syed Hassan (1990) emphasizes the intensified contact between Malays and Arabs in the Middle East as a major factor paving the way for Kaum Muda. In her work on the bureaucratization of Islam in Kedah, she notes the importance of the development of transport links, and thus increased trade, between the two regions. It also meant that the pilgrimage to Mecca (hajj) was more easily accomplished, and by more people. Most importantly for the Islamic reform movement, however, was the strengthening of collegial ties between local religious schools and their Middle Eastern counterparts during this period. These religious scholars (ulama) returned to Malaya with notions of reform: they were critical of the syncretism of Malay religious life and propagated a greater consciousness about *sharia* law.

Purification of Islam

In their quest to purify Islam, the Kaum Muda reformers focused on areas of law and Malay rituals where Islamic scriptures and adat were in obvious conflict with one another. The *bomoh*, the ritual specialist whose powers derive from a knowledge of spirits, demons and Hindu deities, was, for example, strongly criticized by Islamic reformers. *Ilmu hitam*, black magic or knowledge, was defined as non-Islamic and wrong by Kaum Muda. Magical practices were expunged from state ritual in Perak in 1885 (Mohd Taib 1989). However, belief in supernatural beings, sorcery and witchcraft continued to be essential features of Malay life. Wazir (1992) notes that the pressure from local religious authorities in the 1970s further compelled various states to gradually prohibit animistic community rituals. However, animistic practices on the personal level were performed as before in spite of this policy. In need of help, people continued to relate to *pawang* and *bomoh* as authorities. *Bomoh*s responded to these attacks from religious and local leaders by recasting their knowledge and practices in Islamic terms. Some developed and specialized in *ilmu putih*, white magic or knowledge, in which only spells that did not contradict Islam were used. Verses from the Koran were added to spells, making them useful as a defence both against Islamic and non-Islamic evil forces (Mohd Taib 1989: 140).

Challenging traditional authorities

Formal education in precolonial Malay society had been almost exclusively in the hands of village religious teachers (*ustaz* for male and *ustazah* for female) or the village ulama. Lessons were conducted in homes or at the village prayer hall (*surau*) and sometimes in the larger *pondok* schools. The *pondok* was a form of religious boarding school established by an ulama who then assumed the role of principal teacher. Village teachers and ulama were often those who had performed the hajj, which gave them added status and authority. Nonetheless, according to Roff, '… very few could claim more than the most rudimentary and dogmatic knowledge of Islam, clouded in the haze of traditional Malay spiritual beliefs' (1994: 85). These teachers, he wrote, could do no better than to teach, '… uncomprehending recitation of the Kuran, some elementary exegesis of the Kuran and the *hadith*, and Malay-Muslim ethical and behavioral precepts' (ibid.: 84).

Roff also reminds us that, for the vast majority of rural Malay, the village ulama was the transmittor of the faith, as well as a person who was also of great cultural importance. The ulama was not only imam of the mosque and chief religious functionary at all important junctures of life – birth, circumcision, marriage and death – and at the *kenduri* held to mark each of these special occasions, he was also the companion of the *bomoh* during the villagers' physical and spiritual crises. Thus, the ulama's authority reached far beyond the realms of religion.

Kaum Muda's criticisms of local Islam were at the same time a challenge to the basis of customary authority and to the traditional elite involved with the religious hierarchy. This was an important issue in the conflict between Kaum Muda and the Kaum Tua. Reformers criticized Kaum Tua for giving more authority to the ulama than to the Koran and the Hadith, held as sole authorities by Kaum Muda. The idea that each person must use his own reason (*akal*) to determine the truth in religious, or worldly, matters was at the bottom of Kaum Muda's rejection of the blind acceptance of intermediary authority prevailing in Malay religiosity.

The reformed school system and its gender implications

The perfection and purification of Islam advocated by Kaum Muda was not simply an end in itself. Embedded in their ideas of religious reform was a social vision of an improved Malay society. Reformers held that such social change was retarded by traditional Islam as it was practised in the Malay states and a reformulation of Islam was seen as a possible response to the economic and social changes that Malaya was facing at the time. Kaum Muda propagators '… proposed rationalized reformulations of Islamic practice which would better enable them and their coreligionists to compete in the modern world' (Roff 1994: 78). One such example was their support for Malay women to have better access to education.

The fundamental idea that each individual can, and must, use his reason to determine the truth about religion or other matters placed education high on the reformers' agenda. In traditional Malay society, however, it was much easier for young men to fulfil their obligation to acquire knowledge than it was for women, since the *pondok* schools were boarding schools and it was not customary for young unmarried women to live outside their homes on their own. According to Sharifah Zaleha Syed Hassan (1995a), very few women went through the *pondok* schools. Those who did could later return to the villages and become village teachers (*ustazah*). Thus Kaum Muda introduced a reformed school system – the *madrasah* – based on a secular Western model, as an alternative to the traditional *pondok* schools.[23]

The *madrasah* offered both secular and religious subjects. What was radically new was not only the *madrasah*'s emphasis on secular subjects parallel to religious studies, but also that they actively welcomed female students. The idea of including women when talking about man's duty to use his *akal* to gain religious knowledge was a radical departure from established Malay religious thinking, where women had never been associated with intellectual endeavour. Sharifah Zaleha points out that the introduction of Islam to the Malays in the fifteenth century generated two mutually contradictory views about women. The first was that there is equality between the sexes: piety, not gender, determines one's status as a Muslim. Women and men are thought to possess the same rights and opportunities to attain salvation. Each individual is responsible for his or her own fate in this world and the next, and for his or her good and bad deeds. The second view, however, stresses that women and men differ physically, emotionally and psychologically. Women can be described as weak, with a psychological constitution that renders them more emotional and less rational than men in dealing with problems in life. Sharifah Zaleha says:

> On the one hand, the religion advocated ideas concerning equality of the sexes; on the other, it stressed the obvious differences between them. Both messages induced a certain consciousness in the Malays, which in turn influenced the structure of gender relations. The Islamic contention

> concerning the genetic differences between the sexes had a close affinity with prevailing beliefs and assumptions regarding women; it was instrumental in ensuring continuity rather than bringing about a sudden break with existing tradition which preferred that women be regarded as secondary to men. (Sharifah Zaleha Syed Hassan 1995a: 61–62)

Hence, the reformers were hoping to modify prevailing perceptions and ideas about women by making education more accessible to them, but the Kaum Muda's promotion of the view that *akal* was an element common to both sexes was not widely adopted. Moves to provide for women's education, however, did begin in the first half of the twentieth century. Some ulama, for example, set up religious schools exclusively for girls, while new schools were established for boys and girls by the colonial government and various Christian missions. In the late 1950s, there was a tremendous increase in the number of Malay girls attending these schools.

Sharifah Zaleha's conclusion is that Malay women, in the first part of the twentieth century, reached a certain degree of liberation through education and employment and that this posed a challenge to established norms. It also provided the religious elites with an opportunity to reach the ideal of an egalitarian society that is central to Islamic thinking. But neither the first wave of religious reform nor the more recent *dakwah* groups have considered making the issue of social freedom for women the basis for realizing social equality. Indeed later chapters in the present book show how Malay women's everyday religious practices are often characterized by an attempt to deal with the same kind of conflicting ideas about gender expressed in religious terms.

Considering the importance of Kaum Muda for the modernization of Malay society, it may be seen as a forerunner to the *dakwah* movement. Kaum Muda was a movement for social reform, and so was *dakwah*, though, as we shall see later with significantly different ideas about women. The *dakwah* movement must furthermore be understood in the context of Malaysia as a plural society, in particular the emergence of postcolonial Malay nationalism and economic development policies after independence.

POSTCOLONIAL ISLAMIC REFORM: THE *DAKWAH* MOVEMENT

Dakwah is the generic, Arabic term for any Muslim (or non-Muslim) missionary activity, but historically, both in Malaysia and in the wider Muslim world, it has come to encompass a whole range of meanings.[24] In its contemporary use in the Muslim world, *dakwah* has taken on a general meaning of renewed commitment to religion by the existing Muslim population, thus not referring exclusively to the conversion of non-Muslims. In Malaysia, *dakwah* also refers to the early 1970s Islamic revivalist movement, encompassing a variety of organizations within that movement, along with their members and activities (Nagata 1980). Two of the most important *dakwah* organizations are Angkatan Belia Islam Malaysia (ABIM, Malaysian Muslim Youth Movement), Jemaah Darul Arqam, or simply Al-Arqam. In addition, Jemaah Tabligh, which emerged in the 1950s, is a low-key, international organization that does missionary work mainly through door knocking and the distribution of flyers.[25] There is also the government-sponsored Pertubuhan Kebajikan Islam Malaysia (PERKIM, Malaysian Welfare and Missionary Organization), which is designed to handle all conversions to Islam and to assist converts. Thus, *dakwah* organizations are diverse both in terms of their objectives and how they operate. What they share is the aim of strengthening the faith amongst Malays by encouraging a stronger commitment to the two most important sources of Islam, the Koran and the Hadith.

In their respective studies of the *dakwah* movement, Malaysian social anthropologist Judith Nagata talks about 'religious revivalism' and the 'reflowering of Malaysian Islam' (1984), while Chandra Muzaffar (1987), a Malaysian political scientist and social activist, prefers the term 'Islamic resurgence'. Concepts like 'revivalism' and 'resurgence' indicate correctly that the form of politicized Islam that we see in the *dakwah* movement is not something entirely new in the history of Southeast Asian Islam. So, as indicators of a continuity of Islam in the region, they are apt descriptions. However, a closer look at the activities, ideas and discourses of the latest form of Islamic movement, both in Indonesia and Malaysia, reveals that they represent a *break*, not a revival, of the past (cf. Horvatich 1993; Brenner 1996; Shamsul 1995; Hussin 1993). There is nothing in the activities or the discourses of the Malaysian *dakwah* movement, or, in fact in the earlier religious reform movement, indicating a rebirth of past religious practices and ideas. The *dakwah* movement emphasizes Islam as a contemporary alternative to Western modernity and it stresses the separation of the orthodox, modern form of Islam from the older, syncretic, localized version. For those reasons I avoid concepts like 'revivalism' or 'resurgence' and prefer to use instead 'movement' or 'reform movement' when referring to the *dakwah* phenomenon.[26]

We have already seen how an earlier phase of Islamic reform in Malaya was characterized by the quest to purify Islam and remove pre-Islamic beliefs and practices. This reformist endeavour began to clarify the differences between adat and Islamic legal systems. In this respect, the *dakwah* movement may be said to build on what the Kaum Muda achieved, but the objective had shifted somewhat. The new religious propagators aimed to improve the quality of faith among Malays and to strengthen the Muslim community, the *ummah*, which basically coincided with the ethnic Malay community. An important context for the formulation and appeal of these aims were the problems seen to face Malays during a growing political crisis and ethnic competition. These issues were central to, and forcefully expressed by, young Malay intellectuals. Malay students at local and foreign universities found in Islam ideas and a medium through which their aim to strengthen Malay ethnic identity could successfully be communicated.

Dakwah at the university

The origins of the *dakwah* movement are closely connected to the student movement in the late 1960s and early 1970s (Zainah 1987; Nagata 1984; Shamsul 1997). The birth of *dakwah* in Malaysia is often associated with the violence of 13 May 1969, as it was in the aftermath of this event that the *dakwah* organization ABIM was formed. Malay youth had been voicing their opinions about Malay poverty and 'backwardness' in relation to the Chinese for a long time. Up until May 1969, these issues had been framed in terms of Malay nationalism. Students had also demanded social reform to address the poverty of rural Malays and criticized the government on the grounds of corruption and bad leadership. In the years preceding the riots, Malay students had also been fighting for the Malay language to replace English as the main medium of instruction.

In the months immediately following the riots, student activism intensified. Muslim students from different campus associations such as the National Association of Muslim Youth and the University of Malaya Language Society came together and decided to set up a non-campus organization, ABIM. The organization was intended as a platform for graduate students to continue political activity outside campus, and its motto was to strive '...toward building a society that is based on the principles of Islam' (Shamsul 1997: 213).

The formation of ABIM indicates a change of discourse and methods used in student activism. In her book, *Islamic Revivalism in Malaysia*, the journalist and women's rights activist, Zainah Anwar (1987) shows that it was in an atmosphere of political crisis in the years following the riots that young Malay intellectuals started to reformulate the problems facing Malays in terms of Islam and the survival of the *ummah*. The solution to 'Malay' problems was thus sought within Islam instead of outside it. Nagata (1980) gives an illuminating example of such a shift in discourse. In the late 1970s, she noted that the slogan often used earlier in the fight for Malay rights, '*bahasa jiwa bangsa*' (language is the soul of the race), was no longer used by the students. It had been rephrased into '*bangsa dan agama*' (race and religion). The idea of Islam as a force for change, as a source of modernity and way to modernization was born.

Why did the students turn to Islam?

Several scholars have addressed the question of why students, at this point, abandoned the old discourse of Malay nationalism and turned to Islam. The anthropologist Clive Kessler (1980) highlights the importance of the University College Act 1971, which prohibited students from participating in party politics or being members of any political associations, on or off campus. In spite of threats of withdrawn scholarships, student political and intellectual life was not suffocated, but remained vibrant. Kessler suggests that Islam thus provided an important 'parapolitical outlet' with a certain kind of immunity. After the establishment of three new universities, the Malay student population, and hence the pool of potential *dakwah* supporters, had also expanded dramatically.

THE POLITICAL MAINSTREAMING OF *DAKWAH*

As *dakwah* groups in the first half of the 1970s found political support among large numbers of urban Malays,[27] UMNO responded by starting to improve its image to fit the new religious discourse. Chandra (1987) notes that, from the mid-1970s, UMNO began to pay a great deal of attention to Islam in their communication with their constituents, who were reminded that UMNO was a party that had done many good things for Islam. The party also appealed to Malays to understand the danger of religious extremism in a multireligious society, and therefore the importance of supporting the government's supposedly moderate approach to Islam.

Between 1973 and 1975, the government also created two new Islamic institutions: the Islamic Affairs Division in the Prime Minister's Department and the Yayasan Dakwah Islam Malaysia (YADIM, Dakwah Foundation of Malaysia). Their function was among other things to coordinate the missionary activities of the various *dakwah* groups.

The role of Mahathir Mohamad, who became prime minister in 1981, in the further Islamization of Malaysia has been widely recognized. Under his leadership, the co-opting and mainstreaming of the *dakwah* movement was accelerated. Mahathir assumed leadership fully aware of the events in international Islam, the most important of which was the Iranian revolution in 1978. He saw a need to improve Malaysia's status as an Islamic nation within the Muslim world and made the domestic position of Islam one of his main policy concerns. Given the *dakwah* movement's political gains and its impact on Malay thinking and culture, it was clear that the movement presented the government with a challenge to those aspirations.[28] The government, dominated by UMNO, saw the need to take control over Islam in order to improve its international Islamic standing, as well as to keep the Malays unified as a religious/ethnic group in order to secure votes.

In the early 1980s, the government enacted a series of policies relating to Islam, thereby starting to promote its own version of *dakwah*. In the field of education, for example, Islamic knowledge was introduced as a subject in national examinations, a Southeast Asian Islamic Research Centre was established, and the International Islamic University was set up. Plans were also launched to remodel the Malaysian economy into one based on Islamic principles, with Islamic alternatives to pawnshops, insurance companies and banks. Internally, sensitive to the nation's significant non-Muslim population, the government introduced 'moderation' and 'tolerance' as keywords in its promotion of Islam. The government also started to spread their version of *dakwah* to the rural areas through various programmes. Externally, the government was proactive in its approach to political and economic aspects of international Islam.

The next important domestic political move was when Anwar Ibrahim, the ABIM leader, joined UMNO and the government in 1982. This created a split and crisis within the *dakwah* movement. Those who considered Mahathir's version of *dakwah* to be shallow and a mere strategy to secure Malay votes were disappointed with this development. The more optimistic ones thought that Anwar's presence in the government meant an opportunity to create change from within the political establishment rather than from the outside. With Anwar's arrival in the government, Islamic-oriented policies were continually introduced and Chandra (1987) has pointed out a parallel between Anwar's ascendancy from deputy minister to minister of finance and the 'ABIMization' of government policies.

In 1994, Anwar became deputy prime minister. At the same time, the government was changing its attitude towards the *dakwah* groups that had resisted mainstreaming. Having, so far, mainly talked about the problems that 'extremist groups' or so-called cults could cause, the government started to confront these groups openly at this point. Wazir (1990) reminds us that Islamic cults have existed amongst the Malays before the *dakwah* movement and that they were historically regarded as harmless. In contemporary political discourse and policy-making, however, they are defined as 'deviant' (*dakwah songsang*) and 'dangerous'. In 1991, the government declared 70 groups to be 'deviating from Islamic teachings' (*New Straits Times*, cited in Hussin 1994: 169). Such groups were deemed a national security risk and as incompatible with the policy of multiculturalism. Surveillance and banning were features of this new aggressive approach. The most best-known example is Darul Arqam, popularly known as Al-Arqam, an organization that emerged in the late 1960s and early1970s on the outskirts of Kuala Lumpur. The group's leader, Ashaari Muhammad, urged Muslims to relive the lifestyle of the Prophet Muhammad and the organization is associated with strict rules concerning dress code, food habits and devotional acts rather than with a theologically sophisticated discourse (Sharifah Zaleha 1994). Some of the leading figures bought some land outside Kuala Lumpur and established an Islamic village where members attempted to recreate the social conditions and atmosphere believed to have existed during the Prophet's time. They also created a common pool of resources and managed some small-scale businesses producing vegetables, halal noodles and soy sauce. By the 1980s, the group had developed into a movement with 28 communes, or villages, and roughly 10,000 members. Eventually Darul Arqam transformed from an organization characterized by an egalitarian structure into an authoritarian one with a supreme leader. In the mid-1980s, Ashaari came into open conflict with the Malaysian government, and he along with many of the movement's leaders were detained under the ISA. Shortly after this, Ashaari denounced his teachings on national television.

The increasingly hard line taken against supposedly deviant groups and religious leaders has stretched into the twenty-first century and has been fuelled by the events of 11 September 2001, and later, by the Bali bombings in 2002. Deviant forms of Islam in Malaysia have since then been more frequently framed by the discourse on terrorism and national security. New pre-emptive strategies have also developed along with the more traditional ones of surveillance and arrest under the ISA. External influences on young Malay students abroad are perceived as threats. To counteract such influences, the government sends religious scholars and leaders to campuses overseas to teach Malay students about the local form of Islam characterized by tolerance and moderation – Islam Hadhari.

The question of an Islamic state has been actualized since PAS, the Islamic party, won the 1990 elections in the state of Kelantan, thus regaining the local leadership of the state from UMNO. PAS stated immediately that it would work for the realization of an Islamic state in Kelantan and that it had the intention of introducing the Islamic penal code (*hudud*) in the state. From an Islamic standpoint, the party has adopted a severely critical attitude towards, for example, traditional games and cultural performances, and it has banned gambling outlets. UMNO has responded to the political situation in Kelantan by trying to ridicule the Islam propagated by PAS and suggesting that their extreme, as opposed to UMNO's own moderate and tolerant, version of Islam poses a threat to development and to national harmony. In 1996, PAS in Kelantan made headlines in the national press when it proposed to implement separate queues for men and women in the state's supermarkets. The reason given for this public segregation was that it would improve the safety of women as the risk of sexual tension caused by the proximity of men and women standing in line would be eliminated. The national government again took this as an opportunity to ridicule PAS and pointed out the various practical problems that the segregated lines caused for couples and families.

THE APPEAL OF *DAKWAH*

The *dakwah* movement has usually been depicted as an urban and middle class phenomenon. In the 1970s and 1980s, the movement attracted members and supporters mainly from amongst the newly urbanized Malays who had moved from the countryside either for work or education. The growing urban Malay middle class was thus forming the base of the movement. Several scholars have offered suggestions as to why the *dakwah* movement held such a great attraction for these Malays.

Sharifah Zaleha Syed Hassan (1995b) argues that migration to the city meant the loss of the familiar context of kinship within which Malay social and religious affairs were traditionally regulated. Kuala Lumpur, having been a predominantly non-Muslim area, also lacked well-developed Islamic networks, such as mosque networks, a common ingredient in Malay villages. In addition, the existing networks proved to be slow in responding to the new problems and needs of these migrants. Instead, from the early 1970s, a new form of social context – the *jemaah* – developed in Kuala Lumpur and Petaling Jaya. The *jemaah* is described by Sharifah Zaleha as an informal group of individuals who gathered for religious purposes. The *jemaah* were usually organized by someone who was knowledgeable about Islam; they were loosely organized without a fixed membership and gatherings took place in private homes weekly or fortnightly, usually at night or on weekends. These gatherings provided urban Malays an opportunity to meet and discuss the Koran and the Hadith and to learn about Islamic law and history. Both Darul Arqam and Jemaah Tabligh emerged out of two such *jemaah* groups. Sharifah Zaleha thus suggests that the social context of kinship, so important in Malay village life, had in a way, been transformed into the form of *dakwah* organization, reproducing rural social worlds.

Chandra (1987) also considers the changed conditions that rural Malays moving to the city found themselves in. The urban and industrial world they found themselves in brought them into greater contact with non-Malays. While Sharifah Zaleha Syed Hassan (1995b) pointed to the significance of the breakdown of kinship bonds for the development of the *dakwah* movement, Chandra emphasizes the ethnic composition of Kuala Lumpur. Malays who moved into the city were moving into a largely non-Malay and non-Muslim environment. Chandra describes the atmosphere in the city as 'ethnically alien' (1987: 25) to the Malays and he suggests that this experience made Malays acutely conscious of their ethnic identity. The experience of the city environment as 'ethnically alien' together with the government's pervasive ethnic rhetoric and the reinforcement of the Malay/non-Malay dichotomy through various policies, made migrants aware of their ethnic identity as Malays. Their response to this situation was expressed in a religious idiom, including stricter adherence to Islamic dress codes, heightened awareness of Islamic dietary rules and more diligent practice of Islamic rituals such as prayer and fasting. Chandra understands this attachment to outward manifestations of religion as a way for Malays to develop an exclusive identity which, basically, enable them to avoid contact and communication with the non-Malays:

> What impels the Islamic resurgent to go out of his way to emphasize identity through food and dress is the largely non-Malay, non-Muslim city environment. The resurgent becomes acutely conscious of his own ethnic identity because the atmosphere is ethnically alien.... Given the prevailing ethnic dichotomies and the government's pervasive ethnic rhetoric, the migrant slips easily into an ethnic response to his new situation. He begins to express his ethnic consciousness through Islam, since by adhering to its rituals and forms, he can develop an exclusive identity that does not require him to establish contact and communication with the non-Muslims. ... Ethnic identity, then, is protected by a veneer of religion. (Chandra 1987: 25)

The ethnic dimension is certainly useful for understanding the development of the *dakwah* movement in the 1970s and early 1980s. While I do not argue with Chandra's analysis, I disagree with his interpretation of the *dakwah* adherents' emphasis on *outward* manifestations of religion as an indication that the meaning of their actions must lie outside the realm of religion, and thus were about something other than faith or belief. In his view, they become meaningful only in the light of the Malay search for ethnic identity. Again, I am not saying that Chandra was wrong in tracing the ethnic dimensions of the religious resurgence, but I would like to point out that his study gives an image of *dakwah* adherents and the *dakwah* movement that leaves no room for religious experience, faith or belief.

The image of the *dakwah* adherents presented by Chandra stands in sharp contrast to the material presented in this book where women, as we shall see later, express a very different meaning to the correct performance of religious acts of worship and duties. In their religious practices, the body emerges as a means for the realization of a pious self.

DAKWAH AND GENDER RELATIONS

A starting point in this regard would be Aihwa Ong's 1995 study, which showed modernization and Islamization in Malaysia as being highly integrated and gendered processes. She argues that the NEP, besides its effects on ethnic relations, also transformed Malay gender relations. As has been mentioned, one of the NEP's goals was to create conditions for Malays to enter the waged labour market in order to raise their standard of living. The Malaysian government's policy of providing incentives for multinational companies to set up factories in Free Trade Zones was one important strategy. The original intention had been to create a male, Malay working class, but the electronics and other manufacturing industries attracted to these zones demanded young, female workers, mainly because they could be paid lower wages than men. As a result, there was a massive migration of young, unmarried Malay women to the urban, industrial areas, and by the late 1970s, some 80,000 girls had left their villages to work in these factories (Jamilah 1980). This huge, unprecedented female labour migration meant that, for the first time, large numbers of single Malay women were living and working away from their parents and kin, which, according to Ong, posed a great challenge to male authority and a threat to traditional notions of female morality.

In Malay village life, Islamic law defined a man's identity in terms of his ability to provide for his household and to prepare his sons for independent householding. His role was also to exercise control over the sexuality of his wife and daughters. The grounds for this code of morality are found in a set of notions concerning men and women in connection to the Islamic concepts of *akal* (reason, rationality, intelligence, self-control) and *nafsu* (desire, lust, passion, animality). In Malay gender ideology, men were perceived to have more *akal*, rationality and self-control than women. Women were perceived to have more *nafsu* than men, which meant that they were understood to be more susceptible to animalistic lust and thus in need of male control. By extension, all village men were responsible for the moral status of all village women. On the other hand, adat practices and kindred relations provided women a measure of autonomy and influence in everyday life that prevented a rigid observation of male authority. Adat often prevailed over Islamic family law and it created a space where married women could move freely tending to the fields or engaging in trade. Adat also gave married women the responsibility for making decisions concerning the household economy.

According to Ong (1995), the young Malay women migrants became morally, economically and socially independent of their parents and kin. Life in the Free Trade Zones meant that young men and women were mixing and dating, which created something of a moral panic. Factory girls became known as 'Minah Karan' (Fatima Daud 1985), which derives from a common female name – Aminah – and a Malay word for electricity – *karan* (current). The expression 'Minah Karan' (electrified Minah) associated factory women with powerful, dangerous, unregulated sexuality.[29]

Working daughters also contributed considerably to the household economy. The earnings of a daughter were often used to pay for a son's education or for the building of a new house. Female wage labour also created divisions within the Malay household. It strengthened the influence of mothers, since they were the ones taking charge of the money earned by their daughters and redistributing it in the household. It also meant that the young working women earning their own income could choose their husbands independently of their parents' wishes.

In addition to these changes caused by female migration, Ong suggests that the various state family planning programmes introduced during the 1970s and 1980s were perceived as a challenge to the two key elements of Malay masculinity – control of a wife's sexuality and control of her ability to raise children. Together, these factors caused moral confusion over the proper roles of men and women and threatened the boundaries between private and public. In terms of gender relations, they meant a challenge to men's control of women's sexuality and a diminishing of the father's role as a breadwinner. Ong argues that, as a result, male authority was weakened in Malay society and she sees the birth of the *dakwah* movment as a direct response to this breakdown in Malay gender relations and an effort to restore male authority. For the *dakwah* movement, the recovery of the *ummah* became a central goal in dealing with the breakdown in social boundaries that had traditionally defined Malay group identity. Boundaries between men and women, as well as between Muslims and non-Muslims, had to be redrawn. This was done through the promotion and adoption of certain Islamic traditions – prayer, diet, clothing and social life.

In the *dakwah* construction of the *ummah*, attacks on changes in gender and domestic relations were central, focusing on the moral status of mothers, wives and daughters. Unregulated female sexuality was seen as a symbol of social disorder and women were urged to guard their modesty and cover themselves. Many women responded to *dakwah* messages by trading their jeans and t-shirts into more 'Arab'-inspired robes and headscarves and factory floors filled with young women in headscarves. Ong's argument is that the strengthening of the *ummah* also meant a more gender-stratified social system than that which existed in Malay society. Islamic resurgence, in her view, has undermined the adat emphasis on bilaterality while strengthening Islamic tenets that increase male control in the emerging Malay middle class.

Ong thereby places the 'headscarf issue' in the context of power. She argues that Malay women have been donning the scarf as a result of their position in between competing sources of power – the state and the *dakwah* movement. Her understanding of 'veiling', however, has its critics. In her work on young Javanese women and veiling, social anthropologist Suzanne Brenner has pointed out the reductive aspect of this explanation since it '… elides both individual agency and the symbolic role of veiling in processes of self and social production' (1996: 689). The American anthropologist John Bowen (1995) even suggests that Ong's analysis falls into the trap of presenting Malay women who choose to use the veil as being governed by a false consciousness.

This discussion illustrates two different presuppositions of women as primarily 'victims' or 'agents'. Ong's analysis tends toward an image of Muslim women as victims of Islamization whereas the others call for an exploration of the meaning ascribed to veiling by those who practise it.

It is important not to deny the social and political constraints and pressures that may limit or guide women's choices. The material dealt with in this book, however, shows that the dimensions of faith and religious experience as a base for, or an expression of, women's agency, cannot be ruled out.

Figure 2.2. Women walking towards Masjid Jamek in Kuala Lumpur to pray

THE COMPLEXITY OF *DAKWAH*

Clearly, the *dakwah* movement in Malaysia is highly complex. What started out as an intellectual and political movement soon became ideologically divided into a 'moderate' and an 'extremist' version. The moderate version was represented by ABIM and later co-opted by UMNO and the government, while the 'extremist' version is roughly associated with the opposition, and thus with PAS. Anthony Milner (1998) argues that the Islamic movement has divided the Malay community more than it has united it. He emphasizes that it is UMNO that has been strongly *bangsa*-oriented in their efforts to strengthen the economic standing of the Malays. The Islamic movement has, on the other hand, criticized both the concepts of *bangsa* and nationalism. *Dakwah* members perceive Malay nationalism as being artificial, man-made and, in fact, illegitimate in strictly Islamic terms.[30]

So, *dakwah* adherents, as a group, have become pluralized in terms of ideology, but also background. In the early days, the movement attracted mainly urban, middle-class Malays but later expanded to other segments of society. It has also spread geographically from urban to rural areas.

Several scholars have pointed to the fact that there is sometimes confusion as to what is actually meant by *dakwah* in the Malaysian context (Nagata 1995; Kessler 1980; Hussin 1993; Shamsul 1997). They are then referring not so much to the ideological and demographic aspects of the movement as to what *dakwah* is meant to describe. On the one hand, it is often used to refer to specific groups, organizations or institutions created in order to spread the Islamic faith. Individuals can also be referred to as *dakwah*. Nagata (1995) says that a *dakwah* person (*orang dakwah*) is popularly thought of as somebody who is narrow-minded, fanatical and orthodox. *Dakwah*, in this sense, is then a somewhat narrow definition of specific elements in society carrying out specific activities. The other use of *dakwah* is to apply it as a name for a very broad wave of raised Islamic consciousness among Malays. Thus Kessler (1980) has emphasized its importance as an intellectual and cultural phenomenon rather than for its significance as a network of organizations and institutions. Shamsul (1997) points out that '*dakwah*' has taken on a wide spectrum of meanings, from merely being relatively more strict in the observance of Muslim codes to committed activism.

Studies of the dakwah movement show a slight, but interesting, shift in the translation of the concept into English. In 1980, Nagata gives the translation of the Arabic word dakwah into English as a 'call' or an 'invitation'. Almost two decades later Shamsul (1997) translates dakwah as 'to call' or 'respond to the call'. The two translations show different forms (noun or verb) of the same word and as such they do not contradict one another, but the shift indicated by Shamsul when adding 'respond to the call' is significant in the Malaysian context. This shift mirrors the historical development of dakwah in Malaysia, a development that takes dakwah from a small university-based political movement to a general trend of raised Islamic awareness among the Malays. The way the concept is used in today's Malaysia does not only define those who 'do dakwah', those who propagate Islam to others, but also those who are responding to that call by beginning to take an interest in Islam. And there is no fixed boundary between the two aspects.

A way of expressing this subtle difference in meaning is suggested by Hussin (1993) who distinguishes between 'Islamic revivalism' and 'the dakwah movement'. In his use of the terms, 'Islamic revivalism' is a general trend in society where 'the dakwah movement', as a phenomenon, plays an important role. But, as mentioned above, dakwah and revivalism are not identical. According to Hussin, the dakwah phenomenon manifests itself in the activities of Muslim organizations such as ABIM, Darul Arqam, PERKIM and Jemaah Tabligh.[31]

The consequences of a raised Islamic awareness can take on many forms on an individual or collective level. It can result in a stronger personal commitment to Islam, entailing a change in practice. Instead of praying irregularly, a person starts to pray five times a day, and initiates a search for spiritual guidance from God and the Koran. For some, this is a personal process while for others it means reaching out and joining loosely organized study groups. A stronger commitment to Islam can also lead to a desire to affect other people's lives in the direction of Islam. This can be done on an individual level: by gaining knowledge about Islam and leading a pious life, a person can be an example for others, so that those around him or her may be willing to seek change in their lives and may ask for help. A strong commitment to Islam can also result in participation in formal group activity. For some, the commitment leads to more overt political involvement. In some cases, the aim is to change Muslims into better Muslims, and in others, there are explicit political goals such as the establishment of an Islamic state. Thus, in line with Hussin's proposal above, it is important to distinguish between a general process of Islamization of Malaysian society and the phenomenon of the *dakwah* movement which, obviously, has played an important role in the wider trend of Islamization.

However, all agents of Islamization have emphasized the importance of religious education (*tarbiya*) for Muslims. The *dakwah* movement spread the idea that Muslims need to commit more strongly to the teachings of the Koran and the Hadith. This idea implied the need to study the sources in small study groups (*usrah*), which became an important activity for *dakwah* adherents in the universities (Zainah 1987; Shamsul 1995).

In response to these agendas, the government's propagation of Islam has also focused on religious education for Muslims. Compulsory religious instruction for all Muslim school children is one example of this. Another is the promotion of religious 'marriage classes' (*kursus perkahwinan*) with the aim of preparing couples for their religious duties when married. The state-owned mass media are also used to promote religious knowledge and activities. In line with the vision of a moderate Islam within an ethnically and religiously plural society, the government has also reached out to the non-Muslim communities, inviting them to learn more about Islam through conferences and programmes.

The women I focus on here engage in activities that certainly correspond to this upsurge in religiosity displayed by the multifaceted currents of Islamization. However, there are important differences. As we shall see, these women have not just been going along to religious activities and classes organized by various authorities; they have also initiated their own informal religious study groups.

Women's study groups and classes, formed within the context of mosques, workplaces, *dakwah* organizations, or by the women themselves, may all be seen as manifestations of a general awareness that Muslims in Malaysia need religious education. My focus here is not on the differences between these groups. However different these groups might be in composition or form, there are many themes, issues and experiences shared by the participants. They all look to the Koran and Hadith for guidance as they try to practise Islam as 'a way of life'. As informal study groups, I see them as the result of the general process of Islamization that Malaysian society has gone through, but also as important contributors to the Islamization that is still being effected.

NOTES

1   It is, however, interesting to note the reference made in the speech to 'the Hereafter', which may indicate a shift in focus in relation to the discourse of earlier leaders. In an analysis of discourses on Islam by both Mahathir Mohammad and Anwar Ibrahim, Hooker (2004) notes that they make no references to Islam as a means of salvation in the next world. The focus is instead limited to the role that Islam can play for its followers in this world.

2   Figures from the Department of Statistics, Malaysia, cited in Peletz (2002: 35).

3   Although this corresponds to the way that the majority of Malays also express their identity, the picture is complicated by groups of people in East Malaysia who speak Malay and follow Malay adat, but who are not Muslim. There are also non-Malay Muslims.

4   See Susan E. Ackerman and Raymond L. M. Lee (1988) for a general introduction to non-Muslim religious innovation and ethnic identity in Malaysia, and Alexandra Kent (2000) for a study on the Sai Baba movement in particular.

5   Examining the census introduced by the British administration in Malaya, Hirschman finds that the word 'race' appears for the first time in 1891 as an alternative to the word 'nationality'. By 1911, 'nationality' had been completely replaced by 'race'. Hirschman sees a direct connection between the introduction of 'race' in the colonial census and the rising popularity of Social Darwinism which accompanied European technological expansion.

6   In the 1931 census it was clear that the Chinese had become a larger community than the Malays in British Malaya, which included Singapore (Milner 1998: 161).

7   To this was added birthplace; only those who had been born in Malaya or Singapore before independence, or whose parents filled this requirement, could be considered Malay. This was a somewhat narrower definition compared to other suggestions and, as Milner (1998) has shown, there has been continuous disagreement over the scope of Malay ethnicity since before independence.

8   Malaysia, together with Indonesia and Thailand, was ranked in the second tier of Newly Industrializing Economies (NIEs), behind the first tier consisting of South Korea, Taiwan and Singapore.

9   The figures are from the *Mid-Term Review of the Sixth Malaysia Plan 1991–1995* (cited in Stivens 1998: 95).

10 This aim was formulated in the *Mid-Term Review of the Second Malaysia Plan in 1973* (cited in Milne and Mauzy 1999: 52).

11 The Chinese share of corporate ownership had also increased in the same period from 27.2 to 45.5 per cent, while the foreign share fell dramatically to 25.4 per cent (Gomez 2002: 84).

12 See Patricia Sloane (1999), Joel S. Kahn (1996), and Muhammad Haji Mohd Taib (1996) on the New Malay, and Stivens (1998) for a gender approach to the idea of the New Malay.

13 In 1970, 26.7 per cent of Malaysia's population lived in urban areas, whereas in 1998, the figure had increased to 59.8 of a population of 22 million (Government of Malaysia 1999, cited in Abdul Rahman 2001).

14 *The Star*, 5 June 1995.

15 See also Khoo Boo Teik (2003) for a detailed analysis of the 'Anwar affair' and the political crisis that unfolded. He shows that Mahathir's and Anwar's differences over economic policy and management were just one dimension of the events.

16 In the middle of 2008, Wan Azizah left as party leader in favour of her husband who shortly after stood as candidate in the Permatang Pauh by-election in 2008, which he won.

17 Examples of this are saint worship (*keramat*) and the use of charms, spells and divinations as weapons against evil spirits.

18 The image of the relatively autonomous Malay woman, both rural and urban, presented in early ethnographic texts (Firth 1966; Djamour 1965) was reproduced well into the 1980s. Later works, with a focus on rural women, support and elaborate this image of Malay women (Strange 1981). See Stivens (1992) for a valuable and critical discussion on the historical and academic context for the production of this image. See also Khoo Gaik Cheng (2006) for a critical discussion on the relationship between adat and Islam, or between adat and modernity. Through an analysis of Malaysian film and literature produced in the 1990s, she argues that adat is not impermeable to patriarchal interpretations and that adat and modernity are not mutually exclusive. Khoo highlights the fact that adat and Islam have been integrated into each other to an extent that makes it difficult to clearly distinguish between them.

19 See, for example, Clifford Geertz (1968).

20 Mohd Taib Osman (1989: 113) argues that Islam, on the one hand, did influence certain notions in spirit belief through a reinterpretation of good and evil spirits into the Islamic entities of *Jinn Islam*, benevolent supernatural beings, and *Jinn kafir* (the infidel) and *Iblis* (Satan), the malevolent ones. At the same time, the use of Koranic verses as weapons against malevolent

spirits shows that Islamic elements in folk belief are being reinterpreted in terms of the patterns of the ancient religion.

21   In contrast, Dutch colonial rule in Netherlands East Indies had a much more aggressive attitude towards Islam. See Mark R. Woodward (1989).

22   The role of the *kadi* changed as a result of the bureaucratization of Islam. With the new system, only those who had performed the hajj or who had studied at a *pondok* could be appointed as *kadi*. Having been a figure of authority who acted informally in village life, the *kadi* became the link between the sultan, the local ruler, and the congregation (Gullick 1989: 287).

23   Roff (1994) suggests that it was through the medium of the new *madrasah* that Kaum Muda made most of its impact on Malay society as the schools turned out a large number of Kaum Muda-oriented teachers and religious officials who took up posts all over the country.

24   The American social anthropologist Charles Hirschkind (2001) notes that the concept of *dakwah,* as used in the Koran, generally refers to God's invitation to humankind, transmitted by the prophets, to live in accordance with God's will. Hirschkind refers this interpretation to the Koranic verse 14: 46 where *dakwah* makes its first appearance in the text. Hirschkind says that in the historical development of Islam, *dakwah* on the one hand 'came to be used increasingly to designate the content of that invitation' thus becoming interchangeable with the term sharia (the juridical codification of God's message) as well as the term *din* (religion). On the other hand, it came to carry the sense of duty 'to actively encourage fellow Muslims in the pursuit of greater piety in all respects of their lives' (2001: 6).

25   The Malaysian branch is usually described as an exclusively male organization, whereas studies elsewhere (Metcalf 2000) show that women may also be members and activists.

26   The obvious objection to 'movement', which has been pointed out by Roff (1987), is that it conceals the fact that what we are talking about is in fact a plurality of movements, not a single one. For lack of a more precise concept I still use 'movement', but will return to this point later in this chapter, highlighting the plural and complex aspects of *dakwah*.

27   Officially registered in 1970, ABIM attracted large numbers of urban Malay youth and intellectuals. By the mid-1970s, ABIM had also gained a strong position in Malaysian politics.

28   The challenge of the *dakwah* movement increased further when PAS, with new leaders influenced by the IRC, and with the question of transforming Malaysia into an Islamic state on their political agenda, left the ruling coalition and resumed its role as the Malay Muslim opposition. This was perceived as a great political threat by the government.

29   The moral panic surrounding female factory workers faded out in the mid-1980s, but ten years later the same kind of panic emerged, now expressed

in the concept of *boh sia*. The expression, of Hokkien origin, has a strong connotation of sexual promiscuity and was used when referring to young people (of any ethnicity), in particular female adolescents, 'hanging about' or 'loafing' in shopping complexes and in the streets at night, presumably engaging in sexual activities. Girls were thought to sneak out at night to ride motorbikes with their boyfriends. The danger was expressed as a Western lifestyle brought about through capitalism. See Stivens (2002) for a more extensive analysis of this discourse.

30 During my fieldwork, I had some contact with groups that labelled themselves as *dakwah*. These groups tended to have a more mixed composition in terms of ethnicity, with many Chinese Muslim converts. The old saying that to embrace Islam was to *masuk Melayu* (to become Malay), which stems from a time when the religious identity of Muslims was more or less identical with the ethnic identity of Malays, was something they strongly rejected. An example of this is that converts nowadays are not requested to change their family name. In Malaysia, it is common that when converts choose a new Muslim surname, they drop their family name and replace it with 'Abdullah'. Many of those who wanted to convert were surprised to learn that officially, they were allowed to keep their family name since the change of religious faith does not change one's ethnicity. Many converts, however, still choose to use Abdullah in order to avoid any misunderstandings concerning their religious identity in everyday life.

31 There are, furthermore, three main types of *dakwah* activities: 1) those that are loosely organized, with the aim of self-education and a greater realization of Islam, often taking place in a member's home; 2) those aimed at propagating Islam to others; and 3) those that combine self-education with propagation (Hussin 1993).

3

Submission to God
requires knowledge

THE IMPORTANCE OF EDUCATION

As we saw in the previous chapter, Malay women have historically had access to formal religious education: at first, to a limited degree, through the *pondok*s, and later more accessibly through the reformed *madrasah*s. Wazir (1992) also argues that religious education helped, rather than hindered, Malay women's political awakening: religious schools helped spread nationalistic ideas that paved the way for female political involvement in the 1930s and 1940s.

We also saw that there was a strong emphasis on studying Islam in the *dakwah* movement. Malays were urged to become better Muslims through improving their knowledge of the religion and, as Zainah (1987) and Shamsul (1995) have shown, an important part of *dakwah* activities in the 1970s consisted of participation in small study groups. State education in Malaysia has a secular basis. As part of its Islamization policy, however, the government introduced Islamic religious education as a compulsory element for all Muslim students at the primary and secondary level.[1] To complement the normal school curriculum, mosques and *dakwah* organizations usually offer classes on Islam to children. As mentioned, an important part of the NEP was state sponsorship of large numbers of Malay students for further education, especially in the United Kingdom, the United States or Islamic centres in Egypt and Pakistan. The stream of Malay students going overseas for higher education has continued, including hundreds of young Malay women who study at Al-Azhar University in Cairo each year and take up positions as religious teachers when they return (Haji Faisal 1993). In Malaysia itself, the International Islamic University, set up in 1983 in Petaling Jaya[2], attracts foreign as well as local students, both male and female.

Parallel to the various models of formal religious education in Malaysian history, informal religious studies have always been an important part of Malay life. Religious instruction has traditionally been conducted by the local religious teacher or imam. Even though the early ethnographies of Malay village life provide very little documentation of women's religious activities, women and men appear to have had equal access to informal religious studies. In particular, learning to read the Koran in Arabic, from beginning to end (*khatam Koran*), was considered an important rite of passage for both boys and girls as the completion of this generally marked their coming of age.

Although generally well educated, the women in this study had not had any formal religious education. Most of them were born in rural areas and had moved to Kuala Lumpur as young adults. The basic teachings and practice of Islam had thus been transmitted to them by village teachers or their grandparents. As adults they had been touched and inspired by the wave of Islamization sweeping across Malaysian society and, when I met them, they were actively seeking to realize lives permeated by Islam in every aspect. They expressed a desire 'to live in obedience of God's will' and identified their poor knowledge of Islam as the main obstacle to achieving such a life. Hence, these women considered their informal religious education, part of the trend towards women organizing their own religious classes and groups since the mid-1980s, as having a significant place in their spiritual as well as daily lives.

This chapter will present some different kinds of religious classes created for and by women in the mosque, private homes, *dakwah* groups and workplaces. It will also show how these groups were constituted and relate individual women's accounts of how they came to join a particular group. The second part of the chapter will focus on the meaning that women themselves attached to these activities. It will become clear that, for them, the development of a strengthened religious commitment is intimately

Figure 3.1. The cafeteria at the International Islamic University in Gombak

connected to the learning process, and that such learning can be deeply meaningful and may even be embodied.

IN THE MOSQUE

One of the most important visible signs of Islamization in Malaysia is the proliferation of mosques. The immense Masjid Sultan Salahuddin Abdul Aziz Shah (the Selangor State Mosque) in Shah Alam, for instance, was built in 1988 with generous funding from Saudi Arabia. A more recently built mosque, which is also spectactular, is the Putra Mosque in Putrajaya. Both the government and UMNO have substantially funded the building of mosques and *surau*s in the new housing estates continually being built all around Kuala Lumpur. Other mosques have been built with private funding. The result has been that, wherever you go in Kuala Lumpur, you are never far from a mosque.

The mosque that I visited frequently during my fieldwork was built in 1979 as part of the development of the neighbourhood. Initially, the mosque did not have a women's committee. There was, however, a group of women in the community who performed charity work and dealt with death rituals, such as the washing of the corpse (which is done by a woman when the deceased is female). Some women in the neighbourhood also met weekly to study Arabic in each other's homes and, eventually, these two groups more or less overlapped and then merged. In 1989, the women registered an association. The group's activities thus far had nothing to do with the local mosque. The number of women taking part in Arabic study sessions grew and it became difficult to arrange them in homes. In addition, the beginning of the 1990s was also a time when the government was aggressively using the ISA (under which five or more persons can be deemed an unlawful assembly) against groups accused of deviating from Islam. Thus, the women approached the mosque and requested the use of its lecture room for their class. The mosque committee agreed and the women's association moved into the mosque and soon expanded its activities.

Figure 3.2. The Putra mosque in Putra Jaya

General Islamic talks

By the time of my fieldwork, in 1995–1996, the women's committee was organizing several classes in the mosque. In the Introduction to this book, I described one session of the most popular of these, 'General Islamic talks'. This class was conducted once a week by different religious teachers and scholars invited to share their knowledge. The General Islamic talks usually attracted from sixty to a hundred women each time.[3] The reputation of these talks spread beyond the neighbourhood, attracting many participants from all over Kuala Lumpur. Their popularity was usually attributed to the excellent and eloquent teachers, some of whom also gave talks at similar classes in other mosques in the vicinity.

Many regulars chose to come to class quite early to meet up with friends and share news. This was also an opportunity for selling various items such as headscarves, custom jewellery or handbags. 'Gossip' and trading were frowned upon by some members of the committee, however, and shortly before the teacher arrived, a recording of an Islamic chant repeating the 99 names of God was played and the Arabic text of this distributed to those who did not know it by heart. All the women would then sing along until the arrival of the teacher. The singing was intended to create an atmosphere of spirituality instead of idle talk – the tongue often being referred to as the most dangerous part of a woman's body.

Most of the invited speakers had degrees in Islamic studies from local or foreign universities. The content of the classes varied. Sometimes it was a *tafsir* class where one or more verses in the Koran were interpreted by the teacher. *Tafsir* demands a high degree of general Islamic knowledge and Arabic and not all teachers were considered to be equally good at this. The best ones were those who could give deep explanations of the meanings, drawing both on their knowledge of Arabic and written sources other than the Koran. Another popular class was on the Hadith (the collection of reported doings and sayings of the Prophet Muhammad). The attraction of this class also depended on how skilfully a speaker explained and interpreted the Hadith. The popular teachers were those who could suggest how contemporary Muslims should understand these stories. On one such occasion, the story told was one where the Prophet had criticized a woman for wearing too many gold bangles on her arms. The teacher focused on possible reasons for the Prophet's attitude. Since gold, especially in the form of women's jewellery, is an important element in the Malay lifestyle, both as a form of savings and to display status, the participants were not only curious but also slightly worried. If the meaning of the story was that the Prophet had been critical of the woman because she displayed her wealth, some women in the room were possibly in trouble. The women recognized that to flaunt wealth was sinful for men, explaining that it could easily lead to envy and jealousy between Muslims and thus challenge good relations within the community.

One illustration of this involved public discussions of the ubiquitous Malaysian batik silk shirt worn by men on festive and formal occasions. On the one hand, it was considered good for men to wear traditional batik instead of a Western (and non-Islamic) suit and tie since this was a sign of Malay (and Muslim) identity. On the other hand, the correctness of wearing expensive silk was questioned from an Islamic point of view – an interesting discussion where the almost synonymous identity of 'Malay' and 'Muslim' was being challenged from an 'orthodox' perspective.

With this discussion in mind, it is not difficult to understand the ripple of anxiety that the story of the gold bangles created in the room. The teacher argued, however, that there was no support for the notion that a woman's display of wealth was considered sinful anywhere in the Koran or in any Hadith. Instead, the teacher suggested that the Prophet was criticizing the way the bangles had pushed up the sleeve of the woman's dress, exposing her bare arm, thus making it difficult for her to guard her modesty. The women were evidently satisfied with this interpretation, but it did plant small seeds of concern in some. When I continued the discussion with a couple of women after class, one of them said that what had been revealed to them through this story made her think about the dress she was wearing. It was a *baju kurung* of the latest cut, made of beautiful handpainted silk with a red, yellow and green floral pattern. She held up her arm showing the way the sleeve was cut. It was fashionably wide and did not close around the wrist. When she raised her arm as you do when you want to attract the teacher's attention, for example, the sleeve collapsed in soft folds around her elbow, exposing her forearm. It had never occurred to her that the *baju kurung*, the most common garment worn by Malay women in public, could be anything but Islamically correct.

Tajwid classes

Mosques also provided *tajwid* classes to teach the proper pronunciation of Arabic in order to be able to read/recite the Koran. Learning how to read the Koran has always been a very important part of basic religious instruction for Malays. All the women I met had been taught as children how to read the Koran by a grandparent or the local imam. However, they all agreed that it had been different then. The teachers had not been as good and had not bothered to teach them the correct pronunciation. One woman explained to me the great surprise she felt when she realized that her way of reading the Koran was inadequate. When she started university in Kuala Lumpur, she became involved in one of the *dakwah* groups and became aware of her Muslim identity in a new way. She suddenly realized that her way of reading was different from the other students – their way sounding more Arabic – and it was rather a shock to her. As a child, she had been taught by her father. He was the village *ustaz* and had taught all the children in the village to read the Koran. He was a knowledgeable person who had travelled to Mecca and she had never before doubted her father's knowledge or his Arabic pronunciation.

The basic structure of instruction was the following: the women first had to study all the rules of pronunciation, beginning with a single letter and moving on to combinations of sounds. After that, they could begin to read phrases from the Koran and start to focus on the melody of the reading: the pauses, the length of the vowels and the moments of respiration.

There was a preference for small groups of women in the *tajwid* classes since the focus was on pronunciation. If the room was too big or too crowded it would be difficult to hear the teacher and for the students to hear each other. It was quite common for a small group of acquaintances or friends to invite someone who knew Arabic well to teach them how to read the Koran. These gatherings would often take place at one of their homes. The *tajwid* class that I participated in consisted of a group of women who already knew each other. The women had asked the imam at a small, recently built mosque if he would teach them. He agreed, and they met at the mosque for an hour twice a week. Their knowledge of *tajwid* varied; some were advanced but wanted to improve their reading while others needed more basic instruction. As is customary with religious teachers, he did not charge any fees, but the women made voluntary donations to him each month.

The women emphasized the importance of these lessons, since a slight mistake in the pronunciation of a vowel, for instance, could change the whole meaning of a word or a phrase. This was particularly important in the pronunciation of *doa*, which are verses from the Koran used as personal prayers with a specific purpose, in contrast to *solat*, the five daily, ritual prayers.[4] What is significant here is that some women were quite worried that their rudimentary Arabic pronunciation would undermine their chances of God understanding what they were saying – they feared that the meaning of their prayer might be distorted if their pronunciation was wrong. Some women would admit that they often said their *doa* in Malay, to be on the safe side. They felt that, since God was omnilingual, this would be a logical strategy. Nonetheless, most women preferred to be able to say their *doa* in Arabic, as this was God's language.

Rhythm and pace is also considered to be a very important aspect of Koranic recitation. The ability to 'sing' the Koranic verses beautifully is a highly valued and respected skill among Muslims in general. One of the women, Norani, illustrated this for me with the example of the commendable congregational prayers held in the evenings throughout Ramadan (*terawih*), during which the imam recites the Koran from beginning to end. For Norani, this was an important part of Ramadan, something like a yearly revision of the history of Islam. All the laws, all the advice, everything that is in the Koran is recited. If the imam could recite well, Norani found that it was much better than when she read the Koran alone. She could feel it more, she said, and the words were more profound. She also found it much easier to concentrate when the reader performed well. She said (referring to a saying in the Hadith) that a voice should be decorated by the beauty of the Koran. It should not be the other way around – that the Koran was decorated by the beauty of a voice. The idea was that the inherent beauty of the Koran would render the voice of the reader more beautiful. This was also something she had experienced herself.

Arabic classes

After learning to pronounce Arabic correctly, some women aspired to learn the language itself. They organized a couple of weekly classes in the language, one for beginners and one for more advanced students. Women were proud to attend such a class. Learning the language of the Koran in order to be able to read and understand the meaning of the text on your own was considered a very difficult and time consuming undertaking and it was highly respected. Many women who had not yet had the chance to start learning Arabic would state this as one of their main goals.

To begin with there was the obvious problem of translation from one language to another. Arabic, which is a particularly poetic language, is sometimes considered to be untranslatable. In relation to the Koran it is said that the nearest one can get are interpretations of the Koran, through other languages. The problem of translation, however, was avoided if one could read and understand the Koran in Arabic. Many women stated that the meaning of the words would change slightly when read in a language other than Arabic. One of the students, Rafiah, said that since she had learnt Arabic, the words in the Koran had taken on a different meaning. More importantly, when reading the Koran in Arabic rather than in Malay or English, she said that the sense of the words also changed in quality, affecting her actual experience of their meaning. When reading the Koran in Arabic, her experience of its meaning was stronger: 'It is like in some verses when the word *kafirun* in Arabic is used and translated to "unbeliever" in English. To me it is stronger in Arabic. I can't explain.'

To learn Arabic was an important step in the process of improving one's knowledge of Islam. Through Arabic, women said that they could begin to understand Islam in a way that could not have been obtained in any other way. Many women emphasized the fact that individuals had different levels of understanding Islam. There were many ways of doing things among Muslims because there were varying interpretations of the religion. This was true not only for the global Muslim community, but also for Muslims in Malaysia. The women were well aware that religious teachers and even Islamic scholars differed about certain issues and this was often explained as an effect of their divergent understanding of Islam. It was often pointed out to me that this was why it was dangerous to blindly accept as the truth

Figure 3.3.Tajwid class

everything that teachers said at the lectures. The best thing was for each person to learn Arabic for herself and to study the Koran in depth. Then, whenever there was uncertainty about something, the person could look it up in the Koran and go to other authorities for their interpretations and, from there, form her own understanding. One of the more active committee members admitted to me that the passive attitude of some of the women troubled her. She was worried that they just took whatever the teacher said as the truth without thinking things through or checking with other teachers.

Women who had an excellent command of Arabic often stated that this knowledge had transformed their relationship to the Koran, and to God. The deeper knowledge that was gained from learning Arabic was an important source of spiritual change. This was expressed in the words of a woman who had been looking, earlier in her life, for spiritual cleansing in various Sufi groups characterized by their search for the path to truth (*tarikat*) through experience. However, she had not been convinced that *tarikat* was something for her and had instead found spiritual experience through the Koran:

> To tell you the truth, ever since I studied Arabic, and began reading the Koran and actually being able to understand it (something of it, not totally, I still have a long way to go) I have felt the need for this *tarikat* becoming less and less. When you read the Koran it is like God talking to you, I believe, although I have a long way to go. There are words that I do not understand and I read the translation. I can even cry now when I read the Koran. I used to wonder why my grandfather did that. He used to cry, not *cry*, tears would come out. I used to wonder why. So now I understand why. It gets into your heart. It is so full of meaning. So I don't think any *tarikat* session will give me that.

IN THE WORKPLACE

Since the classes in the mosque were usually held on weekday mornings and afternoons, they predominantly attracted non-working women and/or those without small children – mainly women around and above the age of 40 with more time for themselves.[5] For working women who wished to attend religious talks, the easiest way was to go to those held at the *surau* in their workplace. This was very common, especially in government offices and in state-owned companies. Sarah, who worked in a large state-owned company, had been the organizer of such gatherings in her office for a few years. For Sarah, it began in the 1990s. The lunch hour on Fridays had been extended to two hours in order for men to have enough time to perform their obligatory Friday prayers at the mosque. Most women spent the Friday lunch hour at the nearest shopping mall or just having a nap in the office *surau* and Sarah had felt that they could use their time in a better way. She asked some of her Muslim colleagues if they were interested in religious talks, and they were. They started with every second Friday, and recruited a female religious teacher to come and talk and lead their afternoon prayer. Later, they expanded this to every Friday, with different teachers each week. They preferred to have female teachers. In Sarah's opinion, female teachers tended to have a softer, and gentler, approach than male ones. Also, women felt more relaxed with a female teacher. Over the years, the lunchtime religious activities expanded to every day of the working week. Once a week, men and women had a joint class, which was always led by a male teacher. The *surau* was then divided into two parts by a thick green curtain. The men's section was closest to the direction of Mecca; thus, during prayers, the men were in front of the women, but still separated from them by the curtain.

Besides listening to religious talks, the women collected some money each month, which was distributed by Sarah to poor families in a squatter area close to her home. Sarah said that not all Muslim women in her office came to the *surau* to listen to the talks. Some would still go shopping and just come there to pray. And she also had the sense that some women who did go to the *surau* for the talks did not really listen since they would doze off halfway through. Sarah thought that they came just to gain merit, since attending religious talks and listening to the Koran was an act rewarded by merit. She felt sad for those women but continued to encourage them to come and comforted herself with the idea that she was at least helping to provide them with an alternative.

The nature of the office talks varied a lot depending on the wishes of the group and the teachers that they were able to engage. None of the women in the group I joined felt that they had very advanced religious knowledge. They needed someone to teach and repeat the basics of Islam for them. The teacher that they invited was someone who was from the same village as one of the group. Her talks were roughly organized to coincide with, and relate to, significant dates in the Muslim calendar: for example, she spoke about the rules for paying *zakat* (the yearly tithe) and fasting during Ramadan, and recounted the life of Muhammad on his birthday. In the small and rather intimate group, there were also a lot more opportunities for questions and discussions compared to the crowded mosque classes.

Classes in English

Religious classes held in mosques or in offices were conducted in Malay and attracted mainly Malay women. But many Malay women who had grown up during the British administration or before the NEP made Bahasa Malaysia the medium of instruction had been educated in English and preferred classes in that language. One of the teachers at the International Islamic University had seen this need and had started an English language *tafsir* class. With guidance from the professor, they uncovered the meaning of a few pages of the Koran each time. They had started from the first page of the Koran and were more or less halfway through when I joined them. This class had been running for almost ten years.

The class was open to both men and women; most of the participants were Malay and well educated. Most of the women had professional careers but there were a couple of housewives as well. Norhani, one of the women who had been following the class almost since the beginning, explained that she had used English since childhood. Even though she was Malay she had spoken English with her brothers and sisters. Only her parents spoke Malay at home. She attended an English medium Methodist school. She married just before she turned 20, and with her husband, settled down in the northern state of Kedah. She was a housewife then but tried to follow some religious classes. However, she was not very happy with these classes because the other participants were all old men who used to discuss the meaning of one single phrase in the Koran for hours. Another thing was that there was no good translation of the Koran available in English, only a very old English version, which she found very difficult to understand. She felt that she did not learn much from these classes. After some years in Kedah, the family had the opportunity of going to Europe and, when they were in London, Norhani bought some Islamic books in English and an English translation of the Koran. She described this as one of the most important things that had ever happened to her. This first translation, which she read repeatedly until it fell apart, made her discover what she referred to as the first level of meaning of the Koran. Norhani assured me that her understanding was still very limited because there were many more levels of meaning yet to be reached by her. When Norhani and her family settled down in Kuala Lumpur in the mid-1980s, she soon discovered the *tafsir* class, which she finds very helpful in her efforts to deepen her understanding of Islam. While acknowledging that the classes at the mosque were also good, she said that she found it difficult to follow them because they were in Malay.

Other classes in English were provided by *dakwah* organizations such as ABIM and PERKIM. As a student's association, ABIM had a pronounced international atmosphere. The guest speakers were often from abroad and, therefore, English was the language used. PERKIM is the official missionary organization in Malaysia and all converts must go through its classes in order to be registered as Muslims. PERKIM has study groups all over Kuala Lumpur and throughout Malaysia and uses English as its principal medium of instruction so that converts and potential converts may better understand the teachings.

PERKIM provided a class in English in my neighbourhood. The group had been formed in the late 1970s by European female converts. It had started out as a kind of social gathering at one woman's home. In the beginning, they did not have anyone to guide them in religious matters. One of the women said that they were all 'groping with religion' at the time. In the mid-1980s, the group became more organized. They rented a house in the neighbourhood where the gatherings could be held and looked for a teacher. They found an Indonesian who had just completed his studies in Medina and was on his way back to Java. He accepted their invitation to stay on in Kuala Lumpur and teach them.

At the time of my fieldwork, the class was open to both men and women but in reality the group was made up of women. There was a young couple who attended once or twice during the year that I followed the class; besides the teacher, the husband was the only man who ever came to the class. Being a missionary organization, PERKIM mainly attracted Muslim converts. The group was quite small, with eight to ten regular participants. There were two Chinese converts and a few women of Western origin. But some Malay women came regularly because they felt more comfortable with English than with Malay. The most active woman in the group was a Malay woman who had been with the group for about fifteen years. There was one young woman who originated from Sabah and who had been brought up in a Catholic family who took the class with the intention of converting to Islam. She eventually went through with the conversion some six months after joining the class. Apart from the group's ethnic diversity, the women in the PERKIM class had many similarities with the Malay women who joined the mosque classes. They were in their thirties or older, well educated and had formed important ties of friendship and cooperation that extended beyond the class.

This class was held in the evening since many of the women worked. The group would gather at the time of the evening prayer (*maghrib*), and therefore it always began with a communal prayer. This opportunity of worshipping together was important to many of them and, for some, the only time during the week when they did not perform the worship on their own.

How I was taught the method

In the PERKIM class, we all sat with an English version of the Koran in front of us. The teacher would usually initiate a topic that he had prepared but sometimes the class would take a certain turn because there was a specific question from one of the participants. The size of the group created a certain intimacy and the women often raised questions of a personal nature, seeking the advice of the teacher and of each other. One of the first times that I came to the class, Norsiah, who was one of the most active Malay women in the group, showed me the basic principle for understanding Islam.[6] On this occasion, the topic was 'Belief in the hereafter – one of the six articles of faith'. The teacher started by telling us that both believers and non-believers, those who reject the truth (*kafir*) will go to the hereafter. In the hereafter, there is heaven and hell. But how does one enter paradise and how is one to avoid hellfire? Norsiah asked the teacher to show us, and in particular, me, 'the newcomer', how he knew what would happen. The teacher asked us to find verse 3: 185 in the Koran and he asked me to read it aloud.

Every soul shall have
A taste of death:
And only on the Day
Of Judgement shall you
Be paid your full recompense.
Only he who is saved
Far from the Fire
And admitted to the Garden
Will have attained

The object (of Life):
For the life of this world
Is but goods and chattels
Of deception. (Sura 3: 185)

Norsiah then whispered to me that I should ask the teacher how to enter paradise, and I did. We were asked to refer to another verse:

But give glad tidings
To those who believe
And work righteousness,
That their portion is Gardens,
Beneath which rivers flow.
Every time they are fed
With fruits therefrom,
They say: 'Why, this is
What we were fed with before',
For they are given things in similitude;
And they have therein
Companions pure (and holy);
And they abide therein (for ever). (Sura 2: 25)

The teacher commented that this verse shows that the conditions for entering paradise are belief and righteous deeds. He stressed the fact that only belief (*iman*) is not enough, it has to be accompanied by good deeds (*amal salleh*). This was sustained by another verse where belief and righteous deeds are linked together:

For those who believe
And work righteous deeds,
There will be Gardens. (Sura 31: 8)

At this point, the teacher went outside the Koran and said that it was quite common for Malays to neglect the importance of righteous deeds for the next life. He gave us an example of the expression that this sometimes could take. He had recently been at the hospital to visit a sick relative. During the visit, he had overheard a man ask his uncle to say the declaration of faith. The uncle had asked his nephew if he thought that he was going to die. According to the teacher, this was an example of a very arrogant attitude. He explained that it was not enough to say the declaration of faith at the last minute in order to go to paradise. As we had seen in the Koranic verse, faith must be accompanied with practice.

The teacher was by now proceeding by asking rhetorical questions. Having identified who will enter paradise, the next question had to do with what was meant by 'righteous deeds'. What was demanded from a righteous person? The answer was given in verse 3: 134.

> *Those who spend (freely),*
> *Whether in prosperity,*
> *Or in adversity;*
> *Who restrain anger,*
> *And pardon (all) men; –*
> *For God loves those*
> *Who do good;–* (Sura 3: 134)

Norsiah wanted me to realize that everything we were being taught came from the Koran. The teacher was constantly using the Koran as the source and authority for all his explanations and arguments. This meant that the Koran held all knowledge and that the way to God went through the text.

WOMEN AS RELIGIOUS TEACHERS

In the Muslim world, positions of authority such as mufti (a Muslim legal expert empowered to rule on religious matters or *fatwa*), ulama, or imam are traditionally only available to men. The important role of women as mothers is often emphasized in contrast to this. Muslim women are, however, gaining religious legitimacy in areas other than mothering, as several ethnographic studies have shown (Mahmood 1998; Torab 1996; Kamalkhani 1998; Hegland 1998; Rosander 1998).

The uncentralized nature of Islam, and the lack of any ultimate authority for the faith as a whole, has provided considerable scope for individuals to acquire a standing as a teacher or interpreter of the scriptures on the basis of personal characteristics and local acceptability alone (Nagata 1982: 45). In Malay society, the source of legitimacy for religious teachers lies to a large extent in their reputation and the confidence they gain from other Muslims. Formal religious educational qualifications are not required of a person who takes on a teaching role. Instead, the basic skills required of a teacher of Islam is fluent Arabic and the ability to read and comment on the Koran and the Hadith. In particular, a teacher's ability to relate the meaning of Koranic verses or the Hadith to contemporary issues is an important source of esteem and popularity and is especially valued. Personal piety is another important criterion for religious legitimacy.

Malay women have long been involved in both secular and religious education. The teaching role provides individuals with a position from which social influence and acceptability are easily obtained. Teaching continues to be considered an avenue of upward mobility in both urban and rural Malay society. Many of the women that I met, who were active as religious teachers in Kuala Lumpur, had been schoolteachers. Female religious teachers in the urban areas, however, tend to have various backgrounds. Even women with professional careers outside teaching are moving into the arena of religious teaching as a result of a greater commitment to Islam. In some cases, this new direction comes from a life crisis that makes the person turn to religion, to religious studies, and eventually to the role of teacher. Well-educated women who have acquired a command of Arabic and good knowledge of the Koran, and who are considered to be pious, can also be asked for guidance or to impart their knowledge without having claimed to be teachers themselves. Women who have left a professional job in favour of a stronger religious engagement can find an alternative road to social esteem through a new career as religious teachers. One religious teacher whom I came to know had been a successful businesswoman. She turned around completely after experiencing two crises. First, she was diagnosed with cancer and around the same time her only son was killed in a car accident. She overcame the cancer and began to devote all her time to the study of Islam. As she gained more knowledge, other women started coming to her for advice on different religious matters and soon she found herself in the position of *ustazah.* She was asked to come and give talks in the *surau* and was very popular because of her great piety but also for her knowledge of business, economics and politics.

Female teachers with a university degree in religious studies were also becoming more common. In particular, those who organized classes in the mosque preferred to invite qualified religious teachers. They felt a great responsibility to provide those who attended the classes with teachers who had a certified command of Islamic knowledge.

Islamization has thus created an increased demand for religious teachers, particularly in the urban areas, to conduct religious classes in the mosques, in private homes, or in workplaces. Female teachers were sometimes preferred to male ones for practical reasons. As mentioned, this was important in *tajwid* classes so that the teacher could sit closer to her students in order to listen to and correct their Arabic pronunciation. A female teacher also contributed to a more relaxed atmosphere in the group. Given that an important part of a teacher's role was to answer questions, women felt more comfortable when asking a female teacher for advice on personal matters or concerning religious practices in relation to their bodies. Questions were often born out of everyday situations, as in the following example with Norani.

One morning, on our way to the *tajwid* class, Norani and I stopped by a plant nursery to buy a bougainvillea for her front veranda. A Chinese family owned the nursery, so I was quite surprised to hear the manager welcome Norani with the Arabic greeting, *'Assalamualaikum'* (peace be upon you). This was the first time I had heard a non-Muslim use this phrase. Norani was in a *baju kurung* and wearing a scarf, so there was no mistaking her religious affiliation, but there was nothing indicating that this man was a Muslim. There are, of course, Chinese Muslim converts, but at the back of the shop I had noticed a small Buddhist altar with fresh fruit and candles. Norani, however, replied as customary, *'Waalaikumsalam'* (and upon you, be peace) and made her purchase. Later, in the car, she reflected on what had happened. She said she was not at all sure she had done the right thing by responding positively to the Muslim greeting. This had never happened to her before and she was uneasy about it and decided that she would ask the *ustaz* about the correct behaviour in such a situation. When waiting for his arrival she also discussed the incident with the other women in the class. Some had experienced the same thing and said that it was a new trend in town. The prevailing assumption was that the greeting was used in a polite way in order to show that the other person's religion was respected. But none of the women were sure of the answer in these situations. When the teacher arrived he was asked for advice and responded that if a non-Muslim greets you in such a fashion a Muslim should just say 'Good morning' or whatever is appropriate for the time of day. The Muslim greeting phrase was only for Muslims.

This incident shows a situation in which uncertainty about correct behaviour is created, and how Norani, after reflecting on her own action, immediately turns it into a question that she discusses with her friends and with the closest religious authority – her *tajwid* teacher. Many questions that were raised in the context of religious classes were similarly the result of uncertainties concerning a particular behaviour or practice. Sometimes there were questions concerning the Islamic point of view on a certain issue. One such example would be the woman who had had a discussion with an uncle about alcohol and who wanted to know exactly what the Koran had to say about it. The uncle had held that it was only commendable (*sunna*) to avoid alcohol. His attitude was that you were allowed to drink as long as you did not get drunk. She had argued that it was forbidden to taste alcohol or even to use perfume with alcohol in it but she had not been able to convince the uncle. She asked the teacher what to say to such a man. He showed us some verses that could be useful. One of them was the following:

> *Oh ye who believe!*
> *Intoxicants and gambling,*
> *(Dedication of) stones,*
> *And (divination by) arrows,*
> *Are an abomination, –*

Of Satan's handiwork:
Eschew such (abomination),
That you may prosper. (Sura 5: 90)

The teacher made us notice that the important word here was 'eschew' which was very strong. It meant that one should not even go near the things mentioned in the verse. It was not only a command not to drink but even to stay away from places where there is alcohol. He also showed us several other verses where the word 'eschew' was associated with the greatest sins in life. The woman was satisfied and jotted down the verse in order to show it to her uncle.

Disagreements or controversies also provoked questions. The religious teacher was then asked to clarify the problem and give Koranic references, if any, in support of his or her own explanation. In the process of Islamization, stricter adherence to religious practices such as praying and fasting has been emphasized, but also outward appearances and what Chandra (1987) has described as outward manifestations of Islam. Also, a more intense contact with other Muslim countries through student exchanges and broader accessibility to the hajj has contributed to the introduction and elaborations of religious practices. There were often questions, for instance, about the practice of commendable prayers and commendable fasting, performed in combination with the religious duties of ritual praying and fasting.[7]

One woman had noticed that some people, having performed one of the five daily prayers, would get up and change position in the mosque before saying their *doa*. Some even changed position more than once. She had asked one of her neighbours who was a religious person about this and he had explained that it was in order to have more space when you perform your *doa*. When she posed the same question to her religious teacher, she received a different explanation. The teacher said that a worshipper gets extra rewards just for praying in the mosque; the very spot on the floor will grant you extra points. By changing position in the room, the person would get a new set of rewards. Discussing this with the other participants afterwards, she said that she was very happy to have learnt this. This was one reason she came to class, to learn the right way of doing things: if you just listen to what people around you say, you might actually do things that are not Islamic.

FROM WORKING WOMEN TO ISLAMIC HOUSEWIVES?

A large proportion of the women who participated in these classes at the mosque had purposely decided to stop working. Both *dakwah* and government discourses have been focusing on Malay women as mothers and wives. Islamic resurgents held that women's most important role was as mothers and that, as mothers, their principal responsibility was to instil Islamic values in their children. Women were reminded that they had a moral duty to construct and nurture the aspired modern Muslim-Malay community (Ong 1995).[8] This image of women as primarily wives and mothers later emerged in state policy. The government set a new target for population growth, from 14 to 70 million over a period of 100 years, in line with its economic development plans and labour needs. Women whose husbands could afford to support them were encouraged to stay at home and raise at least five children.

When the women in this study did stop working, however, it was not with the intention of staying at home and having children. They had already had their children and did not intend to start all over again. Sometimes, their children were part of the reason to stop working. One woman, a former teacher, said that she had found it increasingly difficult to spend her days teaching other children while not having time to teach her own. But her children were already between 10 and 14 years old when she finally did leave her career. Instead, women stressed that the decision had been based on a wish to devote more time to religion. Their interest in religion had been gradual and had grown stronger in the previous five to ten years. They expressed a need to 'turn back to religion'.

When women told me why they had decided to spend more time on religion, they often expressed it in terms of age: 'When you reach 40 you tend to return to religion. You start to think about death.' This was a natural explanation indicating that religious awareness evolves with age. Women told me that they had received basic Islamic knowledge (how to pray, how to fast, to respect your parents, stories from the Koran and the Prophet's life) from parents or grandparents and most of them were taught to read the Koran by the same person or by the village *ustaz*. Many women said that, despite their religious induction, they had not really understood the meaning of Islam. 'It was all a bit in a haze', was one woman's reflection. As adults they had come to realize that they had largely neglected religion and expressed a wish to make up for this. In addition, women said that the religious education they had received as children was deficient. One common way of putting it was: 'I realized that the things I had been taught about Islam as a child were not enough or not correct. I have to learn again.' These experiences also point to the changes that Malaysian society and the Malay practice of Islam have undergone during the lifespan of people who today are in their middle years.

Leaving work – a difficult choice

These women came from families where secular education had been seen as an important means to a better life. Many had been sent to mission schools and were therefore equally comfortable with Malay and English. Most of them had at least a secondary education and professional careers, many as teachers or as government administrators. To most, a working career was also a source of self-esteem. They enjoyed working, they took pride in having an education, being good at their jobs, and in earning their own income. Some women said that they would have preferred to stop working earlier, but they had hesitated for fear of being economically dependent on their husbands. To drop a working career and stay at home would put a woman in a difficult position in case the husband wanted a divorce later on.

One woman in her early forties had recently retired as a computer programmer with a private company. She started taking part in the religious classes much more actively than before and stated that this was her time to 'return to religion'. She found the classes interesting and planned to start learning Arabic. But she also admitted that she was often bored staying at home. She had been working all her life and she found that she spent too much time in the house. A few months later, she accepted an offer to go back to work on a project since the company could not find anyone else with her skills. She still tried to attend the classes now and then and the company had accepted her request for flexible hours. Another woman had had similar experiences when she stopped working at the age of 38. She said very clearly that her reason for not working anymore was that she wanted to learn more about Islam. She did not do it for her husband, even though he was very pleased with her decision. And she did not do it for her children, although she admitted that taking children to and from school became easier and she had more time to help them with their homework. The main reason was that she wanted to study Islam. But although it was her own choice to stop working, it took her a long time to accept herself as a non-working woman. In the beginning, she had been uncomfortable being called a housewife, feeling that she had lost her social esteem. Used to working all her life, she initially felt inferior as a housewife in relation to working women who, in her eyes, were contributing to society. But she found both intellectual satisfaction and a new path to social esteem through her religious studies and through learning Arabic. She found that her contributions and opinions were valued by the religious teachers and fellow participants in her classes. Her background as a working woman in combination with her knowledge of religion gave her the confidence to take an active part in the classes.

For a third woman, a slightly different problem in her married life made her turn to Islam. After a few years of married life, with two small children and a professional career as a teacher, Rafiah found herself very lonely. Her husband, an example of the new generation of successful Malay entrepreneurs, was in the initial phases of building up a company and worked day and night. The little time he did not spend in the office was devoted to a *dakwah* organization with which he used to travel around the villages to inform people about Islam. Rafiah often found herself alone with the children. This was not the way she had expected family life to be, and she was quite unhappy. She found comfort in religion and, as she did not have much time for herself, she bought cassette sermons and listened to them while she did the cooking. She learnt a lot about Islam in this way and eventually she decided to wear the veil. Her religious studies helped her to cope with her life, and after about ten years, she decided to leave her job and devote more time to Islam. Like many other women, she said that the decision to stop working had not been an easy one, and she spent a long time thinking about it before she took the step. As a housewife she could more easily manage her time and was able to attend religious classes. She started to learn Arabic and, with time, she gained the respect of others for her knowledge and was often sought out by other women for advice both on religious and personal matters. She had also become interested in Islamic jurisprudence and planned to study at the International Islamic University.

STORIES OF VEILING

When women told me their stories of how they had become more interested in Islam, the subject of the headscarf was often brought up as a turning point. For many, the moment when they started to cover up was an important mark of transition. Wearing a scarf was a conscious choice and as such in need of comment and explanations. There were always one or more reasons, and a story, attached to the scarf. Those who were married often said that the decision to veil was in line with their husbands' wishes, but they always added that they had not been forced in any way. Other typical comments and reasons given by women who had decided to cover up were:

- I was ready.
- I had health problems.
- I do it for God.
- My husband is so pleased.
- It feels good and I feel naked without it.
- Everybody says it suits me.

Sometimes it was a combination of these. In the literature in English, modest dressing by Muslim women is generally referred to as 'veiling'. Veiling is useful as a concept as it embraces the great variety of modest female dress throughout the Muslim world. The Malay expression for the English verb 'to cover' is *tutup,* to close. When the scarf is taken off, the verb used in Malay is *buka,* to open. A small scarf that covers the hair and the neck is called a *mini-telekung.* A *telekung* is larger in size and covers also shoulders and the chest. When a scarf is used together with a *baju kurung*, the whole outfit is referred to as a *tudung*. Generally loose-fitting and ankle-length, the *baju kurung* displays variations in tunic length, as well as the style of the neckline and pleats around the waist. A traditional form of Malay female dress since around the 1700s (Sandborg 1993), it is very common today: worn together with the *mini-telekung*, it corresponds well to the Islamic norm of modest dressing.[9]

It was in the streets of Kuala Lumpur and on the university campus that young Malay women for the first time appeared veiled from head to toe, in what was perceived as an Arab style of Islamic dressing. This was a definite break with the Western style of dress that was predominant at the time. For some of the women I met in the various study groups, their religious awakening and change of lifestyle were initially brought about when they came into contact with the university-based *dakwah* movement. Some were at university themselves during the turbulent years of 1969–1973. Others were married to men who had been involved in the movement during this time. In the story of Minah, it is the meeting with *dakwah* teachings that marks the turning point in her life.

Minah

When I met Minah she was a professional woman in her mid-thirties. She was unmarried and devoted much of her spare time to Muslim charity work and to religious studies. She was born in a village on the east coast of Malaysia but was quite young when she was sent to a boarding school on the west coast. Her father had been the village *ustaz* but he had been very particular about providing his children with a good secular education. He was therefore very pleased when Minah was offered the chance of doing her secondary education in an English-medium boarding school. Minah's account of the time she spent at boarding school was a very emotional one. The experience of being on her own, without the family, has stayed with her. Having gone to a Malay-language primary school, she also found it very difficult to manage the schoolwork since she did not know any English at all. It was a difficult time, but she worked hard and in the final year she even received a reward for her accomplishments in English. After secondary school, she chose to further her science studies at university in Kuala Lumpur. Minah told me that it was in her final year at college, in 1972–1973, that something happened to her that made her aware of her Muslim identity. There was a public holiday on account of the Chinese New Year and some students were arranging a day seminar on Islam. A friend of hers was involved and invited her to come along. Minah expressed this as a turning point. She said that it was the first time that she realized that religion was a part of who she was. Overnight, she started to wear a *tudung* and *baju kurung*. She remembered that she only had three sets of *baju kurung* and she wore them out completely in just six months. Before this she used to wear short skirts and T-shirts like everyone else. Minah's newfound identity was, however, not strong enough to last. When college was over and she started to work, she found it difficult to stay with Islam. After about a year and a half she took off her scarf. Her own reflections about this were of two sorts. First, she believed that her awakening to Islam happened too fast, overnight. Second, she described the situation in 1973 as difficult for someone in *tudung*. Almost nobody was covered at that time and people used to stare at her. She said that she felt like an 'alien'. Nobody else at work was covered and she found it very difficult to keep it up without support from someone else. Her interest in Islam was still strong and she took part in religious activities and tried to learn as much as possible about her religion. About fifteen years later, times had changed and Minah was ready again. The *dakwah* movement had spread far beyond the university campus and veiled women had become an everyday sight. Minah started to cover again in connection with performing the hajj. Since then, her commitment to Islam has just grown stronger, making her increasingly secure in her Muslim identity.

A conscious choice

In contrast to Minah's first and dramatic awakening to her Muslim identity, manifested by the decision to start veiling, most women told me that the decision to *tutup* had come gradually and it was often preceded by a long period of pondering whether to 'close' or not.[10] Covering was something that needed getting used to and many women started by wearing a small scarf tied at the back of the neck, leaving ears and neck uncovered. They would 'close' gradually by taking to using a larger scarf that could be draped around the neck or later fastened by a pin under the chin. A larger piece of cloth would also reach further down over the shoulders and chest. There was clearly a certain degree of fashion involved in the choice of scarf and women were conscious about choosing scarves that matched the colour and pattern of their *baju kurung*. But one could also detect a preference for less colourful and plainer scarves by women who had been covering for some years and whose commitment to Islam had grown strong. Women who were just starting to cover would more easily choose colourful and patterned scarves.

My material is dominated by women who were practising veiling and who had done so for some years, often parallel to their participation in religious study groups. Faridah, however, was a woman I met who was in the process of considering whether to 'close' or not. I will include the case of Faridah since it shows to what extent the decision to veil or not to veil was perceived as a conscious and individual choice.

> When I first met her, Faridah did not cover except for when she went to the mosque or for collective religious rituals. The first time I was invited to her house for coffee (after the *tajwid* class) she removed her loosely draped silk scarf, sank down into her cream-coloured leather sofa, lit a cigarette and declared that she was not a staunch Muslim. She had just turned fifty and had returned to Malaysia after almost twenty years in Australia. Her husband, who had passed away some ten years earlier, had been employed by the Malaysian embassy. After the husband died, she had stayed on in Australia for a few years as her two children were almost grown up and well adjusted to Australian society, and she

had not wanted to uproot them again. By the time she decided to move back to Malaysia, her eldest daughter was married to an Australian and had children of her own. Back in Kuala Lumpur she had been encouraged to join the classes in the mosque closest to her house, but she had not liked them very much. She had enjoyed the talks but did not appreciate the atmosphere in that mosque. When she met women from the mosque in the supermarket they had asked her why she did not cover outside the mosque. It was 'a must', they had said. To Faridah, wearing a scarf was a personal issue and she did not like other women commenting on it. Her mother or other female relatives had not covered when she was young, except for wearing a *selendang* on festive or ritual occasions. She had followed the trends of the *dakwah* movement from abroad and had been critical of the women who had adopted an Arab style of dresssing. Over the years, some of her friends had also started to cover up but, as far as she could tell, many did it for the wrong reasons. Many of them were not sincere in her eyes. They were just following a trend or because their husbands wanted them to cover. *Layan suami* (to comply with and always be attentive to their husband's wishes) is an important ideal for Malay women. It was quite common for a woman to explain an action by referring to the wishes of her husband. Faridah did not have a husband to *layan* and she had no intention of putting on a scarf to please everyone else. She considered herself a good Muslim, with or without the scarf. The incident with the mosque ladies had led Faridah to withdraw from that particular mosque and she had joined another class where she found the atmosphere more relaxed. But, however much she had disliked being told how to behave by the mosque women, it had also planted a seed of uncertainty in her. To cover or not to cover became an issue for her in a way it had never been before in her life. She started to discuss it with friends, relatives and people whose knowledge about Islam she trusted, among them the religious teacher of her *tajwid* class.

When Faridah brought up the issue of covering with her teacher, she phrased her question in the following way: 'If you are not covering and somebody comments (negatively) what should you respond?' This was the only time I heard anybody, openly, asking for arguments to support the practice of not covering and the answer given by the teacher was short and did not bring about any further discussion. He simply said that you should not say anything, since you know you are wrong and should not try to justify it by saying that it is too hot or your husband does not want you to. He referred to Koranic verses and to some sayings in the Hadith that showed that veiling is a command by God and therefore required of women.

A few weeks later, Faridah told me that she had come to a conclusion about the *tudung*. It was clear to her that human beings, compared to God, were imperfect. She said: 'Only God is perfect. We always make mistakes.' So, she figured that she would let herself make this one mistake, not to cover. She was diligent in her prayers and fasting. She paid *zakat* (the yearly tithe) without failure and she had performed the hajj a few years earlier. 'It is impossible to do everything right,' she said, and then she added, 'I am not ready yet.'

A SACRIFICE TO GOD

In many of their accounts, the point where a woman started to turn to religion had to do with health problems or some other crisis in life. Judith Nagata (1995) notes that veiling among young university students was often related to problems with health or academic results. In the case of illness, for example, a vow could be taken to start covering if the illness was overcome. The person would then start to cover as a way of showing thanks and gratitude towards God (*syukur kepada Allah*).

Some of the women I met did in fact *tutup* as a way to give thanks to God. One woman, a former nurse, had a heart attack in her late fifties and made a vow to God that if she recovered she would *tutup* and become more diligent in her religious practice. She had not been very concerned about religion earlier in life, admitting that she used to wear mini-skirts and low-cut dresses in her younger days. As she recovered from her heart attack she started to study Islam and later took up a post in a *dakwah* organization. Her life, when I met her, was devoted to God and her commitment only grew stronger with time.

There could be other reasons, such as marriage problems, that triggered a turn to Islam. Unfaithful husbands or a husband who wished to take a second wife were other motives mentioned to me for making a vow to God. One woman had problems with her husband because she had not been able to give birth to a son, which he strongly wished for. After having three daughters, the woman made a vow to God and started to cover. She did not have a son, but she was still grateful to God. Her desire to have a son had made her turn to religion and she found her life more fulfilling after that. She even suggested to her husband to marry a second wife and try to have a son with her, but her husband had also come to accept the situation and was pleased with his wife's interest in Islam.

Veiling – a transformative practice

In interviews and conversations, women thus gave a wide range of reasons for their decision to veil. For many, as we have seen, deciding to veil marked a turning point in life. In this sense, veiling can be seen as a manifestation of faith. But many women also expressed a more dynamic relationship to the practice of veiling. Women had come to experience aspects of veiling that they were not aware of when they first decided to *tutup*. For them, the veil was imbued with new meaning through practice and they talked about veiling as something that made them experience themselves and their environment differently.

It could, as in the case of Zarah, generate a new sense of the body. Zarah expressed that the 'secret' about the scarf was that it 'made a difference' in terms of how she sensed her own body and sexuality. She explained that wearing the scarf in public meant that a woman did not have to worry about her looks so much. There was no point in spending a lot of time doing one's hair for a function if no one was going to see it. But in the privacy of the home, in front of her husband, she did not cover. Since she wanted to look good for her husband, she did spend time caring about her hair and looks. The result was that when she did not wear the scarf, she felt much more attractive than she did when covered. If she had not practised veiling, she would look the same all the time, there would be no difference.

More often, however, women expressed the transformative effects of veiling in terms of religious experience. The practice of veiling was an important part of women's efforts to become pious persons in the sense of drawing closer to God. Women who covered emphasized the veil as something that was required of them by God. To cover was seen as an important everyday act of obedience to God's will. Through veiling they manifested their submission to God, but veiling was also a means whereby an awareness of God was created and upheld. Women explained that when they were covered they were 'closing' their persons to some things in the world, but as they 'closed' to those things, they also experienced that they opened themselves to God. Veiling made it easier to have an awareness of God's existence in everyday life. What was a closure to some aspects of life meant an opening to others. Veiling is thus both a symbol of faith, at the same time as it generates an awareness of God and strengthens faith. The next chapter will deal with a number of other religious duties that the women performed in their desire to create piety.

NOTES

1 Non-Muslim students are provided with lessons on moral education and ethics in place of the Islamic class. They are also invited to join the Islamic class if they so wish.

2 The university later moved to a newly built campus in the Gombak area, just north of KL.

3 There were, however, very few converted Muslims in this class. (Converted in the Malaysian context would indicate that your ethnic identity is not Malay, but Chinese, Indian, Western, Orang Asli or 'Other'.) The mosque in general in was more or less a Malay area. Most converts that I talked to said that they didn't go to classes in the mosque because they were held in Malay and they found it very difficult to follow. They preferred classes in English.

4 The following chapter will give a more detailed account of how women used *doa* and of their importance in everyday life.

5 In my local mosque,women were discouraged from bringing small children to class. The rationale for this was that the classes were meant to be exclusive moments of learning that should not be disrupted. Other mosques did allow mothers to bring their children. The National Mosque in the city centre, for example, was spacious enough for children to roam about while their mothers were attending classes. There would consequently be a larger portion of younger women in these classes than in other, smaller mosques.

6 The following presentation is an extract of what was said during the class. For example, there were many more references to verses than the ones

presented here and the discussion was sometimes sidetracked. I have chosen to condense the class by focusing on the way I was shown how to learn about Islam.

7   The next chapter discusses some of the most common themes of questions relating to the religious practices of praying, fasting and ritual purity.

8   See also Stivens (1998) for a discussion on the image of the new Malay middle-class (*Melayu baru*) emerging in the beginning of the 1990s. This 'new Malay' is clearly '...a male citizen subject, whose wife and children are addenda, inhabiting a space outside of politics' (1998: 92–93).

9   Kirsten Sandborg (1993) notes that the oldest Malay model of female dress is the *kebaya*, which is traditionally much tighter both over the upper and lower parts of the body. During my fieldwork however, the *kebaya* was becoming popular again, but now adapted to Islamic dress codes. The blouse was held together by buttons as in the traditional manner, but the whole outfit was cut longer, and looser.

10 The performance of the hajj was often chosen as the moment for 'closing'. During the hajj, women are required to cover, and it was easy to simply continue with the practice when they returned to Malaysia. Ramadan, the time of the year when there was a strong atmosphere of religiosity, was also a time when many women decided to 'close'.

4

Religious duties and acts of worship

THE FIVE PILLARS

This chapter focuses on women's performance of everyday religious practices, and the importance and meanings they attach to them. Central to these practices are the five pillars of Islam: the declaration of faith (*shahada*), the ritual prayer (*sembahyang* or *solat*), fasting during the month of Ramadan, paying a yearly tithe or almsgiving (*zakat*), and, if possible, performing the pilgrimage (hajj). These correspond to what Muslims refer to as *ibadah*, religious duties. As we shall see, a number of related practices, such as commendable prayers and fasting, may also be referred to as *ibadah*. This suggests a more inclusive sense of *ibadah*, encompassing all activities of life that can be seen as implementations of faith; anything from charity work, interaction with other people in everyday life, to matters pertaining to personal hygiene. This broader understanding of the religious sphere, as Carol Delaney (1991) has pointed out, challenges conventional definitions of religion as consisting primarily of beliefs and practices set apart from everyday life. She emphasizes the need to understand lived Islam as a conceptual system which '...regulates and integrates every aspect of corporeal existence' (ibid.: 25).

Thus, while the discussion of women's religiosity here centres around the five pillars, this chapter will also account for related activities, such as commendable prayers and fasting, which can generate extra religious merit for the performer and is considered a good thing in view of the imagined day of judgement (when deeds will be evaluated by God, and each individual will be rewarded or punished before entering the afterlife). Commendable acts of worship, much discussed and debated in the classes, are also very much connected to the creation of piety in daily life; they are a way for women to create and maintain a stronger relationship with God and were given a central place in the women's lives.

Anthropologists working in Muslim societies have generally paid scant attention to the ways in which the basic Islamic tenets are locally understood and practised. The ritual prayer, for example, has received much less attention than customary religious ritual.[1] As the social anthropologists Nancy Tapper and Richard Tapper (1987) note, this imbalance probably mirrors the divide between Great and Little traditions that, for a long time, dominated the study of religion across disciplines. Religious elements shared by all Muslims were viewed by many anthropologists as part of a Great tradition and therefore less interesting. However, the analytical usefulness of the distinction between Great and Little traditions has been questioned, and there is growing interest in the local practice of Islamic duties and rituals, and interpretations of Islamic jurisprudence and scripture.[2] The anthropological contribution to the study of Islam could be to highlight '... the process by which Islamic ideas and practices have taken on locally specific social and cultural meanings' (Bowen 1993: 6). This process is formed through a combination of ideas and practices given in Islamic doctrine and the social and cultural context in which they are lived (Eickelman 1982).

The Malay women in this study generally expressed their religiosity in terms of a process of accumulating Islamic knowledge. They said that, although they had been taught the basics of Islam when they were young, their knowledge and understanding of the religion had been very limited. When asked what they meant by the basics of Islam, they always referred to the five pillars: 'That there is only one God, how to pray, how to fast and all that.' Often a contrast was made between the past, when being Muslim simply meant engaging in ritualistic behaviour, and their present broader and deeper understanding of the faith. Belief and knowledge were like two sides of a coin – they were aspects of faith. Likewise, faith was implemented and strengthened through the performance of religious duties and other acts of worship.

For Malays, the five pillars, and in particular regular praying and fasting during Ramadan, are referred to as a kind of minimum for defining one's Muslim identity. For the women in this study, all of the five pillars were important, although there were animated discussions and arguments about the conflict between the idea of the oneness of God expressed in the articulation of faith and traditional spirit beliefs still permeating much of Malay life. These women diligently prayed five times a day, as a way of strengthening their faith and establishing a close relationship with God. Fasting during Ramadan was held to be significant both as a social and a religious experience. The pilgrimage to Mecca took on a special meaning in the affluent, urban context. Many women had even performed the pilgrimage a second time, expressing a sense of progress in terms of religious understanding and experience in relation to their second hajj. The structure of the chapter follows the order of the five pillars, beginning with the articulation of faith. The following sections will focus on prayer, fasting and almsgiving in the form of a yearly tithe. Lastly, there is a section on women's experiences of the hajj.

THE ONENESS OF GOD

The *shahada*, or the Islamic confession of faith, 'I testify that there is no deity save God and that Muhammad is the messenger of God',[3] is the foundation for all the other religious duties in Islam and a person who declares the *shahada* in public is embracing Islam. I shall limit myself here to the first part of the declaration of faith expressing the basic idea of God's unity (*tauhid*), the essence of which is that God is the creator of everything. This limitation is due to the fact that the idea of God's unity was much more central in controversy and negotiations about Islamic beliefs than was the idea of Muhammad as prophet. Women often used the idea of God's unity as a marker of boundaries between religious traditions, for example, sometimes in relation to me. Assuming that my Swedish background had made me more in tune with Christian concepts of faith, women often used the Christian idea of the trinity, which would imply the existence of forces external to God's, as a contrast when explaining the Islamic idea of God's unity to me. In the context of ethnically plural Malaysia, the monotheistic idea was at times contrasted to Buddhist and Hindu perceptions of the divine, held mainly by Chinese and Indians respectively, as a way of indicating the supremacy of the Malay/Muslim faith. And as we have seen, pre-Islamic, animistic notions and beliefs in the Malay context have historically come into conflict with Islamic monotheism. At times, they still do.

SUPERNATURAL BEINGS AND EVIL FORCES

Islam recognizes two groups of non-human beings – angels and jinns. Angels play important roles as protectors of human beings and as supervisors of human conduct. Angels are created by God and act only on orders from God. Malays often present a vivid image of the two angels thought to sit on a person's left and right shoulder respectively, taking note of their good and bad actions throughout life. The two angels that Muslims believe come to the dead in their graves, interrogating them about their faith, are also evoked in discussions about mortality and the afterlife. Jinns are equally the creation of God and are described as unseen beings of an undefined character. The Koran does not talk about jinns at any length, but it is generally considered that they can be both good and evil. 'Jinn Islam' are said to be benevolent spirits or jinns, and 'Jinn kafir'[4] are defined as doers of evil. Satan is believed to be either a fallen angel or malevolent jinn.

Chapter 2 showed that the historical relationship between Islam and the pre-Islamic animistic belief systems in Malay society has been characterized by conflict and exclusion, as well as incorporation. Spirit belief has remained an important part of Malay social and cultural life, both in rural and urban areas. The attacks on spirit beliefs and practices by Islamic reformists have, however, led to a recasting of these beliefs into Islamic terms. Mohd Taib (1989) shows the historical merging of the Islamic notion of jinns and the Malay notion of animistic spirits. The notion of jinns has provided Malays with a new frame of reference for animistic spirits. The belief in spirits has thus not vanished. Nor has Western science been a real threat to animism, which exists and is used in parallel to, for example, traditional healing practices. As a result of this, there is a growing demand for what are called 'Islamic *bomohs*' (shamans), as opposed to traditional *bomohs*. *Bomoh*s who have the power to communicate with spirits and who use this power to cause illness or misfortune are not considered Islamic, and their powers are referred to as *ilmu hitam*, black knowledge or magic. Islamic *bomoh*s, on the other hand, are those who keep within the Islamic context, combining their knowledge of the healing properties of plants and herbs and and using verses from the Koran for curing ailments.[5]

Among the women whom I met daily, the idea of black magic as contrary to Islam was firmly rooted. The powers of those engaging in such magic were neither denied nor approved of since, in their eyes, it meant close connection with Satan and evil jinns. Yet belief in Islam and denial of animistic ideas did not prevent people from becoming the victims of black magic – indeed, there seemed to be an ambivalence to the whole issue. As mentioned, the Islamic version of magic included the use of powers considered evil, satanic or from malevolent jinns, and a good Muslim should steer clear of people who had dealings with Satan.

Besides recognition of the Islamically defined evil magic, it was common knowledge that some *bomoh*s used the powers of, and communicated with, spirits whose existence was not recognized from an Islamic point of view. These shamans were believed to derive their powers from communicating with spirits who, according to Islam, do not exist. When talking to people about the use of magic, it was often unclear whether they believed the power to be Islamic or non-Islamic. The two kinds of evil forces seemed to merge conceptually. 'We are not supposed to believe in it, but somehow it seems to work' was a common phrase pronounced whenever cases of black magic were referred to. Even though the existence of animistic spirits was denied in theory, many women had themselves experienced attacks from what was supposed to be the doings of a *bomoh* practising black magic. They claimed that they themselves would never consult such a *bomoh* in order to fight the evil force at work. To counteract evil deeds, in times of illness, trouble or distress, they only relied on natural medicine and/or the Islamic *bomoh*s for help.

Victim of black magic

Iman, a lecturer in her late twenties, was having difficulties at work because she openly challenged the way in which she was being unfairly treated by her superiors. She spoke up about her concerns and was aware that her behaviour did not correspond to the image of the ideally submissive and quiet young Malay woman. When she fell ill, Iman believed herself to be a victim of black magic, connecting it to her work conflicts. Her symptoms included sleepiness and weakness to the extent of barely being able to keep awake during the day. There were moments when these sensations were particularly intense and dangerous. Each time she got into her car and drove off, for instance, a strong feeling of fatigue would overcome her, and she had come close to crashing her car several times. The drowsiness would also attack her in her office, affecting her ability to teach.

A medical doctor she consulted said that he could not find anything physically wrong with her. She did not want to go to a traditional *bomoh*, even though people advised her to. But she did go to religious ones. One said straight away that he could not cure her because 'the power was too strong'. Another gave her some water in a bottle and read a verse from the Koran. Iman recounted that she had been holding the bottle while the *bomoh* was reading and that the bottle had burst in her hands. If she had not experienced it herself, she said, she would not have believed it. Her explanation for the incident was that the power of Satan was so strong. Finally, she went to a well-known Islamic *bomoh* with a very good reputation among religious people. He gave her some water over which he read some verses from the Koran. Then he gave her some good verses from the Koran to say when she was entering a room or stepping into the car. This was to avoid the attacks of drowsiness.

Iman was convinced that the only way for her to fight the evil power was to make use of her strong faith, and she was convinced that praying was her best defence. She was very clear about whom she was fighting against – it was Satan. And therefore she prayed every day in her office. She refused to go to the *bomoh*s who used what she referred to as black magic because they were allies of Satan. She saw prayer as a vital means to counteract evil. Thus, through praying, Iman was actively integrating the idea of black magic, with its roots in pre-Islamic animistic notions, into an Islamic frame of reference.

Discussing spirits of the dead

Women denied the existence of non-Islamic spirits (*hantu-hantu*) and, in particular, the spirits of dead people with reference to the Islamic view. However, at the same time, there was much confusion in relation to certain ritual practices connected to death. The custom of visiting the graves of relatives after Ramadan included giving water and food to the dead by leaving these gifts at their graves. People also used to read the chapter called 'Yasin' from the Koran and offer prayers (*doa*) by the grave, asking God to forgive any sins committed by the dead and to accept them into paradise. Most people were under the impression that these customs were Islamic and were surprised and somewhat shocked to learn that this ritual had animistic roots since it suggested that communication with the spirits of the dead was possible. Reading the Koran by the grave was seen as an attempt by the living to transmit rewards to the dead in order for the dead to enter paradise, something that is unacceptable in orthodox Islam. Women were taught that, in Islam, rewards are certainly gained from reading the Koran, but that it is only the reader who reaps such rewards, as rewards cannot be transmitted to somebody else. They explained this as having its base in the idea that there are no, and can be no, intermediaries between the believer and God. Religious teachers thus discouraged people from placing water or food and reading the Koran by the grave by referring to these practices as part of adat or tradition, and even contrary to the teachings of Islam. To say a prayer (*doa*) for the dead, however, was accepted and encouraged. Saying a *doa* did not mean communication with the dead – it was a direct communication between God and the supplicant. One could never be sure that God would accept the *doa*, but praying for the dead had a value in itself. It reminded the living that all beings are mortal and that there is life after death.

This sort of discussion sometimes became quite animated in the study groups. On one occasion, in one of the smaller and more intimate groups, a young woman told us that she had been back in her village the week before because her stepfather had died and the family had gathered for the ritual held 40 days after death. Perhaps because I was in the room she saw the need to explain the reason for holding this ritual. She said that the seance was to remind the spirit of the dead person that he really was dead, in case he was not sure, and added that spirits could 'hang around' for 40 days and therefore had to be reminded to leave for the afterlife, just in case. After this account, the young woman looked a bit hesitant and said: 'That is what we [Muslims] believe, right? That the spirit stays in the house for 40 days.' The question was directed to Zainah, the woman in the group who was considered to be the most knowledgeable in Islam, and her reaction was immediate. She declared that this belief was in direct conflict with Islam and explained that according to Islam, when a person dies, the spirit leaves the body and goes straight to the next life. She became quite upset and continued with force, tapping the Koran in front of her while saying firmly: 'What you learn here, you practise!' The sharpness in her voice caused a little stir in the group. A few of the other women nodded in support but nobody commented directly. After a second or two, one woman reflected on what had just been said by asking: 'If the spirit leaves the body straight away after you die, why do we go to the graves with water and food after Ramadan?' The question was answered by Zainah who said that this was a tradition that belonged to Malay adat. She stated clearly that it was not an Islamic tradition and supported this by explaining that, in Islam, there is no point in trying to talk to the dead, ask things from them or give things to them. She repeated that the spirits of the dead do not stay on in the world of the living and that the grave contains only the body of the dead, not the spirit. She emphasized that it was quite all right to visit the graves but that there was no point in bringing things for the dead. When you visit the grave, the only thing to say is: 'Peace be upon you.' To emphasize the stupidity of believing that the grave was anything more than a vessel for the corpse, Zainah told us the story of an educated man, a doctor, who had had himself buried like the dead for five hours. His wish had been to meet God and he had believed that the two angels would come to him in the grave, but of course they didn't. Zainah used the story to stress that the grave is just a place where the body is kept, and that the spirit of the dead leaves the body and goes to the next life. 'This is where you will meet God,' she finished. The women laughed at this story, but some of them were surprised to hear that the tradition of visiting the grave after Ramadan with food and water was a Malay custom rather than a Muslim one and they asked Zainah to clarify this for them.

Zainah continued by saying that it is legitimate to believe in jinns because they are referred to in the Koran. She opened the Koran and showed us one of the first verses in it, which, among other things, says that those who believe in God also believe in the unseen – in jinns. But Zainah also reminded us that the Koran doesn't talk about jinns more elaborately and that it is difficult to actually know anything about them. In relation to this, Zainah warned us about some *bomohs*, as well as of those people who claim to be *ustaz* and who say that they perform 'white magic' and are able to communicate with jinns. She said that some of them play with Satan. She also reminded us that in Islam there is no mediator between the individual and God and that the important thing is that all beliefs must have their source in the Koran.

In the cases of Iman as well as the discussion on spirits above, we have seen how the concept of the oneness of God is used to draw a boundary between Islamic and non-Islamic beliefs and practices; between what to believe in and what not to believe in. A wider meaning of the oneness of God often referred to is to be aware of God in everything. This idea forms the basis for the ways in which the women made meaningful their performances of religious duties and acts of worship, including praying.

PRAYING

In Islam there is a distinction between 'ritual prayer' (*sembahyang* or *solat*) and 'private prayer' (*doa*). Ritual prayer, or the ritual of worship, is performed five times in twenty-four hours. The first time is just before sunrise, followed by noon, in the afternoon, after sunset and lastly at night. The Koran does not state the number of obligatory prayers, nor does it give any prescriptions as to how ritual worship should be performed. The structure of ritual worship, as it is performed by Muslims today, is based on what is considered to have been customary in Muhammad's lifetime (Schimmel 1992: 39). Anthropologists, notably Bowen (1989) and Mahmood (2001b), have, on the other hand, shown that in spite of the high degree of conformity as to how the ritual prayer is performed in the Muslim world, there may exist great local variations in terms of the understanding and experiences of prayer. Bowen undertakes an exploration of local sociopolitical meanings of the ritual worship in Indonesia. He analyses three cases of disputes over ritual procedure, finding that all three dissimilar disputes were deeply intertwined with national politics. Working with material from a women's piety movement in Cairo, Mahmood, on the other hand, is more interested in the act of worship as ritual action through which an experiencing body is produced and an embodied subject formed. She finds that, for the women in the movement, the ritual prayer played an important part in the formation of pious selves. Both of these studies show that text-based presumptions about prayer do not exhaust the meaning of ritual prayer in any given context. Taking its cue from Mahmood, the following is an attempt to capture the meaning of prayer for the women in this study.

Ritual prayer in the Malay context

The Arabic word for ritual prayer is *solat* and the Malay word is *sembahyang*. Among *dakwah*-oriented Muslims in Malaysia there is a preference for the Arabic word, but *solat* and *sembahyang* were used interchangeably with the English 'prayer'. In a conversation in English, any of the three words can be used when a person wants to indicate an intention to pray. Briefly, the ritual of worship begins with an act of ablution, followed by a series of two, three or four ritual cycles (*rakaat*) in the direction of Mecca. In order for the prayer to be valid in the eyes of God, the worshipper needs to state the intent (*niat*) of the act each time he or she is about to pray, thereby cultivating the consciousness of the act. The number of ritual cycles to be performed in each act of worship is fixed and depends on the time of day. In each cycle, the worshipper executes a fixed sequence of movements including standing, prostrating, kneeling and sitting. Each movement is accompanied by Arabic recitation, including verses from the Koran, in which the worshipper praises God, affirms the oneness of God and asks God for guidance.

Since the exact time for each prayer depends on the solar position, the time for prayer varies from day to day. In Malaysia, they are announced in various ways. The daily prayer times are published in the newspapers and posted up on notice boards in mosques and prayer halls. The call to prayer (*azan*) is broadcast from the minaret of mosques by the muezzin.

As the muezzin often uses a loudspeaker, and there are mosques in most neighbourhoods, the call to prayer can generally be heard throughout the city. The house that I was staying in during my fieldwork was situated some five hundred metres from the mosque in the immediate range of the *azan*. Each morning, I was pulled out of sleep by the beautiful musical voice of the muezzin. The *azan* was softer in the early mornings, becoming louder and performed with more gusto later in the day when the streets were noisy and busy.

The *azan* was also called on television and radio. The state-owned channel interrupted its broadcasts to play a recorded call to prayer to images that corresponded to the phrases of the *azan*. The *azan* consists of the profession of faith with some short phrases added to it. During the first strophes, they showed moving images of mosques and men coming to the mosque to pray. Men in white were lining up in a big mosque. When the phrase 'let us pray' came, they all fell to their knees touching the floor with their foreheads. At the phrase 'let us pursue in victory', there was an image of the half-completed Petronas Twin Towers, taken from the ground. This image of Malaysian prosperity and modernity was followed by an image of the Kaaba, surrounded by hundreds of thousands of pilgrims, taken from above. The whole sequence showed very few images that included women. Islam was here connected to Mecca, to Malaysia's economic success, to the Muslim community, and to men.

Ritual purity

In order to pray, a Muslim has to be clean in the sense of being ritually pure. For women, menstruation and childbirth require that the whole body be washed from head to toe. The water must not have been touched by anyone. The bath is accompanied with a *doa*. After having sexual relations, both men and women need to wash in this manner before they can pray or touch the Koran. Sleeping or fainting, as well as relieving oneself (in the form of gas, liquid or solid matter) from the lower part of the body are considered minor pollutions and require a minor ablution. This means that the face, part of the head, the arms to the elbows and the feet to the ankles are washed.

In Malaysia, women remove their skirt and headscarf and wear a special white *telekung* and sarong for praying. Any make-up is thoroughly removed before prayer and put on again afterwards. Perfume is not considered polluting unless it contains alcohol and does not have to be removed before praying. One female religious teacher used to say that the important thing is to be clean and beautiful before God. She emphasized that it was equally important that the white prayer *telekung* was clean and ironed as was a silk *baju kurung* worn to the office. She criticized the habit of neglecting to take care of the prayer *telekung*, reminding the women that praying meant a direct relationship with God and they should want to look and smell their best to please Him.

In relation to the topic of ritual purity there were often inquiries about how strict it was necessary to be in the observance of washing before worship. The basic rule said that touching a person of the opposite sex, or going to the toilet, required a new ablution before praying. In practice, by avoiding these two actions, it was thus possible to 'rationalize' by not performing the ritual washing again between the midday and afternoon prayers, or between the afternoon and evening ones. One question concerning this was what to do if one *unintentionally* touched a man. Some said that you should wash all over again, while others said that this was too strict. Another question was whether the same rule applied for non-Muslims to which the answer was no, it only applied to members of the opposite sex, regardless of faith.

The confusion sometimes felt by Malays concerning these rules was also transmitted to non-Malays. Once, during Ramadan, I was travelling in a taxi with a friend, in between worships. We had visited one of her relatives in the afternoon. Instead of going home, we wanted to go straight on to the mosque and break the fast there. We were running a bit late, and my friend wanted to avoid washing again, so she asked the driver (a Chinese man) to place the change on the seat for her to pick up, explaining the rule about not touching someone of the opposite sex if you wanted to keep an earlier ritual ablution valid. The taxi driver was very pleased to hear this; it had angered him when female passengers had requested this before, since he had thought that some Muslim women did not want to come into contact with him because he was Chinese.

Places of worship

Women, for whom it is not obligatory to attend congregational prayers at the mosque, can pray at home or, if they are working, in the prayer room in their workplace. Malay women are not formally excluded from the mosque on Fridays but most mosques are filled to the brim with men on this occasion. There is simply no room left for women. All the mosques that I visited in Malaysia had separate prayer sections for women. In some mosques, the women's section was a separate room, or built as a gallery overlooking the men's and thus women were guaranteed space even on Fridays. Other mosques simply divided the prayer room into two halves by using frames or sometimes just a white line of separation on the floor. The women's section was always behind the men's with respect to the direction of Mecca. In these cases, the two halves were not fixed in size; many women complained that during the Friday noon prayers, the women's section shrank or even disappeared completely, in order to accommodate all the men in the room.[6] Indeed, the crowds of male worshippers on Fridays meant that some mosques were filled to overflowing, with part of the congregation praying on the street outside. While women acknowledged the problem of space, many still felt excluded from the mosque on Fridays. They cited the words of the Prophet, who is reported to have encouraged women to come to the mosque at any time to worship, or to discuss things or seek his advice. Many women also preferred to pray in the mosque because it meant praying as a congregation. There was also a preference for the mosque because it was considered serene and calm, a place where one could more easily concentrate on prayer.

The ritual prayer can, however, be performed anywhere as long as the place of worship is clean. Teachers often underlined this by saying that one could even pray in a toilet, as long as it was clean. A small prayer rug would further guarantee the cleanliness of any place. In their daily lives, women sometimes found themselves experiencing a conflict between their religious and social obligations. The classes on Islam were a place where such questions could be discussed and addressed. One woman was worried that she sometimes did not have the time to pray, for example, when she had to attend functions with her husband, a police officer. The problem was that the functions tended to start around 19.30–20.00 and *maghrib*, the

Figure 4.1. Friday noon prayer at the National mosque in Kuala Lumpur

Figure 4.2. Friday noon prayer at Masjid Jamek in Kuala Lumpur
Photo: Jan Mellqvist

evening prayer, was sometimes around 19.20–19.30. The woman explained that she and her husband were often expected to be at an event before the VIPs and ministers arrived. Considering the traffic in town, this meant that they had to leave their house before the beginning of *maghrib.* Arriving at the reception, she sometimes found that there was no prayer room *(surau).* Many of the other women nodded and admitted that they had had the same problem. The *ustaz* understood the difficulty but said that you can pray anywhere. He himself had prayed in a billiard room and the toilet in an airport. As long as it clean there is no problem, he explained. The women then protested that it was much easier for a man. As women, they had to remove the make-up that they had put on for the function and then put it all back again. They also had to carry around a bag with the *telekung* all through the reception. All this was very inconvenient, but since it was also very bad to miss a prayer, they all agreed that they had to try and do it anyway.

Another woman in the group added that she sometimes missed the afternoon prayer (around 16.30) because she had to go shopping. Sometimes, the queues in the shops were very long and if there were traffic jams on the way home she would not be back in time. This was another problem well known to the rest of the group and they were all taken aback by the harshness in the teacher's voice when his response was that it was a sin to miss a prayer on account of queues or traffic. He advised them to anticipate the time needed for shopping and travelling in order to be back in time. He reminded them that when they had to travel far, they were permitted to skip prayers or combine them, but shopping was not a good reason for failing to pray.

Women who had to move about a lot during the day and who spent much of their time in the public sphere were quite used to finding places in the city suitable for worship. Their daily schedule was often planned with consideration to the *solat* times and the location of mosques or prayer rooms. Most of the big hotels as well as shopping malls in Kuala Lumpur also have prayer rooms where anyone can stop and pray. If no such place was within reach, the women would pray wherever they were. Some busy women carried a small bag with a *telekung,* and sometimes a small prayer mat, and armed with these esssentials, they could turn any space into a place of worship.

This is exactly what happened when I was with a group of women on an afternoon excursion by bus. They had carefully planned the afternoon with consideration for prayer times and their evening household duties. But the bus broke down on the way back and our return to the mosque, from where the excursion had departed, was seriously delayed. After the bus was repaired, we were caught up in the massive Kuala Lumpur afternoon traffic jam. The women were starting to realize that the evening prayer time was approaching much faster than the bus could move and the period within which the afternoon prayer should be performed was coming to an end. One choice was to hope for arriving just in time for them to rush home and perform the prayer before the call for the late evening prayer. But here, religious duties clashed with household duties because many of those on the bus had to prepare dinner for their families, and some had planned to pick up some groceries on the way home. Those who realized that they would not have time for all this, and whose earlier ablution was still valid, decided to pray in the bus. Since we were travelling, they simply prayed in their seats. Others, who had more time or who needed to perform the ablution, waited until we arrived at the mosque and hurried in to pray there. Thus, while an unforeseen delay had prevented the women from arriving in time, they each found ways to deal with the problem.

Creating a desire to pray

In the religious life of the women I met, ritual worship stood out as the most important practice. It was emphasized that the ritual prayer is an act of submission in the sense of accepting that God is the creator of everything. It is a ritually well-defined moment when the worshipper is in direct contact with God. Women used to say that praying five times a day was really a very small thing for God to demand of his believers, and the ideal attitude towards prayer was that it was desired by the worshipper. How the desire to pray was cultivated becomes clear in the following example. It shows how Fati, a woman whose faith had weakened during a crisis, was advised by the women in her study group on how she could regain her desire to pray.

Fati was a Malay woman in her early forties who had recently returned to Malaysia after many years of living in Australia. She was divorced and had moved in with relatives in Kuala Lumpur. Fati did not cover and used to come sporadically to one of the study groups that used English since she felt more comfortable with that language than with Malay. One day, she explained to the group that her faith had grown weaker ever since she moved back to Malaysia. In Australia, her faith had been strong, but in her present situation she felt that her relatives – who had a rather lax attitude towards praying – affected her in a negative way. They did pray sometimes, but not five times a day, and Fati did not consider them to be bad people. But because of their way of practising Islam, Fati felt that her own faith was becoming weak. She found it difficult to pray when no one else in the house wished to do so, so she admitted that she sometimes skipped prayers. The group showed great concern for Fati's problem and one of the women encouraged Fati to think about what it was she was saying in the prayer, what the meaning of those words really were. She flipped open the Koran to Fatiha, the opening chapter, and went through it line by line. She said that when one reads it slowly, with concentration, and thinks about the meaning of the verse, then praying becomes easy. Fati recognized that she would usually say the phrases in the prayer quickly without really thinking about their meaning, like a habit. The other woman said that it was not good when praying became a mere habit. She reminded Fati that praying to God was a kind of submission to him, a means of obeying God who had created everything and who was merciful. She also suggested that Fati should distance herself from her relatives and look for people with stronger faith who could support her. Fati was worried that this meant that she had to leave her family, but the other women assured her that it did not have to come to that. As family, even though they were not very religious, they should be respected. But the women also emphasized the need to have other people with faith around. The study group was one such example. And after class, that evening, Fati stayed on and prayed with a few of the other women.

Besides the important aspect of being part of a community of people who believe in and practise Islam, this example shows that women emphasized ritual worship both as an end in itself, in the sense that ritual prayer is a prescribed duty for Muslims, and as a means of achieving piety. Fati herself sometimes felt that neglecting to pray was an expression of her weakened faith. The same kind of relationship between praying and degree of faith was seen in the case of Iman above who fought her battle against evil forces with prayer; her strong faith made it easy to pray. But when we look more closely at the way in which the women in Fati's study group encouraged her, they emphasized praying as a *means* to strengthen faith, as a way to create a personal relationship with God. The important thing is the creation of a *desire* to pray. In order to inspire this desire, they remind Fati to look for the meaning of prayer and they point her to the Koran and to the words that are pronounced in prayer. Praying, when it was performed with sincerity, with full awareness of the meaning of the words pronounced, was seen as a means to strengthen faith, not merely as an end in itself.

The awareness of God, or the desire to submit to God's will, was also cultivated outside the study groups, in everyday life, and here the practice of personal prayers, *doa*, plays an important role.

PERSONAL PRAYERS

Doa, as personal prayers and a direct form of communication with God, are not obligatory and do not have the ritual character of worship, nor do they have the same restrictions as ritual worship – they can be uttered anywhere, at any time and in any language. [7] There are, however, certain verses in the Koran that can be used as *doa*, and as we saw in the previous chapter, women preferred to say *doa* in Arabic and attended *tajwid* classes in order to improve their Arabic pronunciation and recitation of the Koran.

Other than for worship, *doa* are used to accompany ordinary actions and behaviour. There were different *doa* for different situations, each of them aiming to draw the divine into everyday life. Many *doa* used in this sense were pronounced explicitly for safety or protection: for example, as a way to keep Shaitan (Satan) away when entering the toilet, for safety when departing on a journey, or in connection with intercourse as a means to secure the health of a possible baby. One of my friends would say the very first verse in the Koran each time she started her car or even each time she was about to enter a crossroad or started moving after having waited at a red light. The *doa*, in these contexts, was usually pronounced aloud but in a soft and low voice. Often, the first phrases were pronounced aloud and the rest in a lower voice close to whispering, or even silently. Other *doa* were used in order to make it easier to receive knowledge, and all study groups commenced with participants saying a *doa* (usually Fatiha) together. It was also very common for people to say a personal *doa* after having performed the ritual worship. This could be a general *doa* asking God for guidance, protection or well-being. It could also be something specific, such as good health or as thanksgiving (*syukur*).

Many women said that they would recite a verse from the Koran when they felt that virtues such as patience were being challenged, such as in long queues at the bank or post office, as well as the daily traffic jams. They said that these were good occasions for uttering a verse from the Koran repeatedly to stay calm. Instead of letting the stress of the moment take over, it was better to use the occasion to focus on God and the saying of a *doa*. Repeating the words of God made them realize that a traffic jam was a tiny thing to get worked up about. Through the words of God, the virtue of patience was reached.[8] *Doa* are thus used in a wide range of contexts, both in connection with ritual prayers and as an element in ritual purification, but also as a complement to everyday activities, especially to cultivate patience. Women surrounded themselves, and their bodies, with God's words. The words of God were furthermore incorporated into the body as *doa* and were also used in healing practices and for asking God for good health. 'Islamic *bomohs*' used *doa* as an important part of their treatment, together with herbs. Patients were given one or more *doa* to read over a glass of water. Sometimes at the mosque or in collective rituals at home when the Yasin was recited in the presence of bottles of water, the water acquired healing powers. This water was called *air Yasin* and given to those in bad health. Many healthy women also started their day by reading the first verse of the Koran over a glass of water and then drinking it as a way of asking God for good health and keeping illness away. When I asked what happened to the water when they recited a verse over it, the women said that the word of God went into the water, and by drinking the water, the words got into the body. They were drinking the word of God.

Polluted hair and water

So far, I have emphasized the non-ritual aspect of *doa*, but sometimes the recitation of Koranic verses were elements in ritualized behaviour, for instance, in connection with the prescribed ablutions. This was particularly evident when a person was going from a state of pollution to a state of ritual purity. At the end of the confinement period, the mother's body needed to be ritually purified by a full bath, accompanied by a *doa*. The same kind of procedure was required of both men and women after sexual relations. The issue of ritual purity, particularly concerning the ritually clean female body and its boundaries, gave rise to a number of disputes over correct procedure.

As has already been mentioned, the female body was considered 'polluted' during menstruation. Cutting fingernails and hair washing were therefore to be avoided during this time. When menstruation is over, the whole body and every strand of hair has to be ritually cleansed from head to toe by taking a bath and saying a *doa*. The question that arose had to do with the hair that fell during menstruation and what to do with it. There were two variations of this question. In the first one, modern life and the Islamic ideal were opposed to each other. Many women found it difficult not to wash their hair during menstruation. Modern life made it impossible, they said. They could not go to work with greasy or smelly hair and saw no other way than to wash it. But the question then posed was: What was one to do with hair that fell while bathing? Was that hair still polluted or could it be thrown away? Other women had that problem even if they did not wash their hair. Some women had problems when they wore a *tudung* for many hours of the day, which sometimes caused hair loss when combing, especially during menstruation, since the body was weaker then. They too posed the question of what to do with the fallen hair. They had heard that some religious scholars advised women to collect the hair they dropped during menstruation in order to ritually wash the strands during the purification bath at the end of their period. This was not something the women had ever considered doing before, and they were worried that they had been ignorant of this rule, and had acted wrongly as Muslims. Some of the teachers that I met agreed with the conclusion that the hair should be kept and washed later. But most were of the opinion that this was not necessary. Their reasoning was that once hair had dropped, it was no longer part of the body and thus not polluted and could be thrown away.

Many women followed the advice given by the *ustaz* or *ustazah* that they considered 'theirs'. This could be the teacher who was leading a particular class they followed regularly or, for instance, the teacher engaged to come and instruct their children about Islam and guide the family in Islamic matters generally. The expression 'my *ustaz*' was very common and women, when giving an opinion on a particular subject, were often asked by the others who their teacher was. Most of the women in this study, however, knew several teachers in different contexts and sometimes encountered contradictory opinions. One woman did not have any particular teacher that she considered 'hers'. She attended several classes and took part in religious activities both at work and elsewhere, going to different mosques and thus getting to know various groups. She had heard the two different answers about the hair dilemma and had decided to go along with the idea that you do not have to keep the fallen hair. She was, however, very careful when combing her hair during menstruation so as not to lose too much.

The dilemma about hair washing was caused by the modern lifestyle and its demands, including the fact that women now worked outside their homes. The old tradition of simply not washing your hair while menstruating was no longer acceptable. Sometimes, however, modern life and technology provided solutions rather than complications to pious women seeking to ensure compliance with Islamic obligations. To take two examples, in Malaysia's hot and humid climate, air conditioning at work prevented women from getting too hot in their headscarves and long dresses, while the modern shower in urban houses prevented pollution. Many women found the shower very convenient for taking the ritual cleansing bath at the end of their period and after intercourse rather than the *mandi*, the traditional bath. With a traditional bath, water was kept in a large container and scooped up and poured over the body. The problem was that some drops of that water could easily, when being flung or poured over the body, fall back into the container and pollute the water. With the modern shower there was no such risk of pollution.

FASTING IN THE MONTH OF RAMADAN

Ramadan, or the fasting month, is the ninth month of the Islamic lunar year. Throughout the month of Ramadan, Muslims are not allowed to eat, drink or have intercourse during daytime. Fasting begins at dawn and lasts until sunset. In Malaysia, it is emphasized that fasting should not be done only as a tradition: the quality of the fast is very important. It was said that some people do not get anything from fasting – only hunger and thirst. Those are the people who only abstain from food and drink, neglecting the other aspect of the fast, to 'fast' with the mouth, ears and hands. This means that Muslims should restrain from saying bad things, thinking bad thoughts, and doing bad deeds. Those who do this can be said to fast both with their body and their mind. Even better are those who 'fast with their heart', in the sense of using the fasting period as an opportunity for introspection, to look at one's life, and to ask Allah for blessings and for forgiveness.

Schimmel (1992) indicates that in the Muslim world generally, fasting is the most strictly observed duty. This is also the case in Malaysia where there seems to be a virtually universal observance of the fast during Ramadan. Even those who are not so diligent in performing other religious duties like to fast during Ramadan. It should also be mentioned that the state, through surveillance of public places during Ramadan, underlines the importance of fasting. Any Muslim person seen eating or drinking during daytime may be questioned and punished by a fine or imprisonment for not observing the fast. Even those who are not obligated to fast are extremely cautious and do not eat or drink in public for fear of being spotted by religious officers who patrol the streets of Kuala Lumpur during Ramadan.

Most of the religious classes still running during Ramadan focused on the meaning of fasting and on the paying of *zakat*, and the rules of fasting and *zakat* were repeated. We were asked to read the Koranic verses 2: 183–185 from which one could learn that fasting during Ramadan is a command by God[9] and that Ramadan is the month when the Koran began to be revealed to Muhammad. Ramadan was also the time to ask and receive forgiveness from God. 'Ramadan is forgiveness on sale,' as one of the religious teachers expressed it. It was beyond his imagination how anybody would want to miss this offer.

In Islam, there are a number of general rules as to who may or may not perform the fast. A person must be a Muslim, sane, of age (usually when reaching puberty)[10], and clean/dry. For women, the last criterion meant they were not allowed to fast when having their period, or in confinement or breastfeeding. A menstruating woman had to break fast until she was dry again. When breaking the Ramadan fast on account of menstruation, women would usually remark 'Today I do not fast', or 'Today I do not have to fast' to explain why they were drinking or eating during the day. The reply to my question about why they did not need to fast was that God understands the difficulty of fasting for menstruating women: they are more tired than usual and need to eat and drink. The fast must not cause any health problems. Small children, very old or sick people were given the same kind of dispensation. The loss of fasting days during Ramadan because of menstruation should, however, be 'paid back' in the form of fasting for the equivalent number of days as soon as possible after Ramadan, at the latest before the next fasting month. It was quite common to pay back the lost days by fasting on Mondays and Thursdays spread out over the coming months. Mondays and Thursdays were auspicious days because they were the days that the Prophet Muhammad was said to have had the habit of fasting.[11] It was, however, considered a 'good thing'[12] to do it right after Ramadan.

There were also guidelines for situations when the fast was rendered invalid. This was something that inspired a number of questions during Ramadan. One question had to do with receiving medical treatment. Was one allowed to swallow medicine? And how about seeing to your teeth during Ramadan? Did the blood that you incidentally swallow during dental treatment affect the fast? And, if so, what about your own saliva that you sometimes need to swallow? Did fainting or vomiting invalidate that day's fasting? The basic answers to these questions were that medicine that had to be taken orally did in fact render the fast invalid. People who were too sick to fast and who were on medication could, however, compensate the lost fasting days by paying *fidiah* (the equivalent of a bowl of rice).[13]

Injections did not invalidate the fast, but it was considered better to go to the dentist after Ramadan. If dental treatment was urgently required, there was no problem with swallowing blood, or saliva for that matter, since it came from the mouth. The fast is only accepted if the person who is about to fast states his or her intention (*niat*) of fasting the following day.[14] Fasting must not endanger health and those who fall ill (or menstruate) during Ramadan can fast later when they have recovered.[15] Pregnant or nursing women and people who are travelling must also compensate for lost days by fasting the equivalent number of days later. People who are prevented from fasting altogether on account of bad health or old age, must pay *fidiah* for each non-fasting day.

Breaking fast

Following the Sunna, the fast should ideally be broken with some water and an odd number of dates or at least with something sweet. The meal that follows is, in Malaysia, often an elaborate one with rice and various side dishes, followed by fresh fruit and sweet cakes. Women spend a lot of time cooking during Ramadan, something that is experienced as difficult, not because of the hard work but because of the temptation that the cooking creates. Menstruating women also make sure not to eat in front of those in the family who are fasting so as not to put them through unnecessary temptation. Many women also avoid cooking themselves during this period and prefer to buy curries and desserts from the foodstalls that increase dramatically in number during Ramadan. In the late afternoons, the street markets are crowded and busy and the dishes offered during this time of the year are richly varied. Eating out is also very popular during Ramadan, particularly among the young. Restaurants start to become crowded half an hour or so before the *azan* calls for the breaking of the fast; it is impossible to get a seat anywhere if one waits for the *azan* itself. Fast-food outlets such as Kentucky Fried Chicken and McDonalds are as popular as the open-air stalls serving local dishes such as satay.

The Norwegian social anthropologist Ingrid Rudie notes from her fieldwork in rural Kelantan that 'Ramadan is the period in which Islamic togetherness is maximally strengthened in family and community' (1994: 177). She bases this mainly on the importance of sharing the meal that breaks the fast in the evening. To break fast (*buka puasa*) together with family and friends was very important for the women I met during my fieldwork. In the urban context, relatives do not always live in close proximity to each other and, during Ramadan, there is a good deal of travelling from one part of town to another in order to break fast with a brother or sister's family. The cooking of lavish evening meals during Ramadan was criticized by some women, as well as men, who did not approve of the tendency to turn the breaking of the fast into feasting. They said that feasting should not begin until *Hari Raya* (Eid), which is the celebration that marks the end of Ramadan.[16] They also emphasized that the Muslim community would be further strengthened by the tradition of breaking fast at the mosque where a meal is served in the evening all through Ramadan.

When comparing the material she collected in 1965 to the situation that she encountered in 1987, Rudie makes the reflection that fast-breaking parties in homes had decreased in both number and size over the years, but that breaking fast in the mosque was becoming more common. Although my material does not cover the same timespan, my impression, from what people told me about their lives in Kuala Lumpur, is that mosque activity in general had become increasingly lively over the past 20 years. This indicates a process of consolidation of the Muslim community, which has also been one of the main goals of Malaysian Islamization. The process of strengthening the *ummah* is not only significant in relation to the breaking of the fast and the sharing of a meal. Other practices are equally important in this respect. In the next section we shall see that Ramadan also offers an extraordinary occasion for praying as a congregation, in particular through *terawih* prayers, which many women valued highly and enjoyed performing.

Terawih

After the evening meal it was very common to perform the *terawih*. *Terawih* means 'prayer in the night' and can be performed at any time during the year but it is only called *terawih* during Ramadan. In Malaysia, it typically consists of a series of either eleven or twenty prayer cycles (*rakaat*).[17] My informants gave me the impression that *terawih* reached the wider Muslim community in Malaysia only during the last two decades, and can thus be connected to the *dakwah* movement. Most of them could not remember *terawih* having been practised by parents or grandparents and they had themselves been introduced to it when settling down in Kuala Lumpur. Most of the women that I knew took part in the *terawih* prayer with great pleasure and preferred to perform it in the mosque rather than at home. They explained to me that it was perfectly fine to do it at home but they stressed the spiritual experience of praying late at night, in the mosque.

In connection with the *terawih* prayers in the mosques, the Koran is read aloud from beginning to end, chapter by chapter. Ideally, the whole Koran is completed within the fasting month. It was often said that Ramadan is a special time for reading the Koran since this was the month when the Koran was revealed to Muhammad. The first revelation occurred on a special night referred to as *laylat al-qadr*.[18] People in Malaysia talked about this night as the night when the sky opens and an angel comes down to earth. The exact night is unknown, but it is thought to occur during the last ten days of Ramadan. A person who stays up that night to pray might be touched by God and receive God's blessings. Some women narrated experiences that they connected to this belief. It was, however, stressed that such experiences could not be actively sought after.

At any time, reading chapters or verses from the Koran would give you merit 'points' whenever you did it, but doing so during Ramadan was particularly valuable. Not all mosques offered a reading of the whole text for practical reasons. People were still working during Ramadan and could not stay up all night. Therefore, readings were sometimes confined to nightly recitals of the last chapter of the Koran, which contained only short verses.

Some women found the reading better performed in a particular mosque and made a habit of praying there each night during Ramadan. When talking about their Ramadan experiences, women usually emphasized the sense of togetherness and of spirituality that was created out of these long nightly prayer sessions. One woman said to me:

> As you see, Ramadan seems like any other month here [in Malaysia]. Nothing much. It is these *terawih* prayers that make the whole year different. When everybody goes to the mosque and prays. The atmosphere, that is what I like. I can

do it at home, yes. If my husband is sick or when the children were smaller and they couldn't go to the mosque then we prayed at home. It doesn't matter. But going to the mosque, making the mosque alive, when it is otherwise empty. It is something I look forward to.

Khatam Koran

Religious classes and study groups generally kept going during the first two weeks of Ramadan. After that, the focus was on reading the Koran and praying. The long period of fasting also started to make people tired and they preferred to be less active during the second half of Ramadan. Classes did not resume until a couple of weeks after Ramadan since the celebration of the end of the fasting month, *Hari Raya*, was for many an occasion to take a holiday and visit family and relatives in other parts of the country.

The religious classes in the mosque paused during the whole fasting month and the women concentrated on perfecting their reading of the Koran instead. They met in the mornings in the same lecture hall that classes were held, only now the desks and chairs were stashed away.[19] The women organized themselves in groups of eight or ten and took turns reading one page each. The following day they would pick up where they had left off the day before so that by the end of two weeks they had completed reading the Koran from beginning to end. When one of them was reading aloud, the others followed the text silently and corrected any mistakes in her pronunciation. They all agreed it was a good opportunity to improve their reading.

When the group had almost completed reading the whole Koran, with only the last few shorter chapters left, a small celebration was held to mark the occasion. On one such occasion that I witnessed, all the women who had taken part in the reading gathered at the mosque. A big white cloth was spread in the centre of the floor and twelve women were chosen, by drawing lots, to each read one of the very short chapters at the end of the Koran. The readers sat around the white cloth in the sequence of the chapter assigned to them. The rest were seated in a wider circle around them. The imam was also present. He started the ceremony by giving a short sermon and leading a *doa*, and then the women read the final chapters of the Koran, thereby completing the reading that had begun two weeks before. After the imam left the room, the president of the women's committee thanked all the women for their participation and everyone was presented with a small gift, in this instance, a navy blue silk scarf. The event was drawn to a close by the distribution of packed meals of yellow glutinous rice and the popular Malay beef *rendang* (a curry). Those who were fasting took the food home to eat later. Most of the women stayed on after the ritual and performed the collective prayer in the mosque.

While the importance of reading the Koran during Ramadan was widely accepted, I also heard some guarded criticism of the way the Koran was treated as 'a ritual' rather than read for its content. A mere recitation of the Koran without reflecting on its meaning was not approved of. Women often told me that it would be better to read only *one* verse, and to really understand its meaning, than to read the Koran from beginning to end and not understand a single word. Some commented that this mechanical way of treating the Koran was typical of Malay adat (as opposed to religion, or *din*) and something that should be abandoned. As with the discussions about men's silk shirts, such comments can be seen as a way of indicating the separateness of a Malay vs a Muslim identity.

Commendable fasting

During my fieldwork, women were involved in a controversy that had to do with the commendable fasting (*puasa sunna*) that could be performed in the month following Ramadan, the month of Syawal. In Malaysia, this fast lasting six days is called *puasa enam* (six-day fast, also *puasa sunna Syawal*). On *Hari Raya*, the first day of Syawal, fasting was forbidden (*haram*), while the second day of that month was considered a very good day to fast. Some people who had the habit of fasting on that day would continue to fast for another five days, thus performing the *puasa enam*. This performance, or any of the other suggested commendable fasting occasions, was a very good thing. Not only did it show that the person had a strong commitment to Islam, it also gave extra rewards to the performer. It was mentioned that the rewards given for *puasa enam* were equivalent to one whole year of fasting. (The neglect of performing acts of commendable fasting does not affect a person's 'reward account' or merits (*pahala*) in a negative way, nor does it incur any sin.)

The issue was whether it was possible or not, in some way, to combine *puasa enam* with the specific female practice of 'paying back' lost days of fast during Ramadan. The commendable act of paying back the lost days of fasting because of menstruation right after Ramadan was apparently in conflict with another 'good thing' to do, the *puasa enam*. It seemed impossible to achieve the maximum of rewards for both periods of fasting. Many women therefore posed the question of which fast they should perform first. Religious teachers offered different answers. Some held that the 'pay-back fast' had priority since it was compulsory, as it was done to compensate days of non-fasting during Ramadan, which is one of the five pillars of faith. *Puasa enam*, however, was only voluntary and therefore less important. It was suggested that the *puasa enam* be carried out after the period of 'pay-back fast', but still within the month of Syawal. For women who had lengthy menstrual periods, this was not so easy to accomplish. Let us take Zarah as an example. Her ten-day period meant that, if she were to pay back the lost ten days immediately after *Hari Raya*, she would be sure to have her next period before she could perform the *puasa enam*. The end of Ramadan typically involved visiting a lot of people, and visiting meant sharing food. *Hari Raya* celebrations tended to stretch out over weeks or even a month since there were so many relatives and friends to visit and receive. Therefore, even those with shorter periods found it difficult to perform both their pay-back fast and the *puasa enam* during the month of Syawal.

One solution would be to combine the two different fasts into one, which was the answer that some *ustaz* would give. One could state the intention (*niat*) that the fast was a combination of the two, and it would be counted as such. Other teachers did not agree. They said that it was not possible to *niat* such a thing and that the two different fasts were counted separately. Yet others agreed that one could not *niat* a combination of fasts, but that the fast performed in the month of Syawal would be counted as both *puasa enam* and pay-back fast 'automatically'. Thus, while paying back lost days of fasting, women would gain the rewards for *puasa enam* at the same time.

For many women, this was an important consideration. The idea of receiving rewards, or 'points' as the women more popularly expressed it, for religious deeds (or being discredited for misdeeds) was always present in their minds. There were good deeds, bad deeds and others that did not affect the account at all. Different deeds would be awarded different 'points'. Referring to the image of the two angels sitting on each shoulder, women often talked about their 'account' and the angels 'keeping the books' for them. God would revise the 'account' on the day of judgement, when it would be decided who could enter paradise and who could not. The women that I met had not always been pious and suspected that their 'accounts' were in the negative. Many talked about 'making up for past sins' and were eager to gain as many points as possible and were thus keen on anything to do with rewards. It should be noted, however, that while they were strongly concerned about 'points' from God, this was also something that they joked about. One woman told me about her first hajj, performed in the company of her brother and his wife. After having gone around the Kaaba (the site most holy to Muslims containing a sacred black stone), she found her sister-in-law in deep concentration, staring at the square building. When asked what she was doing, the sister-in-law replied with laughter that she was busy collecting her points.

ZAKAT

Ramadan is also the time for paying *zakat*. *Zakat* literally has two meanings. One is 'growth' or 'increase' and the other is 'purity'. The giver of *zakat* increases his or her store of religious merit and at the same time the giving leads to growing prosperity in this world since it is used as an instrument for the redistribution of income and wealth. The second meaning is that the giving of *zakat* purifies the sins of the giver (Abdul Aziz 1993: 29). Schimmel (1992) expresses the same ideas when saying that the meaning of *zakat* is self-purification and that it is considered a loan to God.

There are different kinds of *zakat*. *Zakat fitrah* is a compulsory tax for all Muslims who have the means, and a part of the performance of Ramadan. This *zakat* must be paid before the end of Ramadan and in Malaysia it was set to RM 2.50 (about USD 1) for each person in a household. The other type of *zakat* that was of relevance for the women in my study was the *zakat* that must be paid in relation to personal wealth.[20] In Malaysia, the Shafi'i Islamic school of jurisprudence states that '...salary earners are not obliged to pay *zakat* if their incomes are consumed and nothing is saved or kept idle (beyond a certain limit) for the duration of one year' (Abdul Aziz 1993: 1). This means, however, that *zakat* must be paid on any savings (2.5 per cent), either in the form of money or other valuables. Most of the women that I knew were either wage earners or housewives and paid *zakat* on their savings, which was often in the form of gold. To '*zakat* gold' was a common phrase. This meant that the worth of gold that a person kept as savings, excluding the gold that she wore on a daily basis, was the basis for the calculation of *zakat*. The state, as well as various *dakwah* organizations, disseminates information through radio and television on who needs to pay *zakat*, how to calculate the amount to be paid, and where to pay it. In spite of this, I often met women, particularly women without higher education, who were confused about the whole matter. This was also reflected in the number of questions about the payment and calculation of *zakat* that religious teachers had to answer during Ramadan.

Most of all, women were afraid of not giving enough as *zakat*, of not having calculated the correct amount to pay. This fear was not directed towards the religious authorities but towards God. Women who did not have any wealth except for a few gold bangles on their arms were eager to '*zakat* their gold' even though it was not necessary. They would calculate the worth of the gold and give 2.5 per cent of the amount as *zakat*. During Ramadan I accompanied one woman when she went to donate some money to a private orphanage outside Kuala Lumpur. This woman was not wealthy and was the sole breadwinner in her family, providing for her two daughters with her factory-worker's salary. She knew about the orphanage and the family who ran it. The old man who had founded the orphanage was also a very religious man who was referred to as *ustaz*. He accepted the donation and said a *doa* over it, asking God to accept the money as payment of *zakat*. Before arriving at the orphanage, the woman was visibly nervous and repeated several times: 'I am so scared! I do not know if it is enough. I do not know if God will accept. I do not have wealth, but I want to pay *zakat*'. She was worried that God would not accept her small sum of money.

Afterwards, going back in her car, she was relieved, but still repeated that she hoped God had accepted her donation.

In Malaysia, all aspects relating to the administration and distribution of *zakat* are handled by the individual states through their respective Religious Councils or Majlis Agama.[21] People can go directly to the Council to pay their *zakat*. In Kuala Lumpur, during Ramadan, there is also a *zakat* office, as well as a table for the collection of *zakat fitrah*, at the National Mosque. Many women, however, preferred to give *zakat* directly to orphanages, or to a mosque that they wished to support. Religious teachers often advised women to give *zakat* through the official bodies but also underlined that the important thing when giving directly to someone in need was that the giver stated the intention (*niat*) of the gift. Only then would God accept the gift as payment of *zakat*. The Koran specifies eight categories of beneficiaries of *zakat*:

> *Alms are for the poor*
> *And the needy, and those*
> *Employed to administer the (funds);*
> *For those whose hearts*
> *Have been (recently) reconciled*
> *(To Truth); for those in bondage*
> *And in debt; in the cause*
> *Of God; and for the wayfarer:*
> *(Thus is it) ordained by God,*
> *And God is full of knowledge*
> *And wisdom.* (Sura 9: 60)

Zakat givers show a preference for donating to children who have lost their father or both parents. Once, I visited a small village outside Kuala Lumpur that only had a small prayer hall, not a mosque. This particular evening was consecrated to a special *buka puasa* and *terawih* prayers to raise and distribute donations for the needy in the village, mainly orphans.[22] The family who took me to this event lived in a nearby village but were very supportive of that particular prayer hall. The land that the prayer hall was built on had been donated by the father of the present imam and thus stood free from the influence of UMNO. The imam's father was also a close friend of the family. The imam was in his late thirties and had recently returned from Cairo where he had studied at Al-Azhar University. He was praised for his piety, a piety that my friends said could be seen radiating from his face. The quality of this man's religiosity was something that made my friends eager to donate money to this particular mosque.

THE PILGRIMAGE TO MECCA

The hajj, or pilgrimage to Mecca, is the last of the five pillars of Islam and is to be performed on the condition that the person who undertakes it has the means for it. Briefly, the pilgrimage is an assembly of rituals performed in Mecca and its surroundings, in the 12th month of the Muslim lunar year, when pilgrims commemorate past events in the Islamic history.[23]

Large numbers of Malaysian pilgrims visit the holy city of Mecca each year. Historian Mary McDonnell (1990) shows that the number of pilgrims from the Malay Peninsula, and later, independent Malaysia, has grown dramatically from approximately 2,500 in 1885 to 25,000 a century later, in 1985.[24] In the background to her exploration of inner and personal changes of more recent Malaysian pilgrims, McDonnell sketches the historical changes in the social composition of those who went for the hajj from this part of the world. In 1900, it was mainly wealthy, elderly men who were part of the traditional elite that went for the hajj. From the 1920s to the 1960s, there was a steady trend towards participation by new groups of people: elderly peasants, the emergent middle-class intelligentsia, students and women. There was also a corresponding shift to a predominance of pilgrims coming from urban areas rather than the countryside. After the Second World War, Malay power shifted to the urban centres and the hajj became increasingly associated with the urban middle class. Turning her attention to female pilgrims, McDonnell found no material from before the 1920s on Malay women who had performed the hajj. In the late 1930s, however, it became common for wealthier rural men to take their families along for the hajj and, as a consequence, the number of female pilgrims began to rise. In the post-war period, the number of women increased further and, since the 1970s, female pilgrims have outnumbered male ones by five to six per cent.

In Malaysia, many of the practical aspects of the hajj are regulated and organized by a special government agency called Lembaga Tabung Haji (Tabung Haji, Pilgrimage Savings Corporation). The agency has mobilized cash savings and as a result Muslims can now participate in the hajj without having to sell their land or houses as was common before the Second World War (McDonnell 1990). The agency is also the link with the Saudi Arabian authorities. Today there are a number of travel agencies tied to Tabung Haji that provide pilgrims with comprehensive travel packages, which include registration, visas, transportation, accommodation arrangements, as well as medical or special care. They also organize preparatory courses for those performing the hajj for the first time.

The duration of the pilgrimage has also shortened drastically since the Second World War. At the beginning of the twentieth century, the hajj was financially and physically exhausting, sometimes taking a whole year to complete; many never returned. Those who returned were accorded greater social and religious authority derived partly from being persons of means, and partly from having undergone a spiritual experience and being more knowledgeable about Islam (Peletz 1996).

Pilgrims today, on the other hand, perform a four-week journey with all the necessary travel and living arrangements organized for them. The pilgrim can continue living as usual upon return to Malaysia. Pilgrims are generally much younger today and have a relatively brief stay in Mecca, thus the pilgrimage per se does not necessarily mean increased knowledge. The pilgrim's social status and religious authority is no longer automatically enhanced and this is mirrored by the fact that a young *hajjah* does not usually call herself *hajjah* and is not referred to as such by others. An older *hajjah*, on the other hand, often use her title. In her case, it is age rather than her identity as a returned pilgrim that increases her authority. The significance of the pilgrimage has thus changed rather dramatically over time, reflecting the fact that Mecca is now accessible to a large proportion of Malaysia's Muslim population.

McDonnell (1990) presents an analysis of Malaysian pilgrims who performed the hajj between 1981 and 1984. The study explores the personal changes that pilgrims experienced and shows that people expected to become close to God, increase their knowledge about Islam, become better persons and be honoured within their community. They felt that the hajj would help them to control negative emotions such as jealousy or hatred, and that they would be able to pray better. They also indicated that another positive aspect of the hajj was to have the experience of belonging to the community of Muslims.

All the women participating in the various study groups described in this book had performed the hajj at least once. Most of them had gone to Mecca in the 1970s and 1980s with their husbands or parents, or a brother. Many women described the hajj as a spiritual turning point in life and many had started to wear the *tudung* then. Putting aside the financial planning that was needed before undertaking the hajj, the decision to perform the pilgrimage was often connected to a personal life crisis. Having recovered from a serious illness was one reason often stated for going. The journey was then performed as a kind of thanksgiving to God. The hajj could also be undertaken because of illness and with the hope of being cured. Women often recounted stories about how their health problems had suddenly vanished during their hajj. The death of someone close to them was another reason for going to Mecca, as a way of dealing with grief and finding comfort. Women who had other personal problems, concerning marriage, for example, told me that performing the hajj was a way of finding their way in life. One woman said that she went on the hajj in order to receive guidance from God in a marriage conflict. She hoped that the moment she faced the Kaaba would be one of revelation, and that she would then have the necessary guidance to make the right choice.

However, many women also recognized that they had not been ready to perform the hajj the first time. They felt that they had been too young and without the proper knowledge to really appreciate the pilgrimage. Many women described their second hajj as a deeply transformative experience. They had been better prepared, both emotionally and intellectually. A strong component in all these stories was that the first time they had simply performed the rituals, while the second time they had understood the meaning of the rituals, and thus felt closer to God.

For most of the women in this study, then, their first hajj had marked a new awareness of religion in their lives. They also emphasized the emotional experience of praying together with Muslims from all over the world. Sometimes it was a turning point in life towards a more active practice of Islam. Many women had started wearing a headscarf when they returned from their first pilgrimage. The second hajj, however, usually meant that they had progressed in terms of their religious knowledge and that their experience was thereby more powerful. While the first hajj was, for most of them, the beginning of their religious commitment, the second one implied a deepening of that commitment.

Spiritual vacation

Affluent Malays often choose to go to Mecca at periods other than during the month designated for the hajj. Many go for a shorter stay (usually two weeks) in the holy city in order to perform a set of rites known as *umrah*, also referred to as the 'lesser hajj'. Those who can afford it go as often as once a year. Some Malaysian companies run on Islamic principles put aside part of their yearly profit in order to send all employees on *umrah*, as a bonus. This is sometimes humorously called a 'spiritual vacation', the joke being that Mecca was described as extremely hot, dry, not very clean and crowded – not really a place one would want to visit on holiday.

ISLAM AS A WAY OF LIFE

A central theme in this chapter has been the concern that women show in relation to the correct performance of their religious obligations and that all aspects of their behaviour in daily life accord with Islamic rules. Importantly, it also shows that what they value is the experience of spiritual growth emanating from such performances. This concern for correctness based on conformity to the life of the Prophet Muhammad has led some scholars of Islam (Graham 1983; Denny 1994) to characterize the religion as an orthopraxy, as opposed to an orthodoxy. The women in my material, however, emphasized the concern to comply with God's will as the basis for their striving for correctness in ritual and other acts of worship. The concern was for a particular act to be performed in a way that would give the person rewards from God. By ensuring correctness in religious practices, women could create, and maintain, a relationship with God. This was a somewhat different interpretation of the notion of 'Islam as a way of life' than the one found in the political discourse of the *dakwah* movement of the 1970s.

As mentioned, the *dakwah* movement in Malaysia has tended to be analysed in terms of the social and political implications of the emphasis that *dakwah* members placed on outward manifestations of their faith. They were using Islam, for example the Islamic rules on diet and dress, to strengthen the ethnic identity of Malays (Chandra 1987) in relation to other ethnic groups in Malaysia. I am quite convinced that Islamization has had a deep effect on ethnic relations in Malaysia and I do not doubt the validity of Chandra's analysis. I would like to focus here, however, on the implicit relationship between practice and belief that permeates his analysis. His assumption seems to be that because there is a radical transformation of *outer* manifestations of Islam among *dakwah* members, the meaning of this behaviour must be sought outside religion. Hence, the religious practices of *dakwah* members are conceived of as surface phenomena that do not correspond with changes in their personal religious experience or conviction.

In my study, however, the women were actively seeking to realize a personal life informed by Islam, and thus God, in every aspect of their lives as an end in itself. They used the Arabic expression of Islam as 'a way of life' (*ad-deen*) continuously. For them, it meant a personal aspiration toward piety achieved through religious instruction and correct religious practice. Islam meant being aware of God in everything, to think of everything as God's creation. It meant striving for a life where all actions and thoughts were oriented toward the fulfilment of God's will. Women taught each other to use everyday situations as a way to become aware of God's presence. The following incident during a class in the mosque one morning illuminates this.

> The morning class had just begun when one of the light bulbs in the ceiling lamp suddenly went out. The crowd of women immediately giggled and stirred. The teacher took up the thread of her lecture by saying that what had just happened could be a lesson for all present. Instead of reacting with giggles, she

suggested that it could be used simply as a moment to reflect on God's presence. She stressed that God, of course, had nothing to do with the bursting of the light bulb. Instead, she suggested that the event should be used as a *reminder* of God. In this example, what the teacher was trying to make the women see was that everyday situations, in fact any situation, can be used to cultivate a conscious faithfulness toward God. I suggest that it is in the framework of the cultivation of a conscious faith that the meaning that women ascribe to the practice of religious duties and acts of worship should be understood. The context of worship also addresses the issue of the body, since it is the material body that performs such acts of worship.

Cultivation of piety

Feminist theologist Sarah Coakly presents a way of conceiving the relationship between religious belief, practice and embodiment that is useful for understanding how Islam is lived by devout women. To her, devotional practices, are not '...optional frills attendant on metaphysical theories acquired somewhere else; rather it is the very medium of such belief, ultimately transcending the thought/action divide' (Coakly 1997: 8–9, with references to Csordas 1990 and McGuire 1990). She holds that religious beliefs may be seen as embodied through religious practice, and she suggests that the practices may be said to precede the beliefs.

In Islamic traditions, the living body's materiality is regarded as an essential means for cultivating conduct defined as virtuous and for discouraging conduct defined as vice The idea, as social anthropologist Talal Asad (2003) describes it, is that the more an individual exercises a virtue, the easier it becomes, and consequently, the more the individual gives in to vice, the more difficult it becomes to act virtuously. In this view, conscious intentionality is seen as the key. Rites of worship are, in this respect, necessary for the cultivation of the virtues and sensibilities that are required of Muslims. Rites of worship, as we have seen, also require, at their commencement, the silent enunciation of the person's intention (*niat*) in performing them. According to Asad, this enunciation of intention '... is an integral part of the rite, a form of conscious commitment initiating acts of worship that must itself be cultivated as an aspect of one's continuous faith' (ibid.: 90). The point here is that a conscious faith in God does not elicit outward forms of conduct. It is rather the sequence of practices and actions that a person is engaged in that determines the person's desires and emotions. Action, it can therefore be said, does not issue forth from natural feelings but creates them (Mahmood 2001b). The body, then, should thus be understood as the 'developable means' (Asad 1993: 76) through which forms of being and action are realized.

Using these ideas, one can say that Malay women were creating and maintaining a relationship with God through a disciplining of the body in daily rituals and acts of worship. The practice of accompanying daily activities with *doa* or recitation of Koranic verses further shows a creative striving by the women to craft themselves as religious persons through the words of God. We have also seen that virtues such as patience and a desire to fulfil religious duties were disciplined through acts of worship, in particular through prayer and fasting. Soft and gentle ways were seen as consequences of piety. A life lived in harmony with the rules and obligations drawn from the Koran and Hadith also required a certain disciplining of both body and mind. When such harmony was reached, piety could even take on a physical form in the form of light (*noor*) radiating from someone's face.

In the next chapter, attention will be turned toward collective rituals performed by women as part of their everyday religious practice.

NOTES

1   Richard T. Antoun (1976) notes that Geertz, in *Religion of Java*, spends 96 pages on various aspects of the non-Islamic peasant rituals and only 10 pages to describing Islamic ritual. See also Abd el-Hamid el-Zein (1977) on the neglect of everyday Islamic ritual in anthropology.

2   See, for example, Marjo Buitelaar's anthropological study of Moroccan women's participation in Ramadan (1993) and Bowen's work on the Gayo (1989, 1993).

3   The English translation from Arabic is taken from Schimmel (1992: 34).

4   Kafir is an Arabic concept meaning 'infidel'. It is used to refer to people who do not believe in the existence of God.

5   There are also bomohs who do not use their powers in a bad way, but who still communicate with the spirits for curing purposes. They might also use

verses from the Koran, thus mixing traditional knowledge with elements from Islam. They were not usually referred to as 'Islamic'.

6   Performing the Friday noon prayer at the mosque with the congregation is a duty for Muslim men. People in Malaysia often said that if a man neglects to pray in the mosque on three consecutive Fridays he is not considered a Muslim anymore. Pressure to participate in congregational prayers was very strong and a few young men admitted that they had sometimes hid in the toilet in order not to be spotted in public at the time of the Friday noon prayer.

7   *Doa* are also an important element in religious celebrations and in rituals performed by the community. This will be discussed further in the following chapter, which deals with urban women's collective rituals.

8   On revisits to the field in 2005 and 2006, I noticed that large electronic signboards had been placed along the roads in Kuala Lumpur and along highways leading out of the city. These signboards showed a mix of advertising, traffic information and information about the next call to prayer.

9   Verse 2: 183 begins with the words: 'O ye who believe!' which indicates that the verse is a command by God. The verse then continues: 'Fasting has been prescribed to you, that ye may (learn) self-restraint,.'

10   In Malaysia, children start practising the fast much earlier. They often begin by fasting half the day, and later they might attempt to fast for two weeks or so. Children were proud of being able to go through with the goal set up and looked forward to the next year when they would be able to fast a little bit more. It was not uncommon for children of ten or eleven to try to fast throughout Ramadan.

11   Fasting could be performed on other days as well but should always be initiated on a Monday or Thursday.

12   A practice that was considered a 'good thing' to do was usually referred to as Sunna, thereby indicating that the act was based on a model derived from the Prophet Muhammad's life. 'Good thing' also referred to the amount of religious merit the performer of the deed accrued in the process of doing it.

13   The Islamic tradition tells that *fidiah* is the meal (a bowl of rice) for one person and should be given to somebody who is poor. Today it is most often paid in the form of money, but it is not uncommon to donate rice or other staple foodstuffs to orphanages.

14   Some religious teachers said that the *niat* must be said aloud. Others said that there was no need to do so and that the important thing was that the intention was stated in the person's heart.

15   Fainting renders the fast invalid and the lost day of fasting must be compensated by one day of fasting after Ramadan. Vomiting was not considered to render the fast invalid, unless it was caused voluntarily.

16 *Hari Raya* is, in Malaysia, the most important religious holiday. In many other Sunni countries, the day of sacrifice (called *Hari Raya Haji* in Malaysia), which is held at the end of the annual hajj period, is the most celebrated day. For Shiites, the most significant day is the *Ashura* festival in the month of *Muharram* when the martydom of Imam Hussein is commemorated.

17 In some mosques there were 11 prayer cycles, and 20 in others. There was no open contradiction between the two ways, but those who did 11 were sometimes critical of the speed that the others were thought to have when praying. Stressing the quality of the prayer, they held a slow, concentrated and beautiful way of praying as the ideal. Their reference for this was that Muhammad had sometimes stayed up all night to pray. The quality of the prayer was stressed rather than the quantity of cycles.

18 Buitelaar (1993) notes the uncertainty among religious scholars as to whether or not the Koran was actually sent down in its totality on the night of *laylat al-qadr.*

19 In the evenings, the same hall was the designated area where women could break their fast. All the bigger mosques would serve food every night during Ramadan and, on this occasion, people were always seated on the floor.

20 There are also a number of zakat rules for the various kinds of agricultural produce and livestock owned. For more information on this, see Abdul Aziz (1993).

21 Except in Kedah, where there is separate Zakat Office directly responsible to the sultan.

22 Converts make up another group of people who qualify for receiving zakat. At this *buka puasa* there was a young European woman who had converted to Islam. She was a university friend of the daughter in the family and she was spending Ramadan in Malaysia. After having broken the fast together there was a small ceremony when donations were distributed to the families in need. To the surprise of the young woman, she was included in the group of people who received donations.

23 See Roff (1985) for a more detailed description of the pilgrimage and a discussion about the hajj as a rite of passage.

24 McDonnell notes that the growth of the number of pilgrims can be seen in relation to the increase in population in the same period, but that 'if we examine Malay pilgrims as a percentage of the Muslim population of hajj age (35+ years), it becomes clear that the percentage performing hajj is increasing at a faster rate than the hajj age segment of the Muslim population' (1990: 111). The increase is further explained both by international and domestic factors. The heightened prestige that Saudi Arabia gained in the eyes of Muslims in relation to the oil embargo in 1973 was one such factor. Domestically, the increase in pilgrims should be seen in relation to the growth of the ethnic Malay population as well as advancements in travel and Tabung Haji's facilitation of making the pilgrimage to Mecca.

5

Transforming rituals
Claiming public religious space

This chapter deals with women's organization of and participation in collective religious rituals, *majlis doa*. Such rituals form an important part of women's religious and social lives in Kuala Lumpur. The *majlis doa*, as a women-only religious gathering, is a modern, urban phenomenon, and its emergence is closely connected to the increase in female religiosity described thus far in the present book. It reflects in many ways the recent changes in Malaysian society and how Malay women are creating more clear-cut religious identities and authority for themselves in that process. At the same time, negotiations about boundaries between Islam and adat become acute in relation to the *majlis doa*. Such negotiations, as we shall see, are also highly gendered, and I shall argue that women's *majlis doa* constitute gendered, condensed manifestations of the contemporary creative relationship between adat and Islam in Malaysia.

It is important to know that the *majlis doa* emerges out of the broad category of rituals known as *kenduri*, historically central to Malay social and ritual life. The *kenduri* itself, as a social and religious phenomenon, has been changing in response to modernization and Islamization. Therefore, this chapter will begin with a brief presentation of the *kenduri* in Malay society and the controversies that it has generated.

THE *KENDURI* IN THE RURAL CONTEXT

The *kenduri* stands out as the main feature of Malay communal ritual life,[1] and shares basic traits with the ritual complex of *slametan,* described in Clifford Geertz's classic ethnography *The Religion of Java* (1960). The *kenduri* is described as a feast, or a communal rice meal, in connection to a ceremonial event, often, but not always, including an element of prayer. In the literature, one finds three main categories of occasions that call for a *kenduri* to be held: religious celebrations, life-cycle crises, happy events, and the fulfilment of wishes. Religious events that call for a *kenduri* are the celebration of the birthday of the Prophet Muhammad and the welcoming of those who return from pilgrimage. Within the second category one finds occasions such as marriage, circumcision, infant hair-cutting, house moving, completion of a new house, long journeys, illness and death. The third category includes, for example, the birth of a child of the desired sex (Scott 1985) or the winning of a football game (Carsten 1997). There is also a category of *kenduri* held for the well-being of the village, for example, to ward off a drought (Scott 1985).

A *kenduri* is usually initiated by an individual or a family. It can also be organized collectively, and held at the mosque (when the purpose is explicitly religious), or elsewhere, for the well-being of the village (Rudie 1994:180). Regardless of who initiates a *kenduri*, the feast always requires communal co-operation when it comes to work and expenses. When a family makes preparations for a *kenduri*, it requires the help of neighbours, friends and relatives. This is also work that is expected to be reciprocal. The *kenduri* is described as a costly affair and the hosts often rely on help with expenses in the form of gifts and loans from kin and neighbours. Guests also make some kind of contribution in the form of food such as uncooked rice (Carsten 1997) or, more commonly today, money (Rudie 1993).[2]

Ingrid Rudie's (1994) detailed description of *kenduri*s in Kelantan shows that the practical arrangements are mostly women's responsibility. Women prepare the ingredients, cook and serve the food, as well as do the washing up and cleaning. The shared meal is described as consisting of cooked rice and side dishes, the number of which varies, according to the degree of lavishness. The side dishes would ideally be meat dishes accompanied by vegetables, although chicken is sometimes used as a cheaper alternative to meat. The meal may be accompanied by sugary drinks and concluded with the serving of sweet cakes. The women have to prepare the entire feast and prepare the decorations, while men perform the religious element of the ritual, the prayer, which is concluded by the sharing of the rice meal. The men eat before the women. The meal is consumed quickly, and as soon as guests have finished their meals, they leave and make room for other guests.

The number of guests in a *kenduri* varies with the scale of the feast. Sometimes, only neighbours and close relatives in the area are invited. For larger *kenduris*, the neighbourhood is more widely defined, and kin from distant villages are also invited. Attendance at *kenduris* must be reciprocated. A large *kenduri* can easily entail the invitation of two to three thousand guests. For Malays in general, the hosting of *kenduri* in connection with life crises and rites of passage is an important means towards the acquisition of social status and prestige.

Within the framework of an ongoing Islamization, there is a continuing dispute over the religious validity of the *kenduri*, which make these feasts a focal point in negotiations over distinctions between Islam and adat. As we saw in Chapter 1, Islamic reformers have since the 1920s, been critical of those elements in Malay custom that are said to be contrary to Islam. 'Well-being' *kenduris*, for example, held to secure the harvest, were seen as drawing too much from pre-Islamic, animistic ideas to be in accord with Islamic teachings, since animism challenges the central Islamic idea of divine unity.

Reformers have, however, had a permissive attitude towards *kenduri* in general since the ritual is perceived as having a strengthening effect on the sense of the Muslim community. Instead of forbidding it, efforts have been made to purify the *kenduri* of its Hindu and animistic elements, as well as to reduce aspects meant to increase social prestige through what has been perceived as 'wastefulness'. Certain categories of *kenduri* give rise to explicit critique from Islamists, and weddings are particularly vulnerable.

WEDDINGS

Malay marriages are made up of a sequence of events beginning with a betrothal party, followed by a religious ceremony, and closed by a feast (the *kenduri*) that marks the presentation of the couple to the community.

The initial betrothal party traditionally takes place in the home of the bride with close relatives and friends as guests. According to Rudie (1994), the betrothal ceremony can be seen as a female confirmation of the marriage promise, since women from both families play leading roles in it. Rudie notes that the practice of betrothal had diminished in the community that she studied and that most families that organized weddings during her fieldwork did not perform the betrothal at all. This was also my experience in Kuala Lumpur. None of the marriages that I attended involved a betrothal ceremony.

In contrast to the betrothal party, the formal religious ceremony (*akad nikah*) can be seen as the male confirmation of the marriage. It consists of the imam's recitation of the marriage service (*khutbah nikah*) and the signing of the marriage contract by the husband and the male guardian of the bride. In addition to the couple, this ceremony usually involves the couple's close family. The religious ceremony marks the point at which the couple is legally married to each other and the imam will also make sure that the groom has sufficient religious knowledge to perform his responsibilities as a husband. The ceremony is concluded by prayers. The *akad nikah* is also the occasion when the marriage money (*mas kahwin*, literally 'marriage gold') is handed over and the exchange of rings can take place. The *akad nikah* may take place the day before, or a few days before, the wedding party (the *kenduri*) when the married couple is presented, but sometimes several months can pass in between. The *kenduri,* which concludes the marriage, is by far the most disputed, manifesting the tension between Islam and adat present in the performance of *kenduri*s in general and wedding rituals in particular.

Basically, one could say that customary weddings are contrasted with more Islamic weddings. But there are also weddings labelled 'modern' which lean more toward Western models in terms of dress and entertainment.

The most significant, and therefore the most contested element, of the traditional Malay wedding is the *bersanding,* which literally means 'enthronement' or 'sitting in state'. During the *bersanding,* the bride and groom are presented as a royal couple. They are seated on a dais, elevated above the rest of those present, and they are dressed in royal style with suits made of brocade. The bride does not cover her hair and wears a tiara. The cultural roots of the custom of *bersanding* are traced back to the Hindu influence in the Malay Peninsula and are thus regarded as not in accordance with Islam. In the customary weddings, there is often some sort of entertainment in the form of music, singing or traditional dances. Since weddings are costly, they require a long period of planning and preparation; a well-organized wedding tends to demand several months of preparation.

The ideal Islamic wedding, on the other hand, typically consists only of the *akad nikah*, preferably taking place at the mosque, immediately followed by a 'simple' tea party, in contrast to the 'wasteful' character of customary wedding feasts. Preferred clothes for the couple are a white *baju kurung* and scarf for the bride and *baju Melayu* for the man. Elements defined as non-Islamic are thoroughly avoided. As the American social anthropologist Michael Peletz phrases it: 'The Islamic wedding is purified through elimination' (1997: 254). Siti's wedding is a clear example of this process of purification.

Siti's wedding

When a young woman, Siti, who attended an English-medium Koran class with me, invited me to her wedding, she also commented on the form the wedding would take. Siti was half-apologetic that the event would not be as Islamic as she had wished for herself. Siti was Chinese, and had converted to Islam some three years earlier, as she had fallen in love with a Malay man whom she intended to marry. Before she was ready to convert, her fiancé was tragically killed in a car accident. Siti continued with her religious studies, finding comfort in Islam, and had gone through with the conversion. When I got to know her, she had recently met another man and they planned to get married. His family, however, was critical of their son's choice of wife and they refused to take any part in it at all. But Siti had a very close relationship with her first fiancé's parents who treated her as their adoptive daughter. They stepped in and offered to sponsor the wedding for the couple. Traditionally, weddings are particularly important for parents, since they constitute a good opportunity for the acquisition of status and also for reciprocating indebtedness to others. For this reason, the parents of Siti's deceased fiancé had wished for a more customary Malay wedding. Siti and her husband, however, had opted for the Islamic version. As it turned out, the wedding was a compromise reached between Siti and her former fiancé's parents.

The day after the religious ritual was held in the mosque about one hundred guests were invited to lunch in a hotel just outside Kuala Lumpur. This was already a much more elaborate and costly event than the couple had wished for. On the other hand, the parents had accepted the couple's choice not to sit in state (*bersanding*) and after all the guests had arrived, the couple entered the room and took their places at the table where both Siti's own Chinese and her adoptive Malay families were seated. Siti was dressed in a white, lace-covered *baju kurung* worn with a white, transparent *selendang*. The groom wore a white tunic and trousers with a piece of turquoise brocade worn wrapped around his waist (*baju Melayu*), which is the male counterpart of the women's *baju kurung*. There was no entertainment or music during the meal, which was terminated with a few prayers and some information about the couple's future plans. As customary, all guests were offered a small gift placed next to each plate. In Malay tradition, this gift is often in the form of an egg or something made with egg as its base such as sponge cake. Most people I talked to, including Siti and her husband, were aware that the egg was a Hindu symbol of fertility. So instead of eggs they had chosen a small porcelain basket containing some sweets for the guests to take back. This choice communicated a distancing from explicit Hindu associations at the same time as it embraced Malay tradition.

Malay weddings in Kuala Lumpur can be more or less traditional, modern or Islamic depending on the composition of traditional, modern and Islamic elements and the intention of the wedding can be communicated on different scales. In the case of Siti's wedding, the hotel reception, absence of a *bersanding*, centrality of prayers, and careful choice of gifts marked it as a ritual event where elements of modernity, tradition and Islam were intrinsically combined. This kind of inventive combination of elements, which was also the subject of much discussion, were similarly found in women's performance of the *majlis doa*.

MAJLIS DOA

Majlis is a word of Arabic origin used in the sense of a gathering or congregation. *Doa* is the Arabic concept for commendable prayer as opposed to the compulsory five daily prayers. *Doa*, then, is a prayer where a person can ask God directly for something – anything from general guidance to protection from unpleasant things. There are fixed verses in the Koran to be used for these various purposes, but as we saw in Chapter 4, a *doa* can also be expressed in individual words in any language.

In the urban context, the *majlis doa* is a collective ritual held in somebody's home. It usually lasts about two hours. The basic structure of the event is that it contains an element of prayer (*doa*), reading of the Koran, and the repetition of God's name (*tahlil*). The gatherings are always concluded by the sharing of a meal consisting of rice, side dishes, drinks and sweets. They are usually held by individual women or by an individual family and, rarely, by individual men.

During my fieldwork I came across various reasons for the performance of *majlis doa*. Generally, they were held to ask for God's protection, guidance and blessings in various situations, most commonly severe illness, house building or renovations, or before children sat for examinations or left home for university. Life-crisis events in connection with birth and death were also accompanied by a *majlis doa*. Another reason could be to mark a change of spiritual direction in life. One woman who had experienced a series of misfortunes had decided to start leading a more religious life. She intended to start attending religious classes and to be more active in the women's section of her local mosque. She highlighted this decision and the new course of her life by giving a *majlis doa* in her home. The *majlis doa* could also be given as a thanksgiving ritual, showing one's gratitude towards God for hearing earlier prayers. Two or more reasons could, of course, also be combined in the performance of a *majlis doa* held in one's home. It could also be given for none of the above reasons, but simply for itself, and some women arranged a prayer meeting in their homes regularly once a year.

When the initiative for the gathering was taken by an individual woman, the *majlis doa* was performed in the home of the host and the guests were all women. Most mosques in middle-class and upper middle-class areas

147

had a group of women whom members of the community could call on to come and help them perform a *majlis doa* in their homes. The invited guests were usually a mix of relatives, neighbours, friends and women attending the same Arabic class. Mutual obligations in terms of attendance were of course created. When a *majlis doa* was announced in the mosque, the hope was that as many women as possible would show up. The explicit reason for having a well-attended gathering was that the chances of your *doa* being heard by God were greater the more people there were. Also, this increased the chances for one of them to have a really beautiful way of pronouncing the words and God would be pleased and grant you what you wished for. Another idea was the significance of the number of times that a particular verse or chapter in the Koran was read. The prayer meetings usually contained recitations of Yasin. Yasin is often considered to be the 'heart' of the Koran and memorization and recitation of this chapter was considered very good and meritorious. There was a common idea that Yasin should be read at least forty times when somebody had died. Some said that a thousand times was better. Instead of having one person read forty or a thousand times, one could have many people gathered together reading simultaneously. For example, twenty people could each read Yasin twice, adding up to forty times. But apart from the religious advantages of having a crowd, a well-attended gathering was also a good social sign for the hostess. Since the ritual was always concluded with a meal consisting of rice and as many side dishes as could be afforded, along with sweet cakes and fruit, the *majlis doa* could be a quite costly affair. The ability to host, and feed, a large number of participants was an indication of wealth.

The gatherings always had the same basic structure. Since it was a special occasion, women arrived dressed in their good *baju kurung*, often with elaborate headscarfs, perhaps trimmed with lace or embroidered. Entering the room, each person exchanged greetings (*salam*) respectfully with those already in the room before sitting down on the floor near the wall. The hall was usually cleared of furniture on these occasions and the floor covered with carpets to make it more comfortable. A special place was often marked, using a piece of cloth and cushions, for the woman who was going to lead the *doa* as well as for those in the inner circle of the women's committee. If a member of the household was ill, there would be bottles of water placed in front of them, to be turned into 'Yasin water' and given to the sick person to drink. The woman called upon to lead the prayer and the reading of Yasin was someone known to have a good voice and who could recite the Koran beautifully. Contrary to the religious classes, where teachers were either male or female, the religious authority in the prayer meetings, when performed by women, was always a woman. The reading of the Koran and the prayers commenced and would usually go on for about an hour. After the reading, the meal was served and eaten quickly while everyone chatted and exchanged news about each other.

MAJLIS DOA – A CONTESTED SPACE

The tension between Malay adat and Islam, expressed in the realm of weddings, can also be seen in the context of the *majlis doa*. Indeed, in some ways, the *majlis doa* may be seen to represent the transformation and Islamization of the *kenduri* in the urban context. The following example of a child's hair-cutting ritual (*akika kenduri*) illustrates this transformation. The example also shows the uncertainties that are generated, even among participants, about the religious status of the *kenduri*.

It was Faridah, a woman in her early forties whom I had met at the mosque, who brought me along for the hair-cutting ritual. She was related to the family organizing the gathering through her husband. Before going to this ritual, Faridah had given me a *baju kurung*. The outfit came from a very tall relative of hers and Faridah indicated to me that it was a more appropriate dress for the *kenduri* that we were about to attend than my usual, certainly modest but more Western outfits. I was not required to wear a headscarf, as was the case in the mosque, even though a majority of the women who participated in the ritual, including herself, did cover their hair. There were about 50 women in the hall. As we entered the room we gave *salam* to each one of the women present and then sat down where we could find an empty spot. The room had been cleared of all its furniture in order to make room for the many visitors, and we sat on the floor covered by Persian carpets. While waiting for the rest of the guests to arrive, Faridah took the opportunity to underline for me that this kind of ritual was 'just culture, not religion'. She explained that although they would pray and read the Koran, the ritual was not to be considered an Islamic custom.

The ritual started with a prayer and Koran reading. This part of the ritual was led by a woman who was appreciated for her religious knowledge and her skills in reciting the Koran. She was also among the oldest women present, and her status was accentuated by the fact that she was the only one who was sitting on a cushion. Next to her, on both sides, were seated the Yasin-group from the local mosque. There was also a small choir of five women who sang verses from the Koran. They were regularly asked to come and participate in *majlis doa*. The prayer and Koran reading was followed by the actual hair-cutting ceremony where all the women stood in a circle and the baby, wrapped in a yellow cloth, was brought in by the maternal grandmother. The child, who had just turned one,[3] was taken around inside the circle of women and those who wanted to, snipped off a thin lock of hair from the baby. A couple of close relatives cut some hair. The whole ceremony was performed with much giggling, and many women did not seem to know what to do next. Faridah pointed out that the cutting of hair and the yellow cloth that the child was wrapped in during the ceremony were actually Hindu elements, and again she emphasized that it had nothing to do with Islam. After the ceremony, there was a meal of rice and various curries (meat and chicken) and vegetables served. Sweet drinks and cakes were also offered. Everyone ate rapidly and said farewell to the hostess before leaving the house.

This ritual occasion stands out from all the other prayer meetings that I attended in Kuala Lumpur during my stay there. As such, it is revealing because it shows ritual practice, as well as religion, in transition. It was the only hair-cutting ritual that I came across and it was one of the very few *majlis doa* gatherings where any clear symbol derived from the Hindu past was being used.[4] All other *majlis doa* I attended turned out to be more adapted to Islamic ideals than this one. And perhaps this is why I was not requested to wear a *baju kurung*, a distinctly Malay outfit, to these other prayer meetings. However, it was not only the *kenduri* that was open to criticism for its non-Islamic character and elements; even the *majlis doa*, although clearly religious in form and content, was subject to questioning from within the Islamic framework. But there are differences. Whereas criticism of the *kenduri* has focused on the use of non-Islamic elements within the ritual context, criticism of the *majlis doa* has primarily been directed towards its religious validity in general. In fact, as we shall see, the *majlis doa* prove to be at the heart of the dispute over the religious boundary between Islam and adat in Malaysia.

Criticisms of the majlis doa

The *majlis doa* and its religious legitimacy was questioned not only by *dakwah*-oriented teachers and scholars but also by ordinary Muslims. There was also, as the case above shows, some uncertainty among the women themselves.

On the one hand, the women's performance of *majlis doa* was discussed and thought about as being part of an explicitly religious realm. Women themselves explained their increased performance of the *majlis doa* in terms of women's generally increased knowledge about and engagement in Islam. At the same time, there was a notion of the non-Islamic character of the ritual. In spite of its religious character – with prayer and Koran reading – the rituals were very much associated with Malay adat. In this context, adat, or Malay custom, was used mainly as a counterpoint to Islamic practices and beliefs. Rituals, or elements in ritual, were understood to belong to the sphere of adat rather than Islam and women were well aware of ceremonies or elements in a ceremony that did not have Islamic roots. Some women (and men), mostly those who identified themselves more with the international community of Muslims rather than with the ethnic group of Malays, were very critical of the practice of the *majlis doa* and of the *kenduri,* in general. They said that even though these kinds of gatherings, in general, could not be said to contradict Islam, they were not supported by the scriptures either. Some women chose to stay outside the *majlis doa* networks because they found that they entailed, from an Islamic point of view, unwanted 'waste products' or 'side effects' such as gossiping, sometimes direct selling, and competition in terms of wealth and status expressed through food, clothes and jewellery. While it was considered good for Muslims to strengthen the *ummah* through rituals and religious gatherings, some argued that if the negative aspects turned out to be as evident as the positive aspects, it was better to steer clear of them.

The element of reading the Yasin in a group was also questioned from an orthodox point of view. Some women held that if they needed to read the Yasin, for whatever reason, they could read it by themselves, alone. They said that there was no need for others to do it. A person sitting for an examination could read the Yasin herself – they stressed that there is no need for an intermediary between a Muslim and God. As a Muslim you have a direct connection to God and there was no point in having someone else communicate with God on your behalf. From this angle, the gatherings were seen as not really Islamic but as more of a social affair. An example that was often given was *kenduri* held at funerals. Islam teaches that there is no point in reading the Koran for a dead person because he is already gone. It is not possible to transmit 'points' or merit, gained from reading the Koran, to another person, dead or alive. So, the significance of that kind of *kenduri* would be merely for the living. In addition, the family who were organizing the *kenduri* had to cook for all the guests and they should not have to do that when mourning. Women who did not agree with *kenduri* in connection with death often took an example from Muhammad as support for their view. It was said that during the Prophet's time, others used to send food to the house of the deceased so that the bereaved family did not have to think about cooking. Another example of this was the thanksgiving feast (*kenduri syukur*). As an Islamic concept, the meaning of *syukur* was said to be thankfulness and gratitude towards God. Such thankfulness and gratitude should best be expressed through faith and obedience to God, and not necessarily through ritual. *Syukur*, it was emphasized, is not about gathering and eating together, but about submission through prayer and obedience to God's will.[5] In this discourse, women suggested that the intention behind the organization of a thanksgiving feast was derived more from concerns for the social aspects of tradition than with the performance of religious duties (*ibadah*). Wealthy people who gave thanks to God for the closing of a prosperous business deal or for making a huge profit were given as an example of this. Some even sponsored their employees for the lesser pilgrimage (*umrah*) as a way of giving thanks to God, but the purity of their intentions was questioned by orthodox Muslims. Sending employees to Mecca was not a bad thing in itself and could, indeed, be praiseworthy in some circumstances. However, if the employers acted more from a desire for social recognition than to please God, their generosity was to be criticized.

Gender aspects of the majlis doa

Women who attended *majlis doa* in Kuala Lumpur were well aware of the fact that their way of gathering had emerged in the urban, modern context. They did not find the same gatherings among women in the rural villages and when they recalled collective religious rituals from their childhood, their descriptions corresponded with the description of the *kenduri* above. They stressed the difference in terms of gender – that women in the city were performing collective religious rituals on their own without the assistance of male religious authorities and they connected this change to their increased religious knowledge. As we could see, the *kenduri* involves both men and women. The men being the ones actually performing the religious elements and the women being in charge of the practical arrangements such as the pooling of resources and cooking. The *majlis doa*, on the other hand, were exclusively female, with the women both as organizers and as performers of the ritual. (In some cases the husband performed a separate ritual the same day or on another occasion.) It is also interesting to note that it was not uncommon for affluent households to have the food provided for and served by a catering service – very often with male staff, thus also reversing the gender image of the ritual. Furthermore, for the affluent middle class, the pooling of resources had lost in importance. The woman who called for a gathering covered all the expenses on her own – and, of course, expected her invitation to be returned by the participants. On the other hand, *majlis doa* were generally much smaller in size than the village-based *kenduri*. A well-attended *majlis doa* would have anything from 50 to 100 guests. The largest one I went to during fieldwork had about 200 guests.

From this it would seem that the gendered aspect of the village *kenduri* has changed as it has been brought into the urban, middle-class environment. Women now actively perform the religious portion of the ritual and they even have female religious authorities to lead them. This means that, in some ways, women have assumed the role of religious guardians of the household and its members. Now it is not only their roles as mothers that is important, but their role as religious persons. This could indicate that women are taking, and are being allowed to take, a more important role in terms of religion than before, something that women themselves connected to the increasing popularity of Islamic study groups for women in the city. The religious aspect of the ritual was clearly emphasized by individuals who referred to their gatherings using a religious/Arabic term, *majlis doa*, instead of the Malay *kenduri*. The gatherings were only referred to as *kenduri* by women who criticized the practice as something belonging to the realm of adat, as opposed to Islam.

Through the practice of *majlis doa*, women can be said to be reinforcing their religious identities and actively create a basis for greater religious authority, thereby renegotiating the boundaries between adat and Islam. The *majlis doa* thus become a focal point for negotiations of boundaries between adat and Islam. Islamization, and the ways in which women are involved in this sphere, creatively shape this transformation. As a female religious space, the *majlis doa* is also central for renegotiations of gender boundaries.

GENDERED BOUNDARIES OF RELIGION

As we saw in Chapter 2, Wazir (1992) argues that the foundation for the relatively equal relationship between Malay men and women is found in the bilateral norm in adat, the Malay traditional, customary and legal system existing parallel to and intertwined with Islamic practices, ideas and laws. As adat principles favour hierachical differences based on age over hierarchical differences based on gender, adat and Islam in Malay culture provide contradictory and conflicting statements on gender relations, particularly in areas of ritual, economic and political activity. Wazir argues that these conflicts have been resolved, over the ages, at times in the direction of Islam and at other times in the direction of adat. This flexibility in the historical relationship between adat and Islam has made it possible for women to exploit the cultural system to their advantage and to transmit components of the culture which significantly support their own power and autonomy.

Wazir argues that adat continues to be a moderating force on Malay gender relations in regard to the contemporary Islamization and strengthening of male authority. Male dominance and authority is resisted through adat and as long as adat remains a basic source of Malay heritage, women can use it to their advantage to compete with men in Islam, for instance, by 'adatizing' Islam through rituals. She perceives women as excluded from religious contexts and understands their 'adatization' of Islam as a way of resisting male religious dominance: 'Where Malay women's sphere of influence is limited, as in Islamic rituals or politics featuring on Islam, customary rights in adat attempt to mediate the problem by giving women dominant roles in *rites de passage*' (Wazir 1992: 220). Without referring to any wider context or any detailed ethnography, Wazir declares a tendency among Malay women in urban areas to '...conduct both cultural and religious feasts and ceremonies independently from men' (ibid.: 221) as an example of this 'adatization' of Islam.[6] As I understand it, 'cultural and religious feasts and ceremonies' performed by women independently from men is a wide enough category to include the practice of *majlis doa* that I have described above.

I find Wazir's analysis of gender relations in Malay society to be highly illuminating, and I sympathize with her intention to trace the sources of Malay women's agency. However, her analysis also entails two problems. The first problem is that the analysis reduces the importance of women's religious practices to their possible social effects. Agency is understood as a capacity to challenge male dominance and authority. Second, and consequently, the understanding of women's agency that her analysis offers is limited to the idea of resistance against male dominance. I shall discuss both these problems in turn.

Islamizing adat

When Wazir suggests that the performance of women's 'cultural and religious feasts and ceremonies' should be understood as an 'adatization' of Islam, she places women's collective rituals within a realm of popular Islam, low tradition, rather than with official Islam, or high tradition. She thereby follows the path so well-trodden by the anthropology of Islam, where 'official' Islam in an often unreflective way is associated with 'male' and 'popular' Islam with 'female'. Tapper and Tapper (1987) have pointed out the analytical danger with these kinds of equations. They easily lead to the assumption that the religious activities and roles of women in Muslim communities are less important than men's, and, by extension, of little or no importance to the spiritual well-being of the community at large.

Using ethnographic material from Turkey, Nancy and Richard Tapper provide an analysis of *mevlûd* services performed by both men and women, although separately and differently from each other. In the men's service, a supernatural dimension is introduced into everyday life and values. The women's service, on the other hand, is designed to create and confirm the promise of individual salvation offered to all Muslims. Through the ritual, an intimate link is established between each participant and the Prophet Muhammad where his intercession with God is emphasized. The two authors therefore argue that the women's versions of the ritual are of great transcendental importance to the community as a whole, not only for the well-being of women.[7]

Considering the data that I have presented so far, one can see that women who perform religious rituals without male participation are also immersed in the study of Islamic scriptures and practices. Indeed, given that women are increasing their knowledge about the scriptures, it seems reasonable to argue, contra Wazir, that women, in fact, are in the process of 'Islamizing' adat. Furthermore, it is clear that women are taking over responsibility for collective life-cycle rituals and that these rituals are being organized along more orthodox Islamic lines. We can, therefore, question the idea that women's religious practices – of which collective religious rituals form an important part – can be identified with popular Islam in any simplistic way. Through their religious studies, in their daily lives as well as via collective rituals, many women are explicitly striving to become pious, to find enjoyment and fulfilment in a life lived in accordance with God's will. Through these practices, the very distinction between popular and official Islam is being blurred.

WOMEN'S PUBLIC RELIGIOUS SPACE

Women's communal, religious gatherings form a common feature of the Muslim world and have received some attention in anthropological literature. In many cases, particularly in the Middle East where patriarchal ideology limits women's freedom to move outside the household, religious gatherings are said to offer women opportunities to meet socially in each other's homes and in groups that cut across the ordinary kin groupings

(Fernea and Fernea 1972; Betteridge 2001). The religious framework of the gatherings is then seen as a means to justify socializing. But Anne Betteridge (2001), when considering her Iranian material, also notes that this argument does not hold as well for modern, educated women who have greater possibilities to move about more in public and secular contexts. They would not have the same need to frame socializing in religious terms. The emergence of women's mosques, created by female religious leaders among the Hui in Central China as described by Maria Jaschok and Shui Jingjun (2000), is another interesting case in point. Their detailed ethnography shows that the mosque is given meanings beyond a social space for Muslim women. The authors argue that it is the religious values and spiritual meanings that are emerging as central in the activities (religious learning, rituals, collective prayer, etc.) that women perform in the space that women's mosques offer.

The women in Kuala Lumpur who attend prayer meetings are educated professionals or have recently abandoned their working careers. Those who still work are, for example, teachers, lecturers and employees in the private or government sector, while some run small businesses. They do not lack opportunities to meet other women outside the household. Those who have decided to leave their careers and devote more time to religion can be quite busy going to religious classes and attending prayer meetings. One day, after leaving a well-attended *majlis doa* with a small group of women, the conversation turned to this very topic. The women reflected on the fact that they had most weekdays booked by religious studies and then there was usually a *majlis doa* to attend once a week. They joked about their calendars being so full with religious things that they did not have time to enjoy each other's company on other occasions. 'No Koran, no homework, just us!' concluded one woman, inviting the group over for coffee one of the following afternoons.

This is not to say that the religious gatherings lacked a social aspect. Many women valued the gatherings highly as social events. But to reduce the analysis of prayer meetings to socializing would be a mistake. In a recent article, the Iranian social anthropologist Azam Torab (1996) provides an analysis of Iranian Shia women's performances of home-based prayer meetings (*jalaseh*) that have developed out of the post-revolutionary religious revival. At such meetings, women recite the Koran, discuss religious precepts and the meaning of Koranic verses, and they conclude by consuming food and drink. Torab offers an analysis of the meetings that goes beyond the socializing argument. According to her, the meetings, held on a daily basis, can be seen as '... arenas for competing claims by groups of pious women as to how to be good Muslims' (1996: 236). While she recognizes the social support and freedom of expression that the meetings provide women in the absence of men, she emphasizes women's achievement of piety through attendance at these gatherings. The women are constructing ideas of faith in ways that sustain and dignify their actions and also allow a sense of well-being and agency.

In spite of the important historical, cultural and religious differences between Iran and Malaysia, there are clear parallels between Iranian *jalaseh* and Malay *majlis doa*. In both cases, women hold religious gatherings independently of men as well as stress the importance of their respective practices in their striving for piety.

When women take on the responsibility of collective rituals, they are creating a space for religious agency in public. The rituals are hosted by individual women and held in their homes. Participants in the rituals, while including family and friends, consist largely of those from the mosque and religious classes. Indeed, a *majlis doa* is an event that requires the participation of the larger community, and is by no means a private matter performed within the confines of the family.

The next chapter focuses on women's active Islamization, and the changes that this process brings about in male and female relations, especially between spouses.

NOTES

1   James Scott (1985) focuses on the role of the *kenduri* in the relationships between rich and poor peasants in the village. He notes changes in attitudes towards the *kenduri* among rich and poor peasants as a result of economic changes, but there is no detailed description of what goes on in the ritual. Peter Wilson (1967) accounts for different occasions for holding a *kenduri* and gives some information of how the expenditures for the feast are managed by the hosts, and does not get into the actual practice of the ritual. There is

more detail about the different elements that constitute a *kenduri* in Rudie (1993, 1994) and Carsten (1997).

2   Rudie's 1993 article on Malay marriage rituals as a field of debate in Kelantan also discusses how some people, in particular those who have a more modern lifestyle, feel uncomfortable about monetary contributions to *kenduri* since it evokes in them a sense of paying for the food. My observations concerning marriage *kenduri*s in Kuala Lumpur was that guests did not contribute gifts of money to the hosts, but rather brought a gift for the marrying couple and their future home as is common in many Western contexts.

3   Ideally, the ritual should take place seven weeks after birth, but the family had not found the time to organize it before this.

4   As we saw earlier, weddings often included elements from religious traditions that were influential in the Malay world before the coming of Islam, such as Hinduism, Buddhism and animistic beliefs, but weddings are not defined as *majlis doa*.

5   Verse 14: 7 in the Koran was often referred to as one that was good to read as a remembrance of what God means by *syukur*.

6   The only example that she cites in terms of adatization is that of women conducting religious feasts and ceremonies independently from men.

7   See also Gillian Tett (1994) whose material from a Tajik village under Soviet rule provides a case where it is the women, rather than the men, who have been the main 'guardians' of Islam. Tett argues that the religious role of the women was vital for the maintenance of the villagers' sense of Islamic identity during the Soviet era. Men's religious activities were more mosque-based – relating to prayer and rituals concerning death, birth and circumcision. These activities were severely limited during the Soviet era. Women's religious activities, centred in the household and thus conceived as being part of the private sphere, largely escaped state control. Although women's religious practices were considered less prestigious than men's, women were considered more diligent in performing their spiritual obligations than men. Women's domestic religious practices were also associated with what was perceived as central to the village's traditional values. Thus, the concepts 'traditional', 'Tajik' and 'Muslim' all came together in female religious performances. Women's performance of core religious duties, wearing of Tajik dress, adherence to 'Muslim' notions of sexual honour, and beautifully kept 'traditional' households were all important for maintaining the community's sense of its Tajik and Muslim identity.

6

Becoming *mukmin*

MUKMIN – A TRUE BELIEVER

Previous chapters have shown how Malay women actively cultivate submission to God's will through studying religious scriptures and sources, as well as through more diligently performing their religious duties and obligatory prayers. Those who had attained such a state of submission and awareness were perceived as being *mukmin* – a true believer. Through personal narratives and accounts of everyday situations, this chapter will further explore the meaning that women attach to the idea of *mukmin*. It shall show how women's establishment of a *mukmin* identity consequently creates a space for gender negotiation.

Within the context of religious study groups, teachers as well as participants often expressed a concern for the weak religiosity of Muslims in Malaysian society in general. 'Islam in Malaysia is like an empty shell', complained a religious teacher, continuing rhetorically by asking why it was that mosques were so empty in the evenings. He further lamented the fact that while the compulsory Friday noon prayer saw mosques overflowing with praying men, mosques were more or less deserted at other times. For those who desired the establishment of an Islamic state in Malaysia, this lack of religiosity was also used in their criticism of the political leadership and its attempts to bring together Western and Islamic values in policy-making. Religious teachers called for spiritual development among Muslims – a call for Muslims to start taking their faith seriously. In such discussions, reference was often made to the Koranic concept of *mukmin* as an indication of the shift in attitude that was needed.

The meaning that women attached to the concept of *mukmin* was that of a 'devout' or 'God-fearing' person (a person with *takwah*). With reference to Koranic verses[1] where the concept of *mukmin* appears side by side with 'Muslim', women explained that all *mukmin* are Muslims, but not all Muslims are *mukmin*. A *mukmin* was seen in contrast to an ordinary Muslim who, basically, was someone who had Islam as his or her religion, but who had not entered wholeheartedly into the religion. Translated into the Malaysian situation, 'Muslims' were Malays who were born into the faith but who had 'not yet been touched by Islam in their hearts', while *mukmin* were those Muslims who were consciously aware of God in all aspects of life, and who put this awareness into practice. A *mukmin* was thus a person who had aquired the *disposition* of faithfulness toward God and, as we saw in Chapter 4, this disposition was cultivated through the performance of acts of worship.

In the Koran, the concept of *mukmin* appears in both its masculine and feminine forms; the understanding in study groups was that the Koran does not indicate any gender-specific meaning of *mukmin*, and it was never discussed in such terms. This gender-neutral meaning of *mukmin* is supported by Sharifah Zaleha (2001) in her study of emerging civil society in Malaysia, with special reference to Bandar Baru Bangi, a new town in the state of Selangor. She describes *mukmin* as 'Muslims who are highly devoted and capable of demonstrating unreserved belief and faith in the absolute truth of Islam' (ibid.: 85). She indicates that there are two main things that make a person, male or female, a *mukmin*: the *mukmin* seeks to strengthen his or her relationship with God and he or she discharges social responsibility.

The women that I met in the study groups tended to express their strengthened commitment to Islam and their increased religious knowledge in terms of a movement from being Muslims to becoming *mukmin*. In doing so, they were ascribing the concept of *mukmin* to themselves. When they described the process of becoming *mukmin*, they emphasized going through stages: from a practice of the basics of Islam without any deep religious knowledge to a stage where their understanding of Islam had increased through study, developing into a desire to live according to God's will.

The idea of being *mukmin*, for both men and women, was closely connected to the idea that each person was responsible for his or her own salvation. The individual was accountable to God for his or her actions and thereby the equal responsibility that men and women had toward God was accentuated. In this sense, all individuals, men as well as women, were understood as equal in relation to God, an idea that implied that women were required by God to make their own religious decisions just as men were.

At the same time, and as a contrast to the idea of individual responsibility, both men and women often pointed out that men as husbands and fathers were considered to be the religious authority of the family. As such, they were responsible for the religious education and moral status of their families. Men sometimes expressed this idea by saying that it was so much easier for women to go to paradise than it was for men, since women were not responsible for another person's religious practice and behaviour, only for their own. The idea of male authority appears to be in conflict with the idea of individual responsibility, something that manifests itself in relations between men and women.

Some husbands were not only too busy but also simply not very interested in religion. They would perform religious duties such as praying, fasting and paying the yearly tithe, even going to Mecca, but their involvement in religion did not go any further. Conflicts sometimes arose because of the difference in religious knowledge between the spouses. Women felt compelled to criticize their less knowledgeable husbands' everyday actions or argue with them over religious issues. There could also be discussions and disagreements between spouses who were equally interested in religion because of their different understanding of Islam. Husbands and fathers were ideally considered the religious authorities of the family, but pious women, with their growing knowledge, were also aware of their God-given responsibility as *mukmin*. This new awareness opened up a space for disputing Islamic practices and ideas as applied at home. As an illustration, I shall recount in some detail the discussions that took place between a woman, Saliha, her husband, Aziz, and myself on an ordinary Sunday afternoon.

Saliha and Aziz

Both Aziz and Saliha were professionals devoted to their respective careers. They had three children between the ages of eight and fourteen and there was also an Indonesian maid in the household. As I entered the family's detached two-storey house, situated in one of the Malay-dominated areas in Subang Jaya, two things immediately caught my attention. The first was the expensive golf set resting at the foot of the staircase and the second was a large, framed decorative hanging on the wall with the words 'God is great' in Arabic stitched in gold thread on a black fabric background. The golf case had been used that morning when Aziz played his regular round of weekend golf with two friends. The wall hanging had been bought in Mecca the previous year, when the couple went on *umrah* with Aziz's brother and his wife.

Saliha had been 19 years old when she married Aziz, both were from the southern state of Johor. When they married, Aziz was already working as a lecturer in Kuala Lumpur, and the couple bought a house and settled down in Kuala Lumpur. The children came quickly and although Saliha was enjoying motherhood, she also wanted to continue her studies. She explained to me that she 'wanted to have it all', both a family and an education. After her studies, she worked as a bank teller for a couple of years but was not really content with the prospects of such a position. Many of her friends who had gone overseas for higher education on government scholarships were returning home and looking for work in Malaysia, and, inspired by them, Saliha decided to move on. She experienced a certain resistance from her parents when she revealed her intention to have a career. They thought that she was out of her mind to ask for more than she already had: a devoted husband who could provide for her, children and a working life of her own. But Saliha was determined and found a job in the administration department of an international company. When I came to know her she was 35 years old and was doing a master's degree in mass communication to improve her chances of advancement within the company. Aziz supported her desire to pursue a career and was very proud of his wife's energy even though he sometimes complained that she was not at home as much as he wished her to be.

In her new workplace, Saliha had joined a small study group that met during the lunch break each Friday in the women's prayer room. Besides the spiritual well-being that she experienced, she also started to reflect on the relationship between men and women in Muslim societies. She often talked to me about the problems that women had with husbands who did not practise Islam in the proper way, and about problems that women faced in male-biased sharia courts. She was critical of the situation that had developed in Malaysia where it was much more difficult for women to initiate a divorce than it was for men. She felt strongly that, although the Koran transmitted the idea of equality between men and women as a basic value, Malay women and men were by no means treated as equals in Malaysian society.

When I visited them that Sunday afternoon, Saliha was eager to tell the story of a woman in her office who was going through a very difficult period in her life since her husband wanted to take a second wife, something that she was against. The couple had small children and the woman was very hurt by her husband's wish to set up a second household, especially since the other woman was much younger than herself and considered very pretty. Drawing from the Prophet Muhammad's life, Saliha argued that the idea of Muslim men being allowed to marry four wives had been born during Muhammad's time at a time of war, when many Muslim women were widowed and their children fatherless. Muhammad had married war widows to support and protect them. But the situation in Malaysia could not be compared to that of the Prophet's time. Saliha, as well as her husband, could see a trend in Malay society where men who sought to marry a second wife looked only for young women. A young and pretty wife was a clear sign of status for the man and both Saliha and her husband knew of men who had actively been seeking second wives who were not wearing a *telekung*. The reasons for taking a second wife was thus social rather than religious, something which to Saliha was a sign of how badly Islam was practised by Malays.

Aziz then came to men's defence by saying, with a twinkle in his eyes, that he could understand that men were sometimes tempted by women. He reminded us that even women who wear *baju kurung* and *telekung* can dress in a very provocative way, wearing high heels, slit skirts revealing much of their legs, and using make-up and perfume in public. 'These women make it difficult for men to control themselves', he said, and supported his argument with reference to the teachings of the Koran. Saliha immediately snapped back that it should not be forgotten that the Koran also tells men to look down when they meet an unmarried woman, in order to avoid being tempted by her beauty. She complained that men, when referring to the verse in the Koran about women guarding their modesty, somehow forget the following verse about men's responsibility in the same matter. She agreed that it was not good for a woman to dress in a provocative manner, but she also pointed out that the Koran places equal responsibility on men and women for the control of sexuality. Saliha was strongly critical of Malay men in general on this point. Compared to women, she said, men showed their weakness and lack of knowledge in religious matters. This made them ignore the responsibilities laid down by God. Without knowledge, men tended to neglect, not only the proper way of interacting with women, but also the will of God.

Aziz agreed with Saliha's reasoning, but felt differently about his own 12-year-old daughter who was wearing jeans and T-shirts when out of her school uniform and who had her shoulder-length hair uncovered. He said that he would prefer her to wear a scarf when she was older. Saliha, who herself had been wearing the *tudung* since her return from the hajj, said that it would be wrong for him as a father to demand that his daughter wear a scarf. She said that no daughter should put on the scarf in order to please her father. The decision to cover should, by a true Muslim – a *mukmin* – be taken from a desire to please God. She argued that there would be no reward for a woman who covered without sincerity and as long as her daughter did not have that desire it would, in fact, be wrong of her to cover. She saw that their responsibility as parents was to instil Islamic values in their children and to teach them the meaning and correct practice of Islam, but they could never force their daughter to cover. Saliha said that she was sad to see her eldest child, a son of 14, spending hours in his room listening to pop music and reading comics. But she felt that all she could do was to remind him to pray and to talk to him about what to her seemed to be a waste of time. The way she saw it, love for God and its implementation in life must come from her son's heart, not from hers.

CONFLICTING REPRESENTATIONS OF GENDER

As was mentioned in the first chapter, one of the main elements of Malay gender ideology is a set of notions concerning male and female in connection to the Islamic conceptions of *akal* (reason, rationality, intelligence, self-control) and *nafsu* (desire, lust, passion, animality). The concepts of Arabic origin and likely to have been introduced to the region around the thirteenth century with the coming of Islam have become key symbols all over Muslim Southeast Asia, with slight regional variations in semantic content.[2]

The basic idea is that God has given all living creatures *nafsu*, which is understood as the need to satisfy basic needs, such as food, drink, air and sexual activity. Human beings, as well as animals or spirits, need to eat, drink, breathe and reproduce, in order to stay alive. *Akal* is understood as a capacity that God has given exclusively to human beings. *Akal* is what distinguishes humans from animals.

In his study of kinship among matrilineal Malays of Negri Sembilan, a state on Malaysia's west coast, Peletz (1995) notes that the satisfaction of basic needs is associated with the absence of restraint. *Nafsu* (or 'passion' which he prefers to use) is '... experienced and construed in predominantly negative terms, as indexing a lack of restraint, hence weakness, animality, etc.' (1995: 91).[3] It is viewed as negative to show eagerness to satisfy hunger or thirst. To give in to *nafsu* is also associated with the devil's temptation, enforcing the dangers that such weakness can produce. *Akal* is believed to develop in human beings over time, and adults, therefore, are thought to have more *akal* than children. *Akal* may also be cultivated through religious instruction and diligence in religious duties (ibid.: 92). The relationship between *akal* and *nafsu* is that *akal* is what humans use to control *nafsu*.

Malay gender ideology is generally presented as an ideology through which women are seen as more susceptible to *nafsu*, in terms of 'lust/ sexuality' than men. Women are perceived to have more *nafsu* and thereby less *akal*, than men. Drawing from material collected in a Malay village on the west coast, Ong (1995) argues that the associations of women with *nafsu* and men with *akal*, understood as a moral code, is what constitutes the ground for Malay gender differentiation. A basic aspect of maleness in the Malay village context was the idea that men had more *akal*, thus had more self-control and were more rational than women. Therefore, men were assigned the guardianship of the virtue of their sisters, wives and daughters. Men's masculinity depended to a large extent on their moral authority (in combination with economic power) over the women in their households. Extended to a wider social level, the village men were collectively seen as being responsible for the moral status of all the women in the community.

It has also been shown, however, that Malay gender ideology allows a space for a reversed image of the representations above. In the Negri Sembilan case, Peletz argues that there are two sets of contradicting gender representations at work; one 'official' and one 'practical'.[4] The official representations of gender, which emphasize the idea that women have more *nafsu* than men, is in contrast to alternative, practical representations of gender associating men with 'lack of restraint' and women with *akal*. In Peletz' material, men are portrayed as being less reasonable and less responsible than women both in regards to social obligations and money management. Men are depicted as being less trustworthy than women and they are seen as relatively uncommitted to wives, children and other relatives.[5] Men's fondness for gambling and alcohol, and the faults they commit as husbands, are also explained in terms of men being less able to control their *nafsu*.[6] According to Peletz, both men and women support and use this version of the gender ideology.

In a study of Malay women in Penang, the Norwegian social anthropologist Kirsten Sandborg (1994: 240) notes the same kind of reversed images, but she presents them as opposing male and female models, not as 'official' and 'practical' representations of gender as in the case of Negri Sembilan. Without further developing the theme, Sandborg claims that she found men to attribute to themselves greater *akal* than women, ultimately legitimizing their responsibility for decision-making in the family, whereas women saw themselves as more responsible than men, who were held to be irresponsible and desirous.

AKAL OR *NAFSU* – INDIVIDUAL RESPONSIBILITIES

In urban religious classes, the notions of *akal* and *nafsu* were talked about irrespective of gender, and individual responsibility was emphasized instead. Teachers transmitted the idea that *akal* is a human quality created by God. The idea of *akal* developing over time was also supported. Whenever religious teachers touched upon issues concerning the concepts of *akal* and *nafsu*, I would ask them to elaborate on the gender dimension. I was always given the same answer: there was no difference between men's and women's ability to use *akal* and to learn, nor was there any support for the idea that women were equipped with more *nafsu* than men were. *Akal* was basically understood as the ability to learn and it was stressed that the degree of *akal* varied individually. Some people had developed their *akal* well, but it had nothing to do with gender. The important thing about the ability to resist *nafsu* was that it was a precondition of being able to obey God. To highlight the close relationship between the ability to resist *nafsu* and the ability to obey God's will, teachers sometimes used verse 45: 23 in the Koran:

> *Then seest thou such*
>
> *A one as takes*
>
> *As his god his own*
>
> *Vain desire? God has,*
>
> *Knowing (him as such) Left him astray, and sealed*
>
> *His hearing and his heart*
>
> *(And understanding), and put*
>
> *A cover on his sight.*
>
> *Who, then, will guide him*
>
> *After God (has withdrawn*
>
> *Guidance)? Will ye not*
>
> *Then receive admonition?*

From this verse it was argued that for those who do not fight their *nafsu* it is difficult to obey God. Further reasoning from this idea made the association between *nafsu* and Satan significant. Religious teachers used to say that to resist one's *nafsu* meant putting up a fight against Satan: those who obey their *nafsu*, disobey God, meaning that they obey Satan. Difficulties in praying regularly or performing commendable prayers were also signs of a need to fight *nafsu* and Satanic temptations. In an attempt to explain the force of *nafsu* and temptation, one teacher used the example of how it felt when she was eating chili. She liked chili so much that whenever she ate it she could not stop and she wanted to have more and more. But then her mouth would start burning and she would promise herself not to eat so much the next time. It was a constant struggle. It was also emphasized that it was easy to obey *nafsu*, and examples were taken from phenomena in Kuala Lumpur, where people could easily be tempted to attend pop music concerts and football games or see movies. Those queuing up and paying a lot for such attractions were described as ridiculous and weak, whereas people entering the mosque were described as resisting their *nafsu*, thereby obeying God. Ong (1995) has noted that the same kind of discourse was heavily used by the *dakwah* movement in the 1970s in order to explain various modern ills of Malay society, from drugs to communism. The weakness of Muslim societies was explained in terms of Muslims being too weak to resist their baser nature – *nafsu. Dakwah* adherents also made the connection between uncontrollable *nafsu* and working women, urging them to call for a stricter segregation between men and women, both spatially and through the covering of women's *aurat* (the parts of the body that should not be exposed).

Men's weaknesses and women's self-control

In the context of the religious study groups, then, the concepts of *akal* and *nafsu* were not talked about in terms of gender differences. In everyday situations and in conversations that I had with women outside the classes, things, however, were different. When I talked to women about marriage and relationships, men were usually described as the weaker sex, in the sense that they were more prone to giving in to *nafsu*. This was the usual explanation given for men's adultery, drinking and gambling. Other women spoke about men's weakness in terms of their lack of sexual control in the same manner as Saliha did in the conversation recounted above. If men were better at controlling their *nafsu*, it would not be necessary for them to complain about the way women dressed. Women argued that the reason for women being placed out of men's sight during prayer was evidence for men's lack of control. They would not be able to concentrate on their prayers if they had women before their eyes. Women, on the contrary, had no such problems of self-control. Men were simply not considered strong enough to exercise self-control and resist temptation when exposed to it.

The idea that women, compared to men, lacked self-control was quite absent in this discourse. I was also made aware of this in a situation when my own *akal* was put to a test. I had been visiting a female religious teacher, *ustazah* Zainah, living further down the Klang valley from Kuala Lumpur and as I was about to make my way back to the city I was offered a ride with one of the teacher's sons who happened to pass by. He had an appointment in the city and he was happy to have company on the tedious AutoRoute leading to the capital. Even though I was quite familiar with the family I had never met this son before since he had just returned from studies in London. He was Zainah's youngest son and he was married with two small children. I noticed that Zainah was not very supportive of the arrangement and invited me to stay another night in her house, and return to the city the following morning instead. During my fieldwork I had grown particularly close to Zainah and we had developed what I considered to be an emotional and trusting relationship. I followed her commitments as a religious teacher regularly, spent a lot of time in her house, and she had expressed a clear intention to try to make me see what she took to be the truth in Islam. At first I understood her wish for me to stay another night in terms of her usual hospitality and I politely refused the offer since I too had an appointment in the city that same afternoon. As we were about to leave, Zainah took me aside and spoke to me in a worried voice. She made me promise that I would not let her son into my house when he dropped me off. (She knew that my husband was away at the time and would not be in the house on my return.) She was very concerned because she did not really trust her son, she said. And she told me that a man and a woman are never completely alone in a room, even though there are no other people present, because Satan is always in their company. The temptation that Satan would put us through was what she feared, and she wanted to make sure that the situation would not arise.

What I found interesting with this episode was that Zainah appealed to *my akal* to avoid a dangerous situation, not her son's. It was his lack of control that she saw as the major threat, and she showed me how to act in order to resist *nafsu*, thereby keeping Satan at distance.

It was also held that women were less eager than men to remarry after a divorce or after becoming widowed. The fact that men, more than women, preferred to remarry in such situations was explained with reference to men's greater weakness. They could never live on their own, since they had greater sexual needs than women and they needed someone to take care of them. Ainon was a woman who had been separated and had lived apart from her husband for a long time because he was married to other women in other parts of Malaysia. Ainon had not been aware of her husband's other wives when they got married. This had come to her knowledge when her husband decided to go back to another wife after having spent a couple of years with Ainon. Ainon had experienced illness after a miscarriage, something that, according to her, had contributed to problems in their marriage. When her husband left, Ainon became aware of the existence of the other wives, and she also realized her husband did not have any intention of fulfilling his obligations toward her as his wife. She was the youngest daughter of three, and, after being left on her own, she moved back to her parents' house where she cared for them. She was also mothering a three-year-old niece, one of her sisters' daughters, since the sister had become seriously ill after her latest birth. In my company she often talked about her situation and the direction that she wanted her life to take. She sometimes considered asking for a divorce but when talking about it she said, with reference to sexual needs, that it did not really matter whether she was married or not. In her view, men's sexual needs were greater than women's and she found it easy to resist her *nafsu* with the help of prayer and regular fasting. She had, furthermore, been able to assume motherhood through caring for her niece. So, she did not fear a future life without a husband.

In my material, it is clear that *akal* and *nafsu* are seen as elements in both men and women. The responsibility for the control of *nafsu* is placed on the individual. In relation to men, however, there was a tendency for women to talk about *nafsu* as an attribution of maleness. Men were said to have stronger sexual needs, more difficult to control than women's whereas, when women talked about their own capability to control *nafsu* it was connected to the performance of religious duties. Diligence in prayer and fasting were means to strengthen self-control.

Ong (1995) has concluded that the *dakwah* movement's focus on the need to control female sexuality was, in part, the result of efforts to strengthen male authority, threatened by processes of modernization and industrialization. She views the *dakwah* movement's call for a stricter separation between male public roles and female domestic ones as '... a concrete realization of the architecture of male rationality (*akal*) and female eroticism (*nafsu*)' (1995: 177) leading to a strengthening of male control of female sexuality. The reversed image, that women are better at controlling *nafsu* than men, which comes forth not only in my material but also in Sandborg's work (1994), is intriguing. Sandborg even points at this transformation of gendered notions of *akal* and *nafsu* as a rather 'paradoxical momentum' in the politics of the *dakwah* movement. She suggests that the notion of men having greater sexual desire than women may actually be the result of the *dakwah* movement's emphasis on women's responsibility to cover their *aurat* and guard their modesty. This emphasis has produced a shift from the idea of women as 'desirous' to the idea of women as 'desirable'. What has been communicated in the *dakwah* discourse is rather that uncovered women are too desirable for men to be able to resist them, and not that women themselves are desirous. I find this a very good example of how women are agents of, and vehicles for, the constant transformation of Islamic ideas and practices. Through a reworking of the views that men have more *akal* and women more *nafsu*, women may be able to renegotiate their position within Islam.

BECOMING *MUKMIN* – THE STORY OF AISHA

Becoming *mukmin* meant individual responsibility towards God, which exemplified the idea of equality between men and women in relation to God. Being a *mukmin* was also a manifestation of being a person with *akal*, a person who could resist *nafsu*. As an illustration of this I will use the case of Aisha, a woman whose religiosity was manifested, not only in her choice of dress, but also in the quiet certainty of her manners and expression. She was one of those people whose piety expressed itself in her face, recognizable to anyone who met her. Religion had not always been a central part of her life. Her interest in religion had come gradually and, through her religious studies, it had developed into a deep faith and trust in God's guidance. The following story reveals how her strengthened commitment to God, her becoming *mukmin*, created a space in which she could negotiate her relationship with her husband, which brought positive effects to her personal life, as well as her family.

I met Aisha in one of the *tafsir* classes that I attended regularly. She usually appeared in class dressed in Arab style ankle-length dresses in sombre shades of blue, green or gray, with a white scarf covering her head and shoulders. Occasionally, she would wear *baju kurung*, but always of rather subdued colours and patterns. Although she could afford to dress in silk and hand-painted material, she preferred a more simple style. As a good Muslim, she did not want to expose either wealth or vanity in public. The class was held in English, but apart from two or three Chinese converts, the group consisted of Malays. All the participants were well educated with careers as journalists, teachers and government administrators. There were also a few housewives, former professionals. Aisha was in her early 40s and was a teacher. She had attended the Malay Girls' College (Tunku Kurshiah College), which at that point was still an English-medium school, and as a consequence she found it difficult to follow religious talks in Malay and felt more comfortable with classes in English. She was born in another state and had moved to Kuala Lumpur after marriage.

Aisha would often pick up a theme from class and relate it to her own life and through these conversations with her I successively learnt about the course of her life. One day, when the topic of male and female roles in society was touched upon in class, Aisha was inspired to tell me her view on gender relations through experiences in her married life. She began her story by saying that, as a young girl, she was not aware of gender differences. The reason she gave for this was that her brothers and sisters had been brought up in the same way. They all had to help out with household chores and they all received a good education, regardless of their gender. According to Aisha, it wasn't until she got married that she started to realize that men and women are treated differently in society.

Most of Aisha's friends' marriages were arranged and so was hers. Romantic marriages did take place but arranged ones were still more common. In her own case, she says that the arranged marriage was more the result of her own behaviour towards boys than any explicit wish from her family to find a suitable husband for her. She explained that she used to feel awkward around boys and she could also establish a pattern for her contacts with boys: she did not like any of the young boys who tried to approach her and the ones she did like she did not know how to tackle. One of the teachers at university took a liking to Aisha and wanted to help her in this matter. Actually, the teacher wanted her own son to marry Aisha, but he was still in school himself and did not have the means to marry. Instead, she introduced Aisha to another man who was looking for a wife. Aisha was told that this man was a good, intelligent and religious man. She agreed to meet him and shortly after he gave her a ring and they decided to get married.

After the wedding, the couple stayed with the husband's family in the northeastern state of Kelantan. One of Aisha's duties was to cook the family meals with her sister-in-law. When the meal was served, the men would eat first and the women after. Aisha had a difficult time accepting this. She felt bad that she had to do all the work and then eat last and it also meant that all the good dishes were finished by the time it was their turn. She compared this with how it was in her own home, where they all ate together – and she said that this experience made her realize that men and women were treated differently. The conflict with her in-laws became so fraught that Aisha demanded that she and her husband set up their own household. She was determined that she would never set foot in her in-laws' house again.

Like so many others, the couple was drawn to Kuala Lumpur. The husband was offered a job there and he bought a house with a government loan. Their first child was a daughter, followed by two more daughters. Aisha said that her husband was not happy with only having daughters. He wished to have sons, instead. According to Aisha, this was one of the main sources of irritation for her husband and it also manifested itself in conflicts about money. During the first years, he wasn't willing to spend any money on the girls. Aisha liked to buy clothes for the girls and dress them well, but when she asked her husband for money for the children, he would not give her any. So, Aisha spent her own salary as a teacher to buy clothes and other items for the children as well as pay for food. Thus, while her husband paid for the house with his salary, Aisha's earnings were largely spent on food, clothing and other family expenses.

After a few years, Aisha's husband went to do a Master's degree in London for one year. The husband was afraid that the family would be a distraction to him and requested that Aisha and the girls stayed behind. Aisha was not very happy with this, and felt neglected and mistreated by her husband. She remembered her own father's lack of interest in his wife and children and she had hoped that her own marriage would be different. Instead, she saw the same thing repeat itself. It was in this state of unhappiness that Aisha started to turn towards religion. She had seen other women find comfort in religion and, inspired by a woman she worked with, she started to attend the Saturday afternoon *tajwid* class at the National Mosque in order to freshen up her Koran reading. The class was held in the main prayer hall and attracted a couple of hundred women from all over the city. She felt comfortable there and the place was big enough for her to bring the children. They would always find friends with whom they could play while the mothers followed the class. But, because of the large crowd, it was not always easy to hear what the teacher had to say and as a complement to this activity, Aisha used to buy cassette tapes with recorded sermons. She would put them on when she was cooking or cleaning. Over time, her regular listening to such sermons contributed greatly to her increased religious interest and knowledge. She started to wear a scarf at about this time and she became more diligent in her prayers, reaching out to God and asking God to guide her in life.

While her husband was away in London, Aisha continued working as a teacher. During the school holidays, Aisha and her daughters went to visit him. Aisha had tried to save a bit of money each month, in order to have some extra money to spend on their overseas vacation. The problems started immediately. In the taxi from the airport, Aisha's husband asked her to pay for the fare. She gave him the money then but did not feel good about it because it was from her own savings. The next time he asked her to pay, she refused. Even though she was excited about visiting London, she did not feel that the trip had been good, feeling let down by her husband.

On Aisha's return from London, her mother-in-law came to Kuala Lumpur for a visit. Aisha assumed that she wanted to see how her son's family was doing and she showed her the house, which she was very proud of. They had found a nice house on an attractive plot of land. While looking around, the mother-in-law asked how many bathrooms there were. Aisha was happy to show her three bathrooms, one to each room. Her mother-in-law said that if her son would die, his brothers would inherit the house because Aisha did not have any sons. She supported this by saying that it was stated so in the Koran. (At the time Aisha was not aware that this was wrong and she believed her mother-in-law.)

Aisha was stunned and shocked by the implications of what her mother-in-law had said and, when her husband returned from London, she told him what had happened. She also told him that she needed a house of her own and that she needed a car to go to work in. The husband agreed to pay the deposit for a house and a car. It was a lot of money but the way Aisha reasoned it would add up to all the money she had spent on food and clothes over the years, so she thought it was more than fair. She let the house to another family and was pleased to have it as a form of security, in case something happened. Later on, she found support for her way of reasoning in Islam. She had approached a female religious teacher and asked about the rights of a wife and a husband. She had told her about her husband's behaviour concerning money and about the mother-in-law's indication about inheritance. The teacher said that the Koran does not confirm the idea that a wife could not inherit her husband's possessions just because she had not been able to produce a son. She also said that if a wife is earning money herself she is not obliged to spend it on the family. She may do so if she wants to, but she does not have to. The husband did not have the right even to ask for her money. The teacher emphasized that the responsibility to provide for the family is the husband's and that wives should be given an 'allowance' to use for household expenses.

Aisha was surprised to hear what the teacher said. She said that she had had no idea at the time that all that was to be found in the Koran. The experience increased her interest in Islam even more and she was eager to learn more about the Koran. She started to attend religious classes in the mosque and took private lessons in Arabic from a female teacher. She had finally come across the *tafsir* class where I met her. She found this class particularly interesting, not only because of the language, but also because of the teacher whose depth of knowledge and spirituality she admired a lot. She had been following the class for four years when I met her and, during that time, she had also been able to awaken a religious interest in her husband and a few years earlier they had both performed the hajj for the first time. To be engaged in religious education was vital to Aisha and she was also outspoken and had an inquiring attitude in the classes that she participated in. She considered it to be every Muslim's responsibility to seek knowledge and she encouraged her husband to do the same thing. Even though she had come a long way in terms of religious knowledge since she first started to listen to recorded sermons, she emphasized that there was a lot more for her to learn. The most important thing for her was that she had found comfort and strength in Islam, and also the faith to put her life totally in the hands of God, and to accept God's will in all aspects of life. It made her happier as a person and she found it easier to cope with the difficult things in life. Every day she asked God to guide her, to help her make the right decisions and be a good person. This reliance on God's guidance had led her to make what she described as a logical decision – to suggest to her husband that he could marry a second wife and try to have a son with her.

WOMEN AND MEN – EQUAL BEFORE GOD

It is clear that Aisha, by developing an identity as *mukmin*, was finding a way to deal with her her relationship with her husband and her position in the family. Through religious studies, she became aware that Islam grants women both rights and responsibilities with regard to men. By appealing to her husband's responsibilities as a Muslim man, to be the breadwinner of the family, she was able to raise those issues within the Islamic framework. Earlier, we saw how Saliha challenged male interpretations of the Islamic sources, and thereby male authority, when claiming men's and women's equal responsibilities toward God.

In both these cases, where women's rights were brought up, references were made to the idea that men and women are equal before God. This is one of the basic principles in Islam: it is the duty of all Muslims, men and women, to worship and obey God. Men and women have a duty towards God first. If they follow the words of God, there are different roles in society assigned to men and women, roles given in order that society as a whole may work better. They have somewhat different rights and responsibilities towards each other, but their duty towards God is the same – to worship Him. This makes men and women different but complementary towards each other, yet equal before God. It also means that women must follow the will of God first and only secondly, the will of their husbands and fathers.

In these kinds of discourses, the women are creating a situation in which there are three positions – women, men and God. Men and women are equal in terms of their duties towards God. This gives them a way out of what they would say was a Western way of approaching relations between men and women – the women's movement and its claim on equality between men and women in terms of identical rights. This gave them an indisputable argument towards their husbands as well as a moral 'upper hand'. By bringing God into an argument, the injustice was done towards Him, and only indirectly towards the wife. The conflict was thereby grounded, not so much in the relations between men and women, as in the relation between women and God.

In the concluding chapter, I shall discuss the implication of this understanding of pious Malay women's subjectivity on a feminist theory of agency.

NOTES

1   Chapters and verses referred to were, for example, 2: 38, 2: 208, and 22: 35.

2   See, for example, James Siegel's work on Aceh, *The Rope of God* (1969), Brenner (1995, 1998) on Java, and Patricia Horvatich (1992) on the Philippines. For the Malay context, see David Banks (1983), Carol Laderman (1991), Ong (1995) and Peletz (1995).

3   It may be noted that in Sufi thinking there is the idea that one can channel 'desire' into love of God through prayer. A regional example of this idea is found in Siegel's study of Aceh in *The Rope of God* (1969). Wazir (1990) argues that this idea is not actualized in the Malay context, and I never heard anyone refer to it during my fieldwork.

4   Negri Sembilan is characterized by its matrilineal kinship system, in comparison to the bilateral system of Malays in other parts of the peninsula. But Peletz argues that too much focus on descent greatly overshadows the important elements of matrifocality, matrifiliation and matrilaterality significant of all Malay systems of social relations. Furthermore, in regard to perceptions of prestige, personhood and gender, there are basic similarities in all Malay societies. Peletz thus suggests that his finding may have a wider relevance than for the Malays of Negri Sembilan.

5   These ideas permeate the everyday gender discourse on property and inheritance as they, according to Peletz, tie into the matrilineal aspects of Negri Sembilan society that emphasize women's need (greater than men's) of subsistence guarantees, expressed in the favouring of daughters over sons in inheritance of houses and land.

6   See also Brenner (1995) for a similar discussion on contradictory re-presentations of gender in her Javanese material.

7

Conclusion
Feminism, anthropology and agency

Jamilah was 40 and had decided to quit her job as a teacher. She was married and had two children who were university students. With her affluent upper-middle-class lifestyle, Jamilah did not lack anything in terms of money or material comfort. But she was not satisfied with her life and had for several years experienced a growing need to turn to religion. This need was expressed as a wish to devote more time to religious studies. Her decision to stop working and become a full-time housewife was reached after a long period of careful reflection. Jamilah hesitated at first, partly because she was reluctant to be financially dependent on her husband, and partly because she was reluctant to give up her social status as a teacher. She valued teaching and felt that it was a highly rewarding way of contributing to society. Hoping that she would eventually be able to use her teaching skills in a religious context, she decided to stop working.

Jamilah announced this to her husband, emphasizing that it was entirely a personal decision, based on her own needs and on her development into a *mukmin* – a person with a conscious and embodied desire to submit to God's will. She made it clear to me that she did not become a housewife to please her husband, although she was well aware that he would, in fact, be pleased. At the same time, she expressed great happiness when she told me that one of the good things that came with being a housewife was that she could now prepare breakfast for her husband and daughters before they went to work and school. To her, this was a luxury that she had been deprived of as a working woman when she was always rushing in the mornings. In addition, being at home allowed her to put on and listen to recorded sermons while clearing up the kitchen or preparing dinner, and, most importantly, it gave her time to attend religious classes in the afternoon. The pleasure she experienced from caring for her family in the form of cooking was easily combined with her individual choice to quit salaried employment and devote more time to religion.

The choice of Jamilah, and that of other well-educated, professional women, to actively participate in the Islamic movement in combination with the role of housewife may be one which is provocative to Western feminism, since the latter has defined, and stressed, female emancipation very much in terms of financial independence from men. Although the intentions of women like Jamilah are expressed differently, the obvious question from a feminist perspective in regard to her religious subjectivity, however actively produced, is whether it merely results in a reconfiguration of female subordination. Is Jamilah trading in her financial independence for involvement in a religious tradition that emphasizes male authority?

The negative effects of Islamization and modernization on Malay women have indeed been pointed out by scholars who have argued that both state and *dakwah* Islamization projects have actively introduced many aspects of patriarchal Muslim Arab or Middle Eastern gender and family relations, intensifying Malay gender difference, segregation and inequality, and strengthening male authority (Ong 1995; Norani 1998). In the area of family jurisdiction, it has been noted that the application of adat law, which for example grants men and women equal opportunities to inherit property and to initiate divorce, has been heavily circumvented in several of the Malaysian states with the introduction of sharia law, which emphasizes men's rights over women's (Jones 1994; Zainah 2001). In addition to this, Islamic propagators have emphasized women's responsibility as mothers and reproducers of the nation. They have also produced a powerful discourse on women's modesty through dress (in particular the veil), behaviour and restriction in movement.

At the same time, it has been pointed out that wherever the veil emerges as a symbol of politicized Islam, women become important religious and political agents (Göle 1996; Stivens 2000). Women in many parts of the Muslim world openly and explicitly criticize the male-biased interpretations of the Islamic sources that form the basis of sharia legislation and practice in a number of Muslim societies. Women are claiming their rights and at the same time they are formulating an alternative feminism in relation to the Western version(s). The Iranian, Islamic, and explicitly feminist journal *Zanan* (Women), founded in 1992, is an expression of this movement. The journal offers reinterpretations of the Islamic sources from a women's perspective and it claims equality between men and women and irrelevance of gender difference in terms of human rights. The overall aim of the journal is to awaken women so that they will proclaim their rights and thereby bring about a transformation of society (Najmabadi 1998). The emergence of feminist interpretations of Islamic sources is of great significance for a formulation of Muslim reform feminism. The Islamic scholar Amina Wadud-Muhsin's (1992) reinterpretations of the Koran and her argument that equality between men and women is fundamental to Islam, to take one example, have had a profound impact.[1]

In Malaysia, the best known activist group in this respect is Sisters in Islam (SIS). This is a small religious reformist group whose members are urban Malay women with tertiary education. Several are journalists and lawyers. SIS's explicit aim is to reclaim a social justice agenda within Islam and to promote a more egalitarian interpretation of gender status and rights. SIS has published work on a number of topics concerning women's rights within Islam in general (Ismail 1993) as well as on particular issues, such as gender-biased aspects of Muslim family law (Norani 1994) and the implementation of hudud law in Malaysia from a gendered perspective (Ismail 1995).

Ong (1998) describes the quest of 'the Sisters' as a feminist battle, fought in two steps against the ulama's Islamization campaign. The first step is to assert women's intellectual role in interpreting Islam, also an important aim for Muslim feminists worldwide. The right of women and girls to a religious education is defined as a necessary condition for such a role. Muslim feminists emphasize chaste conduct with reference to the concept of *akal* thereby presenting themselves as '... reasoning sisters rather than as passionate mothers, wives or lovers' (Ong 1998: 62).

The second step in SIS's struggle is to enlarge the public space for debates over Islamic truths beyond the control of ulamas. It is by arguing that the ulama's claims are not divine revelations but man-made interpretations that they call for the participation of women in debates about religious truths. To some extent, SIS has been successful in this struggle, but Ong is reluctant to give this success any value in terms of the emancipation of Muslim women in Malaysia. While the rise of feminist public intellectuals has produced a more pluralistic public debate about Islam in modern Malay culture, Ong is concerned that women, in this process, are merely exchanging a lesser form of subordination to men under 'ulama nationalism', than under the state nationalism. 'The Sisters', according to Ong, have, in fact, not yet articulated women's most basic right over their own bodies. In their battle against chauvinist ulama and proving their own moral worthiness as 'reasoning sisters' they have, instead, contributed to the public reproduction of Muslim sexuality as hegemonically male. According to Ong, it is precisely this public notion of sexuality that stands in the way of a number of legislations that would work to guarantee women's rights, for example, the criminalization of violence against women and children in the household and the legal adoption of the concept of 'marital rape'. Ong also makes the connection between the public notion of sexuality as male and the recent and increasing cases of 'baby-dumping' by young, unmarried Malay women. She argues that the public, non-acceptance of unmarried women's sexuality pushes young women who have become pregnant out of wedlock to abandon their children. In relation to SIS, Ong's conclusion is that when they emphasize a presentation of '(...) themselves as upholders of the Faith, they can only support a limited notion of gender equality that is subject to the moral priority of ulama to define what is or is not morally permissible in Malaysian society' (ibid.: 75).

FROM 'WOMEN AND ISLAMIZATION' TO 'WOMEN'S ISLAMIZATION'

While Ong's analysis is important and potent, as it focuses on the power relations between men and women, it runs the risk of portraying women's religious dedication and activities as the result of false consciousness or internalized patriarchy, ultimately pushing women back into the position of victims, which is quite the opposite of what feminist theory strives for.

Furthermore, when the focus is on the negative effects of Islamization on women's lives, however important this is, there is also the danger of 'missing' the meaning that women themselves ascribe to the process of Islamization. With a more generative account of how women actively craft themselves into religious subjects, I suggest that we can better understand women's religious commitment on their own terms.

Thus, through a meaning-centred approach to women's religious involvement and a close ethnographic account of how this was enacted in their daily lives, I have sought to capture the significance it held for the women themselves. In their view, religious studies along with the performance of religious duties and worship were particularly important means through which individual women came to understand themselves as religious subjects. Women were active in initiating, organizing and participating in religious education in various contexts – in mosques, within formal *dakwah* organizations, as well as more informally in workplaces and in homes. All these various classes and study groups were based on the study of the scriptural sources of Islam: women learned to recite, read and understand the Koran. They studied the Islamic sources, engaged in interpretations of them in relation to contemporary life, and expressed a need to review the things they had been taught as children and to deepen their knowledge of Islam. They expressed their learning process as the reaching of new levels of understanding, a process that has no limit.

In tandem with religious education, these women incorporated Islamic ideas and values in their everyday lives through the observance of religious duties and worship. Women expressed sensitivity in relation to correct religious behaviour both in private and public, but, as the material shows, the meaningfulness of religious duties such as prayer, fasting and veiling clearly exceed a mere concern for correctness. I have argued that the performance of acts of worship in everyday life was seen by women as an important means through which they cultivated a conscious desire to submit to God's will. The daily performance of religious duties and acts of worship were thus expressions of piety as well as the means through which an identity as *mukmin* could be developed.

While this study has avoided posing questions about the effects that Islamization has on women's lives, it has asked what effects women's striving towards piety has on the religious practice of Islam in the Malaysian context. In this respect, the material shows that women's educational activities, together with their acknowledged piety, have a number of consequences, both structurally and individually. First, as women appropriated the mosque for the purpose of study and teaching, they created a female space within the traditionally, male-dominated mosque environment. Organizing religious classes for women in the mosque thus brought about change in the gendered space of the mosque.

Second, the acquisition of religious knowledge by women further opened up spaces for women to enter positions of religious authority – for example, becoming religious teachers, either with formal or informal training. Women's increased religious knowledge furthermore has provided them with necessary conditions for assuming the authoritative roles needed for the performance of certain collective rituals. Women in urban areas organized and performed both the religious and social elements of collective rituals connected to life-crisis events. I have argued that these rituals have been 'Islamized' in the sense that participants were drawn primarily from the mosque group rather than from the kin group. Thus, women took on the role of household representatives in the ritual context – a role that has traditionally been assigned to, and fulfilled, by men.

The task of realizing piety sometimes brought women in conflict with a variety of authority structures, including male. Jamilah, for instance, struggled with the secular, national discourse urging all citizens to contribute to Malaysia's development. Her decision to stop working and 'no longer contribute to society', and to follow her desire to devote more time to religion, was a very difficult one.

We have also seen that women sometimes found themselves in a dilemma because of the differences between Malay adat and Islam in terms of religious practices but also perceptions of gender relations. For example, women expressed uncertainty concerning some situations where menstruation constrained them in fulfilling certain religious duties such as commendable fasting. Another example is that of women's negotiations of the gendered representations of *akal* and *nafsu*, which they saw as fundamental to their achievement of piety.

Conflicts could also arise in relation to husbands or kin because of variant interpretations of the Koran or differences in religious knowledge and degree of conformity to Islam and Islamic practices. When women refer to the concept of *mukmin,* they also express the idea that men and women have equal responsibilities towards God. The decision to submit oneself to God's will should also be taken independently of other people and society in order to be good and valid. From a *mukmin* standpoint, women may simultaneously challenge male interpretations of the Koran (including those of their husbands') as well as take on traditional gender roles such as that of a devout housewife. The desire they express here is not to challenge male-dominated gender relations, but to submit to the will of a transcendental God. And as we have seen in the case of Aisha, for example, this desire may, in fact, lead to a transformation in the husband's religious behaviour and attitude as he assumed his religious responsibilities as supporter of his family.

The important thing to remember here is that the logic of these conflicts is not grounded in, and can therefore not be understood solely with reference to, arguments for gender equality or resistance to male authority. The logic of these conflicts had more to do with women's fundamental desire to submit to God's will. This is not to say that women's religious practice and commitment cannot and will not lead to social or political change. What is being emphasized here is that the desire to submit to God's will is an important aspect of women's religious commitment that would be overlooked in an analysis that has the explicit purpose of exposing the social and political effects of Islamization.

FEMINISM AND ANTHROPOLOGY

The difference between these two perspectives on women and Islamization crystallizes what Marilyn Strathern, in her now classic article from 1987, has called 'the awkward relationship' between anthropology and feminism. Strathern argues that feminism and anthropology, as scholarly practices, create different ways of relating to their respective subject matter. She suggests that 'the Other' of anthropology and 'the Other' of feminism are not the same. While anthropology constitutes itself as a discipline in relation to other cultures or societies that are under study, feminism constitutes itself against an oppressive 'Other' in the form of male ideology inherent in social life as well as in academic theory. The aim of feminism is to become conscious of the oppression from 'the Other', whereas for anthropology, the aim is to create a relation *with* the 'Other'.

This 'awkward relationship' is expressed in the issue of the agency of subjects, which is central to both feminism and anthroplogy. For feminism, as I have discussed in the introductory chapter, agency has specific empowering and political connotations, since the agency of women is seen as the key to their liberation from male-dominated gender relations. The conceptualization of agency as resistance has therefore been privileged within feminist theory.

For anthropology, on the other hand, the centrality of agency reflects an ethical imperative in the sense that the doctrine of action has become essential for our recognition of other people's humanity (Asad 1996). The social anthropologist Webb Keane (1997b) points out that the conceptualization of agency within anthropology also seems to demand an account of the conscious agent. He remarks that such an idea presupposes that the agent is a subject that knows itself to possess agency. But, just as as particular forms and objects of consciousness are historical and cultural products, so too is the concept of agency that mediates the agent's self-consciousness. For anthropology, therefore, to seek out agency includes looking for the historical construction of the idea of agency itself. It also means taking into account the fact that agency is context-dependent and that there are diverse motivations for human action and diverse grounds for, and forms of, agency (Desjarlais 1996). Anthropology's reflexive and meaning-centred approach thus allows us to see that agency may not always be something that the people we study want to celebrate or claim for themselves. They may, in fact, instead prefer to find agency in other worlds (Keane 1997a).

This text emerges from both a feminist and anthropological motivation to write against the common image of Muslim women as oppressed victims, and instead to present the pious women of this study as agents. It may be labelled a 'feminist ethnography' in the sense that it tries to present the 'women's point of view', much as feminist anthropologists have been doing for decades. But, when writing ethnography about women who resist identification with the feminist sense of marginalization, the limits of what might be called 'feminist ethnography' is expanded, and pushes feminist anthropology to explore different forms of inequality (Visweswaran 1997).

When applying feminist theory to the material I found the conceptualization of women's agency in terms of resistance, or false consciousness, to be much too limited in dealing with the religious lives of pious Malay women. The material presented has shown women who cultivate religious virtues and attitudes, such as modesty, piety and submissiveness that seem to be contrary to the idea of agency as it has been conceptualized within feminist theory. In this respect, pious women occupy a particularly awkward place in feminist scholarship as they pursue practices and ideals that are embedded within traditions that historically have accorded women a subordinate status (Mahmood 2001a; Saliba 2002).

PIETY AND AGENCY

In my efforts to understand the limitations of the conceptualization of agency as resistance privileged within feminist theory, I have found, as I have discussed in the introductory chapter, McNay's philosophical work on gender and agency illuminating and useful. McNay argues that the conceptualization of women's agency in terms of resistance within feminist theory is closely linked to a specific idea of how women understand themselves as subjects. The subject, in this framework, is understood largely in passive terms primarily as an effect of discursive structure. In this approach, agency is consequently conceptualized as either resistance or subjugation to discursive structures. Feminist theory is here caught in what NcNay (2000) calls the negative paradigm of subjectivation and agency.

The attractiveness of this negative paradigm, for feminist theory, has been that it offers the possibility to analyze entrenched aspects of gendered behaviour without falling into explanations that make reference to pre-social sexual differences. Recall that McNay acknowledges the explanatory potential of the negative paradigm, but she cautions that it does not provide an *exhaustive* understanding of subject formation and agency. Without a more generative account – an account of the more creative and productive aspects of subject formation and agency – we are limited in our ability to conceptualize how people come to understand themselves, and thereby act in new ways, in ways that do not fully correspond to discursive norms.

Following McNay's suggestions, I have tried to emphasize the generative aspects of the process through which women become religious subjects. Through this approach I have hoped to avoid projecting onto pious Malay women an account which, in the words of Valery Walkerdine in her work on English working-class girls, '… portrays them either as proto-revolutionary fodder or duped masses' (1997: 23). I have argued that the process of religious subjectification that the women in this study are involved in cannot be fully captured by the idea that they craft themselves as religious subjects in relation to an imagined oppressive, male, position. Instead, I have tried to show that they craft themselves in relation to the idea of a transcendental God. Becoming religious subjects, for these women, is a creative process through which they actively cultivate themselves as subjects with a disposition to submit to God's will. The pious Malay women that I have come to know in Malaysia are not fighting the same battle as Western, or even Muslim, feminists are. The subjectivity and agency that they produce deserve to be understood in these women's own terms – as active submission and as a way of life.

NOTE

1   Using a hermeneutical approach in her reinterpretation of the Koran, Amina challenges some conventional, and male-biased interpretations of the text concerning gender relations. For example, she argues, that the distinction between man and woman, as it is made in the Koran, is not attributed any difference in value.

Bibliography

Following standard practice, Malay authors are listed in the order of their given name.

Abd el-Hamid el-Zein (1977) 'Beyond ideology and theology: the search for an anthropology of Islam'. *Annual Review of Anthropology*, vol. 6, pp. 227–254.

Abdul Aziz bin Muhammad (1993) *Zakat and Rural Development in Malaysia*. Kuala Lumpur: Berita Publishing.

Abdul Rahman Embong (2001) 'Beyond the crisis: the paradox of the Malaysian middle class'. In Abdul Rahman Embong (ed.) *Southeast Asian Middle Classes: Prospects for Social Change and Democratisation*. Bangi: Penerbit University Kebangsaan Malaysia, pp. 80–102.

Abdullah Ahmad Badawi (2006) *Islam Hadhari: A Model Approach for Development and Progress*. Petaling Jaya: MPH Group.

Abu-Lughod, Lila (1986) *Veiled Sentiments: Honor and Poetry in a Bedouin Society*. Berkeley: University of California Press.

—— (1993) *Writing Women's Worlds: Bedouin Stories*. Berkeley: University of California Press.

Ackerman, Susan E. (1991) 'Dakwah and Minah Karan: class conflict formation and ideological conflict in Malay society'. *Bijdragen Tot de Taal-, Land- en Volkenkunde*, vol. 17, no. 2–3, pp. 201–215.

Ackerman, Susan E. and Raymond L. M. Lee (eds) (1988) *Heaven in Transition: Non-Muslim Religious Innovation and Ethnic Identity in Malaysia*. Honolulu: University of Hawai'i Press.

Allès, Élisabeth (2000) *Une Anthropologie Musulmans des Hui du Henan de Chine*. Paris: Éditions de l'École des Hautes Études en Sciences Sociales.

—— (2003) 'The history of Islam in China: mid-18th to early 20th century'. In Suad Joseph (ed.) *Encyclopedia of Women and Islamic Cultures: Methodologies, Paradigms and Sources*, vol. 1. Leiden: E. J. Brill, pp. 120–128.

Amina Wadud-Muhsin (1992) *Qur'an and Woman*. Kuala Lumpur: Penerbit Fajar Bakti.

Antoun, Richard T. (1976) 'The social anthropologist and the study of Islam'. In Leonard Binder (ed.) *The Study of the Middle East: Research and Scholarship in the Humanities and Social Sciences*. New York: John Wiley & Sons.

Asad, Talal (1993) *Genealogies of Religion: Discipline and Reasons of Power in Christianity and Islam*. Baltimore: Johns Hopkins University Press.

——— (1996) 'Comments on conversion'. In Peter van der Veer (ed.) *Conversion to Modernities: The Globalization of Christianity*. Baltimore: Johns Hopkins University Press, pp. 263–274.

——— (2003) *Formations of the Secular: Christianity, Islam, Modernity*. Palo Alto: Stanford University Press.

Banks, David J. (1983) *Malay Kinship*. Philadelphia: Institute for the Study of Human Issues.

Bartky, Sandra Lee (1995) 'Agency: what's the problem?' In Judith Kegan Gardiner (ed.) *Provoking Agents: Gender and Agency in Theory and Practice*. Urbana: University of Illionois Press, pp. 178–193.

Bauer, Janet L. (1997) 'Conclusion. The mixed blessings of women's fundamentalism: democratic impulses in a patriarchal world'. In Judy Brink and Joan Mencher (eds) *Mixed Blessings: Gender and Religious Fundamentalism Cross Culturally*. New York and London: Routledge, pp. 221–256.

Beauvoir, Simone de (1972) *The Second Sex*. Harmondsworth: Penguin.

Betteridge, Anne H. (2001) 'The controversial vows of urban Muslim women in Iran'. In Nancy Auer Falk and Rita M. Gross (eds) *Unspoken World: Women's Religious Lives*. Belmont: Wadsworth/Thomson Learning, pp. 134–143.

Boddy, Janice (1989) *Wombs and Alien Spirits: Women, Men, and the Zar Cult in Northern Sudan*. Madison: University of Wisconsin Press.

Bowen, John R. (1989) '*Salat* in Indonesia: the social meanings of an Islamic ritual'. *Man*, vol. 24, no. 4, pp. 600–619.

——— (1993) *Muslims through Discourse: Religion and Ritual in Gayo Society*. Princeton: Princeton University Press.

——— (1995) 'The forms culture takes: a state-of-the-field essay on the anthropology of Southeast Asia'. *Journal of Asian Studies*, vol. 54, no. 4, pp. 1047–1078.

Bracke, Sarah (2003) 'Author(iz)ing agency: feminist scholars making sense of women's involvement in religious "fundamentalist" movements'. *European Journal of Women's Studies,* vol. 10, no. 3, pp. 335–346.

Brenner, Suzanne A. (1995) 'Why women rule the roost: rethinking Javanese ideologies of gender and self-control'. In Aihwa Ong and Michael G. Peletz (eds) *Bewitching Women, Pious Men: Gender and Body Politics in Southeast Asia.* Berkeley: University of California Press, pp. 19–50.

——— (1996) 'Reconstructing self and society: Javanese Muslim women and "the veil"'. *American Ethnologist,* vol. 23, no. 4, pp. 673–697.

——— (1998) *The Domestication of Desire: Women, Wealth, and Modernity in Java.* Princeton: Princeton University Press.

Bringa, Tone (1995) *Being Muslim the Bosnian Way: Identity and Community in a Central Bosnian Village.* Princeton: Princeton University Press.

Brink, Judy and Joan Mencher (1997) *Mixed Blessings: Gender and Religious Fundamentalism Cross Culturally.* New York and London: Routledge.

Buitelaar, Marjo (1993) *Fasting and Feasting in Morocco: Women's Participation during Ramadan.* Oxford: Berg.

Butler, Judith (1990) *Gender Trouble: Feminism and the Subversion of Identity.* New York: Routledge.

——— (1993) *Bodies that Matter: On the Discursive Limits of "Sex".* New York: Routledge.

——— (1997) *The Psychic Life of Power: Theories in Subjection.* Palo Alto: Stanford University Press.

Carsten, Janet (1997) *The Heat of the Hearth: The Process of Kinship in a Malay Fishing Community.* Oxford: Clarendon Press.

Chandra Muzaffar (1986) 'Islamic Resurgence: A Global View'. In Taufik Abdullah and Sharon Siddique (eds) *Islam and Society in Southeast Asia.* Singapore: Institute of Southeast Asian Studies, pp. 5–39.

——— (1987) *Islamic Resurgence in Malaysia.* Petaling Jaya: Penerbit Fajar Bakti.

Coakley, Sarah (1997) 'Introduction: religion and the body'. In Sarah Coakley (ed.) *Religion and the Body.* Cambridge: Cambridge University Press.

——— (2002) *Powers and Submissions: Spirituality, Philosophy, and Gender.* Oxford: Blackwell.

Csordas, Thomas J. (1990) 'Embodiment as a paradigm for anthropology'. *Ethos,* vol. 18, no. 1, pp. 5–47.

Delaney, Carol (1991) *The Seed and the Soil: Gender and Cosmology in Turkish Village Society.* Berkeley: University of California Press.

Denny, Frederick M. (1994) *An Introduction to Islam.* New York: Macmillan.

Desjarlais, Robert (1996) 'The office of reason: on the politics of language and agency in a shelter for "the homeless and mentally ill"'. *American Ethnologist,* vol. 23, no. 4, pp. 880–900.

Djamour, Judith (1965) *Malay Kinship and Marriage in Singapore.* London: Athlone.

Eickelman, Dave F. (1982) 'The study of Islam in local contexts'. *Contributions to Asian Studies,* vol. 17, October, pp. 1–16.

Falk, Monica Lindberg (2008) *Making Fields of Merit: Buddhist Female Ascetics and Gendered Orders in Thailand.* Seattle: University of Washington Press, and Copenhagen: NIAS Press.

Falk, Nancy and Rita Gross (eds) (1980) *Unspoken Worlds: Women's Religious Lives in Non-Western Cultures.* San Francisco: Harper & Row.

Fatima Daud (1985) *Minah Karan.* Kuala Lumpur: Berita Publishing.

Fernea, R. and Elisabeth Fernea (1972) 'Variations in religious observance among Islamic women'. In Nikki R. Keddie (ed.) *Scholars, Saints and Sufis: Muslim Religious Institutions since 1500.* Berkeley: University of California Press.

Firth, Rosemary (1966) *Housekeeping among Malay Peasants.* London: Athlone.

Foucault, Michel (1979) *Discipline and Punish: The Birth of the Prison.* Harmondsworth: Penguin.

––– (1981) *The History of Sexuality: An Introduction.* Harmondsworth: Penguin.

––– (1985) *The Use of Pleasure.* Harmondsworth: Penguin.

Geertz, Clifford (1960) *The Religion of Java.* Chicago: Chicago University Press.

––– (1968) *Islam Observed.* New Haven: Yale University Press.

Gemzöe, Lena (2000) *Feminine Matters: Women's Religious Practices in a Portuguese Town.* Stockholm Studies in Social Anthropology 47. Stockholm: Almqvist & Wiksell International.

Goh Beng Lan (1998) 'Modern dreams: an enquiry into power, cityscape transformations and cultural differences in contemporary Malaysia'. In Joel S. Kahn (ed.) *Southeast Asian Identities: Culture and the Politics of Representation in Indonesia, Malaysia, Singapore, and Thailand.* Singapore: Institute of Southeast Asian Studies, pp. 168–202.

Göle, Nilufer (1996) *The Forbidden Modern: Civilization and Veiling.* Ann Arbor: University of Michigan Press.

Gomez, Edmund Terence (2002) 'Political business in Malaysia: party factionalism, corporate development, and economic crisis'. In Terence Edmund Gomez (ed.) *Political Business in East Asia.* London: Routledge, pp. 82–114.

Government of Malaysia (1973) *Mid-Term Review of the Second Malaysian Plan 1971–1975*. Kuala Lumpur: Government Printers.

—— (1993) *Mid-Term Review of the Sixth Malaysian Plan 1991–1995*. Kuala Lumpur: Government Printers.

—— (1999) *Mid-Term Review of the Seventh Malaysian Plan 1996–2000*. Kuala Lumpur: Government Printers.

Graham, William A. (1983) 'Islam in the mirror of ritual'. In Richard G. Hovannisian and Speros Vryonis Jr (eds) *Islam's Understanding of Itself*. Malibu: Undena.

Griffith, Marie R. (2000) *God's Daughters: Evangelical Women and the Power of Submission*. Berkeley: University of California Press.

Gross, Rita (1996) *Feminism and Religion: An Introduction*. Boston: Beacon Press.

Gullick, John Michael (1989) *Malay Society in the Nineteenth Century*. Singapore: Oxford University Press.

Haji Faisal bin Haji Othman (1993) *Woman, Islam and Nation Building*. Kuala Lumpur: Berita Publishing.

Harding, Sandra (1991) 'Representing fundamentalism: the problem of the repugnant cultural other'. *Social Research*, vol. 58, no. 2, pp. 373–393.

Hegland, Mary Elaine (1998) 'Flagellation and fundamentalism: transforming meaning, identity, and gender through Pakistani women's ritual of mourning'. *American Ethnologist*, vol. 25, no. 2, pp. 240–266.

Hekman, Susan (1991) 'Reconstituting the subject: feminism, modernism, and postmodernism'. *Hypatia*, vol. 6, no. 2, pp. 44–63.

——— (1995) 'Subjects and agents: the question for feminism'. In Judith Kegan Gardiner (ed.) *Provoking Agents: Gender and Agency in Theory and Practice*. Urbana: University of Illinois Press, pp. 194–207.

Hirschkind, Charles (2001) 'Civic virtue and religious reason: an Islamic counterpublic'. *Cultural Anthropology*, vol. 26 , no. 1, pp. 3–34.

Hirschman, Charles (1987) 'The meaning and measurements of ethnicity in Malaysia: an analysis of census classification'. *Journal of Asian Studies*, vol. 42, no. 3, pp. 555–582.

Holy, Ladislav (1991) *Religion and Custom in a Muslim Society: The Berti of Sudan*. Cambridge: Cambridge University Press.

The Holy Qur'an, Translation and commentary by A. Yusuf Ali (1983). Brentwood, MD: Amana.

Hooker, Virginia Matheson (2004) 'Reconfiguring Malay and Islam in contemporary

Malaysia'. In Timothy P. Barnard (ed.) *Contesting Malayness: Malay Identity across Boundaries*. Singapore: Singapore University Press, pp. 149–167.

Horvatich, Patricia (1992) 'Mosques, Misunderstandings and the True Islam: Muslim Discourses in Tawi-Tawi, Philippines'. Doctoral dissertation, Stanford University.

––– (1994) 'Ways of knowing Islam'. *American Ethnologist*, vol. 21, no. 4, pp. 811–826.

Hussin Mutalib (1993) *Islam in Malaysia: From Revivalism to the Islamic State?* Singapore: Singapore University Press.

––– (1994) 'Islamisation in Malaysia: between ideals and realities'. In Hussin Mutalib and Taj ul-Islam Hashmi (eds) *Islam, Muslims and the Modern State: Case-Studies of Muslims in Thirteen Countries*. New York: St. Martin's Press, pp. 152–73.

Ismail, Rose (ed.) (1993) *Islam, Gender and Human Rights: An Alternative View*. Kuala Lumpur: Sisters in Islam.

––– (ed.) (1995). *Hudud in Malaysia: The Issues at Stake*. Kuala Lumpur: Sisters in Islam.

Jamilah Arrifin. 1980. 'Industrial Development in Peninsular Malaysia and Rural-Urban Migration of Women Workers: Impact and Implications'. In *Jurnal Ekonomi Malaysia*, vol. 1, pp. 41–59.

Jansen, Wilhelmina (1998) 'Contested identities: women and religion in Algeria and Jordan'. In Karin Ask and Marit Tjomsland (eds) *Women and Islamization: Contemporary Dimensions of Discourses on Gender Relations*. Oxford: Berg, pp. 73–102.

Jaschok, Maria and Shui Jingjun (2000) *The History of Women's Mosques in Chinese Islam: A Mosque of Their Own*. Richmond, Surrey: Curzon Press.

Jomo, K. S. and Ahmad Shabery Cheek (1992) 'Malaysia's Islamic movements'. In Joel S. Kahn and Francis Loh Kok Wah (eds) *Fragmented Vision: Culture and Politics in Contemporary Malaysia*. St. Leonard's: Allen & Unwin.

Jones, Gavin W. (1994) *Marriage and Divorce in Islamic South-East Asia*. Kuala Lumpur: Oxford University Press.

Joseph, Suad (2003) *Encyclopedia of Women and Islamic Cultures: Methodologies, Paradigms and Sources*, vol 1. Leiden: E. J. Brill.

Kahn, Joel S. (1996) 'Growth, economic transformation, culture and the middle classes in Malaysia'. In R. Robinson and D. S. G. Goodman (eds) *The New Rich in Asia: Mobile Phones, McDonalds and Middle Classes*. London: Routledge, pp. 49–78.

Kahn, Joel S. and Francis Loh Kok Wah (eds) (1992) *Fragmented Vision: Culture and Politics in Contemporary Malaysia*. St. Leonard's: Allen & Unwin.

Kamalkhani, Zahra (1993) 'Women's everyday religious discourse in Iran'. In Haleh Afshar (ed.) *Women in the Middle East: Perception, Reality and Struggles for Liberation*. London: Macmillan, pp. 85–95.

––– (1996) 'Women's Islam: Religious Practice among Women in Today's Iran'. Doctoral dissertation, Department of Social Anthropology, University of Bergen.

––– (1998) 'Reconstruction of Islamic knowledge and knowing: a case of Islamic practices among women in Iran'. In Karin Ask and Marit Tjomsland (eds) *Women's Islamization: Contemporary Dimensions of Discourses on Gender Relations*. Oxford: Berg.

Kandiyoti, Deniz (1991) *Women, Islam, and the State*. London: Macmillan.

Keane, Webb (1997a) 'Religious language'. *Annual Review of Anthropology*, vol. 26, October, pp. 47–71.

–– (1997b) 'From fetishism to sincerity: on agency, the speaking subject, and their historicity in the context of religious conversion'. *Society for Comparative Study of Society and History*, vol. 39, no. 4, pp. 674–693.

Kent, Alexandra (2000) 'Ambiguity and the Modern Order: the Sathya Sai Baba Movement in Malaysia'. Doctoral dissertation, Department of Social Anthropology, Göteborg University.

Kessler, Clive S. (1980) 'Malaysia: Islamic revivalism and political disaffection in a divided society'. *Southeast Asian Chronicle*, no. 75, October, pp. 3–11.

Khoo Boo Teik (2003) *Beyond Mahathir: Malaysian Politics and Its Discontents*. London and New York: Zed Books.

Khoo Gaik Cheng (2006) *Reclaiming Adat: Contemporary Malaysian Film and Literature*. Vancouver: University of British Columbia Press.

King, Ursula (1995) 'Introduction: gender and the study of religion'. In Ursula King (ed.) *Religion and Gender*. Oxford: Blackwell, pp. 1–40.

Laderman, Carol (1991) *Taming the Winds of Desire: Psychology, Medicine, and Aesthetics in Malay Shamanistic Performance*. Berkeley: University of California Press.

Launay, Robert (1992) *Beyond the Stream: Islam and Society in a West African Town*. Berkeley: University of California Press.

Lindquist, Johan (2002) 'The Anxieties of Mobility: Development, Migration and Tourism in the Indonesian Borderlands'. Doctoral dissertation, Department of Social Anthropology, University of Stockholm.

Mack, Phyllis (2003) 'Religion, feminism, and the problem of agency: reflections on eighteenth-century Quakerism'. *Signs: Journal of Women in Culture and Society*, vol. 29, no. 1, pp. 149–177.

MacLeod, Arlene Elowe (1992) 'Hegemonic relations and gender resistance: the new veiling as accommodating protest in Cairo'. *Signs: Journal of Women in Culture and Society*, vol. 17, no. 3, pp. 533–557.

McNay, Lois (1992) *Foucault and Feminism: Power, Gender, and the Self.* Cambridge: Polity Press.

––– (1996) *Foucault: A Critical Introduction*. Cambridge: Polity Press.

––– (2000) *Gender and Agency: Reconfiguring the Subject in Feminist and Social Theory*. Cambridge: Polity Press.

––– (2003) 'Agency, anticipation and indeterminacy in feminist theory'. *Feminist Theory*, vol. 4, no. 2, pp. 139–148.

Mahmood, Saba (1998) 'Women's Piety and Embodied Discipline: the Islamic Resurgence in Contemporary Egypt'. Doctoral dissertation, Department of Anthropology, Stanford University.

––– (2001a) 'Feminist theory, embodiment, and the docile agent: some reflections on the Egyptian Islamic revival'. *Cultural Anthropology*, vol. 16, no. 2, pp. 202–236.

––– (2001b) 'Rehearsed spontaneity and the conventionality of ritual: disciplines of *salat*'. *American Ethnologist*, vol. 28, no. 4, pp. 827–853.

––– (2003) 'Anthropology and the study of women in Islamic cultures'. In *The Encyclopedia of Women in Islamic Cultures*, vol. 1. Leiden: E. J. Brill, pp. 307–314.

––– (2005) *Politics of Piety: The Islamic Revival and the Feminist Subject*. Princeton: Princeton University Press.

Martinez, Patricia (2002) 'Malaysia in 2001: an interlude of consolidation'. *Asian Survey*, vol. 42, no. 1, pp. 133–140.

Mazumdar, Shampa and Sanjoy Mazumdar (1999) 'Ritual lives of Muslim women: agency in everyday life'. *Journal of Ritual Studies*, vol. 13, no. 2, pp. 58–70.

McDonnell, Mary Byrne (1990). 'Patterns of Muslim pilgrimage from Malaysia, 1885–1985'. In Dave F. Eickelman and James Piscatori (eds) *Muslim Travellers: Pilgrimage, Migration, and the Religious Imagination*. London: Routledge, pp. 111–130.

McGuire, Meredith (1990) 'Religion and the body: rematerializing the human body in the social sciences of religion'. *Journal of the Scientific Study of Religion*, vol. 29, no. 3, pp. 283–296.

Mernissi, Fatima (1975) *Beyond the Veil: Male-Female Dynamics in Modern Muslim Society*. New York: Halsted Press.

――― (2000) 'Tablighi Jama'at and women'. In Muhammad Khalid Masud (ed.) *Travellers in Faith: Studies of the Tablighi Jama'at as a Transnational Islamic Movement for Faith Renewal*. Leiden: E. J. Brill, pp. 44–48.

Milne, R. S. and Diane K. Mauzy (1999) *Malaysian Politics under Mahathir*. London: Routledge.

Milner, Anthony (1998) 'Ideological work in constructing the Malay majority'. In Dru C. Gladney (ed.) *Making Majorities: Constituting the Nation in Japan, Korea, China, Malaysia, Fiji, Turkey and the United States*. Palo Alto: Stanford University Press, pp. 151–172.

Moghadam, Valentine M. (1993) *Modernizing Women: Gender and Social Change in the Middle East*. Boulder: Lynne Rienner.

――― (1994) 'Women and identity politics in theoretical and comparative perspective'. In Valentine M. Moghadam (ed.) *Identity Politics and Women: Cultural Reassertions and Feminism in International Perspective*. Boulder: Westview.

Mohamad Suffian bin Hashim (1972) *An Introduction to the Constitution of Malaysia*. Kuala Lumpur: Government Printers.

Mohd Taib Osman (1985) 'Islamization of the Malays: a transformation of culture in readings on Islam in Southeast Asia'. In Ahmad Ibrahim, Sharon Siddique and Yasmin Hussain (eds) *Readings on Islam in Southeast Asia*. Singapore: Institute of Southeast Asian Studies, pp. 44–47.

――― (1989) *Malay Folk Beliefs: An Integration of Disparate Elements*. Kuala Lumpur: Dewan Bahasa dan Pustaka.

Moore, Henrietta L. (1994) *A Passion for Difference: Essays in Anthropology and Gender*. Cambridge: Polity Press.

Muhammad Haji Mohd Taib (1996) *The New Malay*. Petaling Jaya: Visage Communication.

Nagata, Judith (1980). 'Religious ideology and social change: the Islamic revival in Malaysia'. *Pacific Affairs*, vol. 53, no. 3, pp. 405–439.

――― (1982) 'Islamic revival and the problem of legitimacy among rural religious elites in Malaysia'. *Man*, vol. 17, no. 1, pp. 42–57.

――― (1984) *The Reflowering of Malaysian Islam: Modern Religious Radicals and Their Roots*. Vancouver: University of British Columbia Press.

――― (1994) 'How to be Islamic without an Islamic state: contested models of development in Malaysia'. In Akbar S. Ahmed and Hastings Donnan (eds) *Islam, Globalization and Postmodernity*. London: Routledge, pp. 63–88.

——— (1995) 'Modern Malay women and the message of the "veil"'. In Wazir Jahan Karim (ed.) *'Male' and 'Female' in Developing Southeast Asia*. Oxford: Berg, pp. 101–120.

Najmabadi, Afsaneh (1998) 'Feminism in an Islamic republic: "Years of hardship, years of growth"'. In Yvonne Yazbeck Haddad and John L. Esposito (eds) *Islam, Gender, and Social Change*. New York and Oxford: Oxford University Press, pp. 59–84.

New Straits Times. Malaysian periodical. Selected issues.

Norani Othman (ed.) (1994) *Shari'a Law and the Modern Nation-State: A Malaysian Symposium*. Kuala Lumpur: Sisters in Islam.

——— (1998) 'Islamization and modernization in Malaysia: competing cultural reassertions and women's identity in a changing society'. In Rick Wilford and Robert L. Miller (eds) *Women, Ethnicity and Nationalism: The Politics of Transition*. London and New York: Routledge, pp. 170–192.

Ong, Aihwa (1987) *Spirits of Resistance and Capitalist Discipline: Factory Women in Malaysia*. Albany: SUNY Press.

——— (1995) 'State versus Islam: Malay families, women's bodies, and the body politics in Malaysia'. In Aihwa Ong and Michael G. Peletz (eds) *Bewitching Women, Pious Men: Gender and Body Politics in Southeast Asia*. Berkeley: University of California Press, pp. 170–192.

——— (1998) 'Sisterly solidarity in the Malaysian public sphere'. In Oh Myung-Seok and Kim Hyung-Jun (eds) *Religion, Ethnicity and Modernity in Southeast Asia*. Seoul: Seoul National University Press.

Parker, Lyn (ed.) (2005) *The Agency of Women in Asia*. Singapore: Marshall Cavendish Academic.

Peletz, Michael G. (1992) *A Share of the Harvest: Kinship, Property and Social History among the Malays of Rembau*. Berkeley: University of California Press.

—— (1995) 'Neither reasonable nor responsible: contrasting representations of masculinity in a Malay society'. In Aihwa Ong and Michael G. Peletz (eds) *Bewitching Women, Pious Men: Gender and Body Politics in Southeast Asia*. Berkeley: University of California Press, pp. 76–123.

——— (1996). *Reason and Passion: Representations of Gender in a Malay Society*. Berkeley: University of California Press.

——— (1997). '"Ordinary Muslims" and Muslim resurgents in contemporary Malaysia: notes on an ambivalent relationship'. In Robert W. Hefner and Patricia Horvatich (eds) *Islam in an Era of Nation-States: Politics and*

Religious Renewal in Muslim Southeast Asia. Honolulu: University of Hawai'i Press, pp. 231–274.

— — — (2002) *Islamic Modern: Religious Courts and Cultural Politics in Malaysia.* Princeton: Princeton University Press.

Raudvere, Catharina (2002) *The Book and the Roses: Sufi Women, Visibility, and Zikir in Contemporary Istanbul.* Istanbul: Swedish Research Institute of Istanbul.

Redfield, Robert (1956) *Peasant Society and Culture.* Chicago: University of Chicago Press.

Roff, William R. (1985) 'Pilgrimage and the history of religions: theoretical approaches to the hajj'. In Richard C. Martin (ed.) *Approaches to Islam in Religious Studies.* Tuscon: University of Arizona Press, pp. 78–86.

— — — (1987) 'Islamic movements: one or many?'. In William R. Roff (ed.) *Islam and the Political Economy of Meaning: Comparative Studies of Muslim Discourse.* London and Sydney: Croom Helm, pp. 31–52.

— — — (1994) *The Origins of Malay Nationalism.* Oxford: Oxford University Press.

Rosander, Eva Evers. 1998. 'Women and muridism in Senegal: the case of the Mam diarra Bousso Daira in Mbacké'. In Karin Ask and Marit Tjomsland (eds) *Women and Islamization: Contemporary Dimensions of Discourse on Gender Relations.* Oxford: Berg, pp. 147–176.

Rudie, Ingrid (1993) 'The ritual work of Malay marriage as a field of debate'. In Vigdis Broch-Due, Ingrid Rudie and Tone Bleie (eds) *Carved Flesh, Cast Selves: Gendered Symbols and Social Practices.* Oxford: Berg, pp. 173–193.

— — — (1994) *Visible Women in East Coast Malay Society: On the Reproduction of Gender in Ceremonial, School, and Market.* Oslo: Scandinavian University Press.

Saliba, Therese (2002) 'Introduction: gender, politics, and Islam'. In Therese Saliba, Carolyn Allen and Judith A. Howard (eds) *Gender, Politics, and Islam.* Chicago: University of Chicago Press, pp. 1–14.

Sandborg, Kirsten (1993) 'Malay dress symbolism'. In Vigdis Boch-Due, Ingrid Rudie and Tone Bleie (eds) *Carved Flesh, Cast Selves: Gendered Symbols and Social Practices.* Oxford: Berg, pp. 195–206

— — — (1994) 'Malay Women: Suffering, Struggle and Strategies'. Doctoral Dissertation, Department of Social Anthropology, University of Oslo.

Sawicki, Jana (1991) *Disciplining Foucault.* London: Routledge.

Schimmel, Annemarie (1992) *Islam: An Introduction.* Albany: SUNY Press.

Scott, James C. (1985) *Weapons of the Weak: Everyday Forms of Peasant Resistance.* New Haven: Yale University Press.

Sered, Susan Starr (1992) *Women as Ritual Experts: The Religious Lives of Elderly Jewish Women in Jerusalem.* Oxford: Oxford University Press.

Shamsul Amri Baharuddin (1986) *From British to Bumiputera Rule: Local Politics and Rural Development in Peninsular Malaysia.* Singapore: Institute of Southeast Asian Studies.

––– (1994) 'Religion and ethnic politics in Malaysia: the significance of the resurgence phenomenon'. In Charles F. Keyes, Laurel Kendall and Helen Hardace (eds) *Asian Visions of Authority: Religion and the Modern States of East and Southeast Asia.* Honolulu: University of Hawai'i Press, pp. 99–116.

––– (1995) 'Inventing certainties: the *dakwah* persona in Malaysia'. In Wendy James (ed.) *The Pursuit of Certainty: Religious and Cultural Formulations.* London: Routledge, pp. 111–132.

––– (1997) 'Identity construction, nation formation, and Islamic revivalism in Malaysia'. In Robert W. Hefner and Patricia Horvatich (eds) *Islam in an Era of Nation-State: Politics and Religious Renewal in Muslim Southeast Asia.* Honolulu: University of Hawai'i Press, pp. 207–227.

––– (1998) 'Bureaucratic management of identity in a modern state: "Malayness" in postwar Malaysia'. In Dru C. Gladney (ed.) *Making Majorities: Constituting the Nation in Japan, Korea, China, Malaysia, Fiji, Turkey, and the United States.* Palo Alto: Stanford University Press, pp. 135–150.

Sharifah Zaleha binte Syed Hassan (1990) 'Towards a syariah-based society: religious rationalization and the development of the Islamic legal order in Malaysia'. *Jurnal Antropologi dan Sosiologi,* vol. 18, pp. 41–53.

––– (1994) 'Beyond orthodoxy: religious reforms and legitimacy in Malaysia'. *Ilmu Masyarakat,* vol. 25, pp. 85–108.

––– (1995a) 'Malay women and social freedom'. *Gemanita,* no. 1, pp. 59–70.

––– (1995b) 'The revival of Islam in post-independence Malaysia: a case study of the Al Arqam movement'. Paper presented at the 1st EuroSEAS Conference, 29 June–1 July, Leiden.

––– (2001) 'Islamization and the emerging civil society in Malaysia: a case study'. In Nakamura Mitsuo, Sharon Siddique, Omar Farouk Bajunid (eds) *Islam and Civil Society in Southeast Asia.* Singapore: Institute of Southeast Asian Studies, pp. 76–88.

Siegel, James T. (1969) *The Rope of God.* Berkeley: University of California Press.

Sloane, Patricia (1999) *Islam, Modernity and Entrepreneurship among the Malays.* London: Macmillan.

Stivens, Maila (1992) 'Perspectives in gender: problems on writing about women in Malaysia'. In Joel S. Kahn and Francis Loh Kok Wah (eds) *Fragmented Vision: Culture and Politics in Contemporary Malaysia*. St Leonard's: Allen and Unwin, pp. 202–224.

——— (1998) 'Sex, gender, and the making of the new Malay middle classes'. In Krishna Sen and Maila Stivens (eds) *Gender and Power in Affluent Asia*. London: Routledge, pp. 87–126.

——— (2000) 'Becoming modern in Malaysia: women at the end of the twentieth century'. In Louise Edwards and Mina Roces (eds) *Women in Asia: Tradition, Modernity and Globalisation*. St Leonards: Allen and Unwin, pp. 16–34.

——— (2002) 'The hope of the nation: moral panics and the construction of teenagehood in contemporary Malaysia'. In Leonore Manderson and Pranee Liamputtong (eds) *Coming of Age in South and Southeast Asia: Youth, Courtship and Sexuality*. Richmond: Curzon Press, pp. 188–206.

The Star. Malaysian periodical. Selected issues.

Strange, Heather (1981) *Rural Malay Women in Tradition and Transition*. New York: Praeger.

Strathern, Marilyn (1987) 'An awkward relationship: the case of feminism and anthropology'. *Signs: Journal of Women in Culture and Society*, vol. 12, no. 2, pp. 276–290.

Tapper, Nancy and Richard Tapper (1987) 'The birth of the prophet: ritual and gender in Turkish Islam'. *Man*, vol. 22, no. 1, pp. 69–92.

Tett, Gillian (1994) 'Guardians of the faith? Gender and religion in an ex-Soviet Tajik village'. In Camillia Fawzi El-Solh and Judy Mabro (eds) *Muslim Women's Choices: Religious Belief and Social Reality*. Oxford: Berg, pp. 128–151.

Thompson, Eric C. (2000) In K.L.-and-Kampung: Urbanism in Rural Malaysia. Doctoral dissertation, University of Washington.

Torab, Azam (1996) 'Piety as gendered agency: A study of *Jalaseh* ritual discourse in an urban neighbourhood in Iran'. *Journal of the Royal Anthropological Institute*, vol. 2, no. 2, pp. 235–252.

Vickers, Adrian (2004) '"Malay identity": modernity, invented tradition and forms of knowledge'. In Timothy P. Barnard (ed.) *Contesting Malayness: Malay Identity Across Boundaries*. Singapore: Singapore University Press, pp. 21–63.

Visweswaran, Kamala (1997) 'Histories of feminist ethnography'. *Annual Review of Anthropology*, vol. 26, pp. 591–621.

Walkerdine, Valerie (1997) *Daddy's Girl: Young Girls and Popular Culture*. Cambridge, Mass.: Harvard University Press.

Wazir Jahan Karim (1990) 'Prelude to madness: the language of emotions in courtship and early marriage'. In Wazir Jahan Karim (ed.) *Emotions of Culture: A Malay Perspective*. Singapore: Oxford University Press, pp. 21–63.

––– (1992) *Women and Culture: Between Malay Adat and Islam*. Boulder: Westview Press.

Whalley, Lucy A. (1996) 'Putting Islam into practice: the development of Islam from a gendered perspective in Minangkabau, Indonesia'. In Mark R. Woodward (ed.) *Toward a New Paradigm: Recent Developments in Indonesian Islamic Thought*. Tempe: Program in Southeast Asian Studies, Arizona State University, pp. 265–290.

Willford, Andrew (2006) '"The already surmounted" yet "secretly familiar": Malaysian identity as symptom'. *Cultural Anthropology*, vol. 21, no. 1, pp. 31–59.

Wilson, Peter J. (1967) *A Malay Village and Malaysia*. New Haven: HRAF Press.

Woodward, Mark R. (1989) *Islam in Java: Normative Piety and Mysticism in the Sultanate of Yogyakarta*. Tuscon: University of Arizona Press.

Zainah Anwar (1987) *Islamic Revivalism in Malaysia: Dakwah among the Students*. Petaling Jaya: Pelanduk.

––– (2001) 'What Islam, whose Islam? Sisters in Islam and the struggle for women's rights'. In Robert W. Hefner (ed.) *The Politics of Multiculturalism, Pluralism and Citizenship in Malaysia, Singapore and Indonesia*. Honolulu: University of Hawai'i Press.

Index

Key: **bold**=extended discussion; f=figure; n=note